TALL PERENNIALS

Tall Perennials

Larger-than-Life Plants for Gardens of All Sizes

ROGER TURNER

TIMBER PRESS
Portland · London

Frontispiece: Attractive plant combinations in
this border at Bressingham Gardens in Norfolk,
where the whole is more than the sum of the parts.
Right: Strong-charactered *Echinops bannaticus*
surrounded by colourful "fillers," *Lythrum*, *Phlox*
and *Heliopsis* at Bressingham Gardens, Norfolk.

All photographs by Roger Turner except those
appearing on pages 75, 78, 90, 112, 138, 228 and
233 by Will Giles; page 64 by Derek Harris/
The Garden Collection; pages 88, 99, 153, 157,
204 and 219 by Andrew Lawson/The Garden
Collection; pages 133–134, 137 and 139 by Peter
Linder; and page 211 by Sue Templeton.

Published in 2009 by Timber Press, Inc.

The Haseltine Building
133 S.W. Second Avenue, Suite 450
Portland, Oregon 97204-3527
www.timberpress.com

2 The Quadrant
135 Salusbury Road
London NW6 6RJ
www.timberpress.co.uk

Printed in China
Text designed by Susan Applegate

Catalog records for this book are available from
the Library of Congress and the British Library.

CONTENTS

ACKNOWLEDGEMENTS

Many people have helped in the preparation of this book by offering suggestions, providing information or answering my queries. However, pressure of space has meant that the minimum height necessary for a plant's inclusion had to be raised, and as a result not every piece of information offered has ended up in the book. Apologies to anyone with whom I corresponded whose name is not included below.

Grateful thanks are due to Anna Mumford, Rom Kim and Erica Gordon-Mallin.

I am also grateful to Barbara Alsop, Geoffrey Alsop, Anne Armstrong, Randy Baldwin, Richard Ball, David Barker, Anthony Brookes, Bob Brown, Mike Brown, Billy Carruthers, Audrey Cary, Joy Caskie, Rev. David Clark, Sarah Conibear, Susan Cunliffe-Lister, Digging Dog Nursery, Gary Dunlop, Sally Edwards, David Fenwick, Tim Fuller, the Garden Collection, Mark Garland, Will Giles, Stan Grainger, Diana Grenfell, Elizabeth Honnor, Laurette Houghton, Nis der Horst, Martin Hughes-Jones, Alison King, Mr. T. Larratt, Hans Peter Linder, Pollie Maasz, Margaret McKendrik, Meg McPherson, Margaret Mason, Robin Middleton, John Millington, Gill Mullin, Veronica Munson, Liz Nicklin, Doreen Normandale, Gill Payne, Paul Picton, Diane Rowe, Stella Sargent, Rachel Saunders, Joe Sharman, Arthur Shipperley, Duncan Skene, Julian Sutton, Dr. Tomas Tamberg, Sue Templeton, Edmond Thomson, Anna Toeman and Don Witton.

The strongly vertical effect created by the foliage and flower spikes of *Veronicastrum virginicum* f. *roseum* 'Pink Glow'.

PREFACE

Some of the most amazing plants in the plant kingdom can be found among the tall perennials. Brilliance of flower colour, architectural outline and quality of foliage are commonplace in this range of plants. Don't imagine you haven't got the space for plants like these. Everyone has space; it simply depends how you want to use the space you have. If you have two square yards available, you could fill it with a few alpines as high as your hand, or instead you could have a clump of elecampane, *Inula helenium*, with bold foliage and brilliant yellow flowers on a plant two metres high.

Space is a question of priorities. Just because your garden is small, there is no logic that compels you to have only low-growing plants. You could equally well have tall ones that would grow up to the light and amaze you and your neighbours. So dig out all those prostrate subjects that grovel on the surface of the ground—dire things like that black, grassy *Ophiopogon planisca-*

Cortaderia richardii, at Bicton Park, Devon, planted in the border, but with enough space around it to show off its size and shape.

pus 'Nigrescens', which is only a few centimetres high and looks like dying seaweed—and plant something bold and attention-seeking instead—whatever takes your fancy in this book.

The chapters in Part I form an introduction to the plant descriptions and offer information and ideas about plant characteristics in general, especially as seen in tall perennials. Most plants look their best when grouped with other interesting and contrasting plants, and the first chapter provides a guide to creating effective plant combinations. The next step is to consider much larger groupings, and chapter two offers detailed ideas on the design of the whole border. Finally, chapter three looks at the practical aspects and provides advice on the successful cultivation of the plants.

Part II concentrates on the plants, and its chapters are organized around the idea of impact. When choosing a plant, one shouldn't think only of the flowers; one should also consider how the plant as a whole will affect the garden. In this book the plants with the highest impact come first, working through to those that we grow for the sake of the succession of colour

Amaze the neighbours by growing elecampane, *Inula helenium*, which is likely to send its flowers up higher than the fence between you and the people next door.

Foliage of gigantic proportions from *Gunnera manicata*, a moisture-loving plant with huge umbrella leaves that will keep the rain off if you seek shelter beneath them.

Tall perennials are plants to look up in every sense of the words. *Rudbeckia laciniata* 'Herbstsonne' reaching for the sky at Waterperry Gardens, Oxfordshire.

and interest that they provide. The plants with the strongest character are described in chapter four, under the heading "Architectural Perennials," which includes some of the most dramatic and attention-grabbing perennials that can be grown. Many of these architectural plants also make good specimen plants. Just as a cedar tree can stand alone because of its striking form and outline, an architectural perennial usually deserves space and air around it so that its shape can be appreciated—pampas grass makes a good example.

However, it is not possible to divide all garden plants neatly into "high impact" on the one hand, and "subtle impact" on the other, as there are too many cases in-between. Some plants create plenty of impact and excitement for the few weeks when they are in flower but are fairly insignificant beforehand and afterwards— *Kniphofia uvaria*, for example, with its hot orange-red flower colour and the arresting "exclamation mark" shape of the flowering stems.

After the architectural plants of chapter four, the next few chapters consider these "in-between" plants, all of which are remarkable in one way or another but are not quite so dramatic as those in the first of the plant chapters. Plants with eye-catching foliage are described in chapter five, "Foliage Plants and Ferns," which covers plants worth growing for their leaves alone, with

Melianthus major is grown for its attractive blue-grey foliage. The plant is not shapely enough to be called "architectural," nor as brilliant in colour as a plant grown for its flowers.

A brilliant splash of colour from *Helianthus* 'Monarch', a vigorous and easy plant in the daisy family.

the flowers as a bonus. However, we have to remember that even if a plant has coloured foliage, it still won't be a match for flowers with all their brilliance and intensity of colour (designed by nature to catch the eye of fast-flying insects).

The next three chapters consider particular ranges of plants, each of which has its own distinct characteristics. Chapter six, "Umbellifers," includes plants in the cow parsley family, with their upright habit and umbrella-like flowerheads, such as fennel, angelica and giant hogweed.

Chapter seven, "Ornamental Grasses," includes pampas grass, *Miscanthus* and other tall grasses, some with good foliage, others with attractive flowerheads, while chapter eight, "Restios and Equisetums," treats an unusual range of plants, mostly from southern Africa, with stiff upright stemlike leafless bamboos.

The remainder of the plant chapters are devoted to perennials which provide colour and a succession and interest through the season. To acknowledge the particular floral characteristics of some plants, two types of flowers have been separated out. Chapter nine considers plants which have flowers arranged in upright flower spikes. Some, such as foxgloves, verbascums and eremuruses, consist of a single spire, but many other tall plants consist of a whole clump of flowering stems, with each stem strongly vertical in shape. Some of these have very many flower spikes and leafy stems, as in *Veronicastrum*, while others have just a few upright stems, but in each case it gives the plant a vertical emphasis which will distinguish it from its lower or more vaguely rounded neighbours. Those which have daisy flowers also have a chapter to themselves in chapter ten, and these tend to be brightly coloured and cheerful in mood.

The last three plant chapters consider the succession of interest that everyone wants from their garden during the summer and autumn seasons: "Early Perennials," in chapter eleven, covering the months of May and June; "Midseason Perennials," in chapter twelve, describing the flowers of high summer (July and August); and finally chapter thirteen, "Late Perennials," those plants which flower from September into late autumn and early winter.

PART I

GARDENING
WITH TALL PERENNIALS

TALL PERENNIALS, in fact, all perennials, have many advantages over other plants. They are rewarding to grow, requiring only a small amount of effort on the part of the gardener, they perform well soon after planting, and they come in a wide range of colours. They are diverse in form and offer every conceivable flower type. They can be acquired at a low cost and, of course, they come up every year. A *perennial* plant is by definition distinct from an *annual* plant, which has to germinate, grow, flower and die all in the course of one season. A *biennial* plant, however, has a built-in two-year life cycle, germinating and growing in the first year, flowering (and dying) in the second. Biennials can sometimes be persuaded to survive a little longer, by cutting off their flowers and preventing them from setting seed, but this only puts off the evil day.

Most perennials are *herbaceous*, a word with various nuances of meaning, but usually indicating that the leafy growth is not persistent, but dies down in the autumn, retiring to an underground rootstock which sends out new shoots the following season. Michaelmas daisies are the classic example. Many such plants leave behind their dead stems, which have to be tidied away in the autumn, although this is not an arduous task. A few plants leave behind dead skeletons which are moderately attractive, and these can be left in place for a while. Others have seed heads which have some value. A few perennials are not herbaceous in the sense just described, but have overwintering stems; examples are cardoon, *Euphorbia characias* and *Helleborus argutifolius*. However, scarcely any tall perennials have overwintering stems.

The great advantage of perennials is that there is always something happening. From the moment the shoots come through the ground in the spring, through the growth of the foliage, to the climax of floral display, and in some cases, on again to interesting seed heads—all this provides interest over the course of many months.

Some tall perennials form a very large clump over time, but others rarely send up

Page 16: Michaelmas Daisies, New England asters, perennial sunflowers and *Solidago* at Barrington Court in Somerset.

more than one or two stems. In the case of verbascums or echiums, the whole plant forms an isolated spire with a distinctive tall and narrow outline, and because verbascums tend to seed themselves, you often get several of them dotted around. With some plants, one or two leggy stems can look slightly uncomfortable—either top-heavy or lamp-post–like—and in this case it is better to plant several plants together as a group at the start. The average clump-forming perennial plant looks best if it is at least as wide as it is tall: a plant which is two metres high needs ideally to form a clump about 2.5 metres across.

When it comes to choosing tall perennials, the possibilities seem endless. To decide whether a plant deserves a place in the garden, it might seem the best thing is to grow it yourself and find out. But to be realistic, it is impossible to grow every available plant and this is why keen gardeners are not only growers of plants but also regular visitors to other people's gardens, devoted readers of gardening books and inquisitive internet image searchers.

Many verbascums are biennial or short-lived perennials. These are growing in the Dry Garden at Hyde Hall in Essex.

Michaelmas Daisies, New England asters, perennial sunflowers and *Solidago* at Barrington Court in Somerset. All these will die right down in the winter, and their dead stems will have to be cut down and tidied away at the end of the season.

The skeletons of fennel, *Foeniculum vulgare*, provide additional interest at the end of the season.

The fluffy white seed heads produced by woolly thistle, *Cirsium eriophorum*, are part of the charm of this plant.

A few perennials, such as the cardoon, *Cynara cardunculus*, are particularly valuable in the garden because of their overwintering stems.

These curious pink spikes coming up through the ground are the young growth of lovage, *Levisticum officinale*, developing in the spring.

The young fronds of the royal fern, *Osmunda regalis*, uncurling. Watching a plant like this develop during the course of several weeks is one of the pleasures of gardening.

One or two isolated stems can look uncomfortable. Tall perennials look much better planted in a good-sized clump made up of several plants.

In any case, we may have a particular kind of garden, and this will mean that some plants are "in" and others will be "out." Having areas of shade or a very dry garden means that the situation has already made some decisions for us. Acid or alkaline soil, coastal winds, or the fact that we live in Alaska, or Auckland, New Zealand, are other unalterable determinants. The garden may also have stylistic characteristics which we want to maintain, and when it comes to style, exclusion is as important as inclusion. If we want a jungle effect, we will need big and bold plants or ones with remarkable foliage. If we are determined to have a classic English herbaceous border, with flowers in soft pastel shades (supposing we wanted all that work), then we must learn to say no to bright brash yellow flowers and yes to other more subtle ones.

A clump of *Miscanthus sinensis* 'Silberfeder' at Bressingham Gardens, Norfolk, about three time as wide as it is high.

A jungle effect created by plants with bold foliage, tall grasses, bamboos and inulas, at Burton Agnes in Yorkshire.

Some tall perennials, such as this rudbeckia, which have most of the flowers concentrated at the top of the plant, look better with something planted in front of them.

The medium-height Michaelmas daisy in this border helps to hide the excess of low-level foliage belonging to *Helianthus* 'Lemon Queen'.

Growing tall perennials means that you will have more plant for your effort and your money. Instead of looking down at your feet to study your plants, they will look you in the face, or in some cases you will have to look up at them. Tall perennials are simply more impressive, more surprising and more rewarding. You may end up with a smaller head-count of different kinds of plants in your garden compared with other gardeners, but at least your plants will come out and grab your attention and that of your garden visitors.

Tall perennials with high-quality foliage, interesting habit or statuesque outline look good from head to foot, and these are good enough to be planted in isolation, either near the front of the border or as specimens. But there are many other tall perennials where the interest is concentrated at the top of the plant, with the lower half or two-thirds of the plant consisting of not-very-interesting greenery. The flowers will be good but something will need to be planted in front of the plant, so that the viewer is not confronted at low level with a wall of greenery.

A succession of interest and colour through the season is one of the joys of gardening, and this is easy to achieve with perennials, tall or not. A walk around the garden for a few moments before setting off to work or taking the children to school will be a fresh source of pleasure every day.

1

PLANT RELATIONSHIPS

The art of plant association consists of putting plants together into pleasing groups. Several good plants in a well-considered arrangement look more attractive than one plant on its own, so most people think. In many ways plant association is like the art of flower arrangement writ large. It may seem natural to concentrate on the attractions of one individual plant, but if we don't consider the context of the plant within the border, it could be like keeping one fish in a goldfish bowl. A better way to keep fish, in my view, is to create an entire aquatic setting, with a range of water plants, a few rocks and a selection of fish of different kinds. In this way you create a virtual watery world. A garden is also a virtual world, and in my view as much attention needs to be paid to creating the setting as to the individual inhabitants of that world.

Of course, there are quite a few gardeners who believe that anything goes with anything, so for them plant relationships are not a difficult art, but whether you are aiming at a random cottage garden effect or something more subtle, there still are several rules that apply to the making of success-

ful plant relationships. And even if you are allergic to rules, I think you will agree that they are straight-forward and make sense.

The first rule we ought to consider is the rule of congruity of scale, which means there has to be a match in size and scale of the two plants in question. It's no good planting a small hosta at the feet of a helianthus, for example, and calling it a plant association, because no one will be able to take in both plants in the same glance. If we want something to relate sensibly with a helianthus we need something to match it in scale, in fact, something at least three-quarters as tall. I have seen *Helianthus* 'Lemon Queen' look good with *Miscanthus sinensis* 'Goliath', a plant even taller than the helianthus; just to one side was a large *Eupatorium* specimen, with a shorter miscanthus, 'Yakushima Dwarf', in front, successfully screening the helianthus greenery.

The second common-sense idea is the rule of simultaneous performance. This states that the plants in question need to flower at roughly the same time, or at least need to be ornamental simultaneously. Would the cloudy panicles of white flowers produced by *Crambe cordifolia* look good with a group of scarlet cannas? Maybe they would, but we shall never know because the *Crambe* flowers will die before the cannas begin. Such things can easily be forgotten when we are planning the garden on the drawing board, or in the depths of winter. Of course we are not dealing with an exact science here because the weather varies from year to year, especially in Great Britain, and this variation may bring one plant forward or hold another back.

The third rule concerns sufficient contrast. A certain amount of contrast is always needed so that one plant can actually be distinguished from the other. A low-growing yellow coreopsis in front of a yellow heliopsis will simply be too similar, yellow against yellow will lack contrast, and so this will not be a successful association. Similarly, if every plant is soft, rounded and shapeless, as many herbaceous plants are, one begins to long for a strong architectural plant to break the monotony.

The fourth rule is one of nature's own, and we defy it at our peril. The rule of similar requirements dictates that all the plants in a group must like the same conditions of soil, climate and so on. Nothing will induce a ligularia to flourish alongside a cistus, for example, since one likes damp, semi-shaded conditions and the other likes it hot

Plants need to be sensibly matched in height and scale if they are to work together in an effective association.

A plant association works only if the plants flower at roughly the same time. This red hot poker is well past its best.

and dry. To tease one of them into tolerating what it hates will only involve a lot of pointless work and produce disappointing results.

But there is an extension of this rule, a mere guideline, in fact, that says that plants have to appear to the eye as though they belong together, from the same habitat or the same world. Some plants can look uncomfortable side by side even if technically they may well survive together. Sedums and hostas, for example, can be persuaded to grow next to each other along the front of a border, but somehow they might not look quite right, since most people know that sedums come from the hot and dry places of the world and hostas from damp woodland habitats.

A similar distinction can be made between horticultural plants and wild ones. Roses, double peonies and tall delphiniums, for example, have been bred by human hands and they belong in the garden border or the cut-flower bed. Other plants seem to have come straight from the wild prairie or the woodland clearing. They may fit into the border, or they may look too rugged or too coarse to associate with "tame" plants bred by human beings. The plant in question may have cheery yellow flowers, but also have foliage reminiscent of some well-known weed. Moorland plants are a similar

Groups of miscanthus varieties in varying heights, with eupatoriums and helianthuses making a pleasing and balanced group.

case—a heather at the foot of a large leafy herbaceous plant never looks quite right. However, one might think that a dwarf pine would look right in a variety of places, since pines are found in a wide range of climates and habitats. But even so, pines are not very horticultural—they look wild and untamed and therefore do not look right in every garden situation. There is one in the famous Red Border at Hidcote in Gloucestershire, but I'm not sure whether it looks ideal now that it has grown so large.

Placing a plant of one kind next to a plant of another kind, usually just side by side, is what plant relationships amount to at the most basic. At Piet Oudolf's nursery in the Netherlands, I found a large dark red eupatorium planted next to *Veronicastrum virginicum* 'Alboroseum', forming a perfectly good plant association. In the best associations

the two plants have a certain amount of similarity and a certain amount of contrast. Too many leafy grasses together, such as *Miscanthus*, *Schizachyrium* and *Panicum*, will look altogether too grassy and leafy. All-grass associations provide far too much similarity and not enough contrast. The same applies to several variegated plants placed side by side—they look more effective separated by plain dark green foliage. However, the association between the eupatorium and the veronicastrum referred to above is successful because the deep pink and the pale pink of the flower colour relate, but there is also contrast of foliage and habit.

In the case of tall perennials, it is also useful to think about the relationship of the plants when one is in front of the other. Here the plant in front may serve a useful purpose, concealing the legginess or leafiness

An off-white veronica placed next to a pastel pink salvia doesn't have enough contrast to create a pleasing plant relationship.

Bright yellow with bright yellow doesn't make an effective plant association, even if the heights are different.

Beth Chatto's gravel garden works because all the plants in it have
been chosen to suit their particular soil conditions.

A pleasing border, but arguably the white rose doesn't fit in well with
the other wilder, less horticultural, moisture-loving plants.

of the taller plant. At the same time the plant behind forms a background against which the lower plant is seen. If a tall artemisia has *Cosmos atrosanguineus* in front of it, the dark red flowers will show up very clearly against the mass of silvery foliage, and both plants will benefit by the association.

Tall perennials don't all have to be relegated to the back of the border; some can be used in among lower-growing plants—for example, acanthuses, digitalises, echiums, eremuruses, onopordums, verbascums, and plants whose only claim to height lies in their tall flower stems, such as beschornerias, dieramas, tall daylilies, kniphofias, *Stipa gigantea* and other specimen grasses. In this way one can have what is called "feature and ground"—a dominant feature plant surrounded by a smaller plant which is laid out like a carpet at its base.

Consideration of colour is the traditional way of organising a large group of plants in a border. This doesn't have to involve a complex or laborious scheme—the simple solution is simply to avoid the worst clashes. Keep the orange colours away from the pinks and all will be well. The brilliant yellow of many rudbeckias, heliopsises, helianthuses and silphiums is also less than ideal alongside pink. A convenient working rule is to have pink-friendly colours in one area and orange-friendly ones in another, the pink-friendly colours being pink, mauve, purple, blue and white. These shades also blend well with coloured foliage in shades of silver, blue-green, purple and dark red.

The orange-friendly colours, however, are cream, yellow, orange, red, burgundy and maroon, and these in turn are happy

Dusky red eupatoriums and palest pink veronicastrums making an effective plant association in Piet Oudolf's nursery in the Netherlands.

Grasses with other similar grasses, lacking sufficient contrast
and creating an altogether too grassy effect.

A pleasing group of grasses of various moderately contrasting kinds, broken up
with a more strong-charactered phormium and a helianthus behind.

with variegated foliage. In practice all the flowers in one genera tend to belong to the pink-friendly on one hand or the orange-friendly group on the other. In the pink-blue-mauve group are plants such as cranesbill geraniums, echinaceas, penstemons, sidalceas and veronicastrums.

Another approach to colour schemes is to divide plants into two categories—the "hot" and the "cool." Using this method, hot and brilliant colours, such as scarlet, red, bright yellow, orange and lime green, go into one group, while the cool shades go into another. The "cool" or pastel colours are blue, white, pale yellow, pale apricot, pale pink, pale mauve and so on. All you need to do is be consistent and this will be another simple recipe for success.

Appreciation of textural effects will also add to the quality of plant relation-ships. Broad leaves contrasted with feath-ery ones, or the shiny against dull, the fine lines of ornamental grasses contrasted with the huge leaves of a rheum, and so on. Too many daylilies (and there are some tall ones) all planted together will be a plea-sure when they are in bloom, but later on all those tufts of lax, grassy leaves will look a mess unless they are broken up by some other stronger, more definite plants that make a stronger, all-the-year-round statement.

No law says that good associations can-not be repeated; in fact, one of the charms of wild habitats is the repetition of cer-tain plants which are characteristic of the habitat. This can be very satisfying to the eye, and such repetition can also be useful in giving a garden an overall theme and a character of its own.

Orange crocosmias with a dusky pink oreganum creating a clash which may not be to everyone's taste.

A hot, fiery scheme at Ness Botanical Gardens, Cheshire, with helianthus,
Lobelia cardinalis 'Queen Victoria', heleniums and rudbeckias.

A cool colour scheme with lime-green euphorbias, verbascums,
Stipa gigantea and various kinds of silver foliage.

2

DESIGNING THE BORDER

Before we consider the placing of the plants in the border, we need to give some attention to the context and general setting of the border within the garden. From which vantage point will the border be seen? And what is there to be seen around it or behind it? What is directly behind the border will be our main concern, because this will form the backdrop against which the plants will be viewed. The background in a traditional English herbaceous border was a yew hedge, which provided both shelter and an evergreen framework of greenery during the winter. There is no colour quite as good as dark green as a backcloth for brightly coloured flowers to show up to advantage, and this is what the yew hedge provides so effectively. A group of good plants with a restless jumble behind them—a tacky fence, a telephone pole, the neighbour's shed or even the average greenhouse—will never prompt you to raise your camera and take a photo, whereas the same plants with a plain, evergreen background will look perfect.

In a small town garden the background will almost certainly be a wall, fence or trellis, but however smart these are, they are never quite as relaxing to look at as the soft, blurred greenery of foliage. For this reason it is a good idea to plant climbers and wall shrubs to soften the appearance of whatever man-made feature forms the background.

Another factor which inevitably affects the choice of plants is the amount of space available, in particular, the width of the border. Narrow borders are fine for low-growing plants, but it is hard to create good plant associations with tall or even medium-sized perennials in a narrow bed. To allow enough room for a series of good plant relationships, a border needs to be at least three plants deep, and for this to work comfortably the minimum dimension from front to back will be 180 cm. Even this allows only 60 cm for each plant. A width of three metres would therefore be better, since it will provide for plants or groups of plants which are 90 cm deep, while also allowing the flexibility of the border being four plants deep in some places. If we want to grow tall perennials in very narrow borders, it is a good idea to choose plants which look good from top to bottom, such as cardoons, macleayas or miscanthuses.

Borders that are backed by high walls or fences will be shaded at certain times of day, even if the border faces due south, and this effect becomes more noticeable the further north the garden is situated. Planted hard against a wall many tall, willowy perennials instinctively lean out to maximize the amount of sunshine they get. Even a three foot wall can have this effect (I have discovered), and when a tall plant leans, it looks uncomfortable, and also leans onto another plant and does it no good. Unlike shrubs you can't hack tall perennials back, so ideally one should allow extra space at the back of the border, so that tall perennials which don't have stiff upright stems can be planted a short distance out from the wall or fence.

A border with paving or a lawn on both sides is two-sided and must look good from both angles. In this case it needs to be nearly double the width. If there is to be a tallish plant in the centre, to give a sense of height, then the overall bed width needs to be between 3 and 5 metres wide if the plants are to look comfortable and not unduly squeezed. Not everyone has this amount of space, it is true.

For the gardener who likes to try a wide range of plants, it is all too easy to end up with a border containing a large number of

One of the borders at Arley Hall in Cheshire with helianthuses, sanguisorbas, Michaelmas daisies, and much more, all backed by a large yew hedge.

The flower spikes of this attractive
kniphofia show up well against
the dark yew hedge behind.

Because of the quality of their
attractive grey-green foliage, macleayas
look good from top to toe.

Perennials look best planted in large groups of the same plant. Plant spacings
carried out to perfection can be seen at Bressingham Gardens in Norfolk.

single individual plants, each one of a different kind. Often one plant will bear down on another, with another one looking as though it's about to be smothered, and this will show that we are trying to squeeze too much in. Perennials look best if they are planted in groups of three or more of one kind, tall perennials in even larger groups. This helps them to merge with one another as a self-contained cluster, and avoids the feeling of overcrowding you get when there is only one of a particular kind of plant. Having several plants of one kind also helps those types of plants which are inclined to flop, to cling together and stand up straight. Overcrowding is not good for the plants themselves

either. Most perennials are from habitats where there is plenty of space. They like light and air around them and don't perform so well if there is jungle-like competition. Tall perennials look particularly awkward if they do not have breathing space.

Ideally a bigger gap should be allowed between groups of plants of a different kind than between a group of plants of the same kind: if a spacing of 45 cm (18 in) is right between plants of the same kind, 60 cm (24 in) will be needed between those plants and the adjacent plants of a different kind. This will allow the cluster of plants of one kind to sit comfortably and also the light and air to get in. However, as the border matures, this

Architectural plants, in this case, phormiums, placed in key positions, with "filler" plants providing seasonal colour, in a garden designed by the author.

will become a maintenance issue as well as a design one.

Once we get down to the serious business of selecting the plants for the border, it is best to pick the architectural plants first, and these can be planted in key positions, such as near the end of the border, or each side of an opening. These strong-charactered plants are best distributed here and there along the border—not all together in one spot.

Once the architectural plants are in place, the next thing to check is that there will be enough evergreen planting to provide cover during the winter months. These days, nobody wants their own garden to be like the old-fashioned herbaceous borders, without a leaf to be seen all winter. In a large garden, where the bed is not within sight of the windows of the house, a herbaceous border may have its place, but in a small garden it is not appealing to see bare brown earth for several months. For this reason the mixed border is the best solution, with a few evergreen shrubs mixed among the perennials. Again, these need to be dotted around the bed, not all clustered in one place. Sarcococcas are very effective for this purpose, in dark glossy green. But one of the most useful, I find, is the grey-leaved Jerusalem sage, *Phlomis fruticosa*, or one of

Echiums providing architectural statements at the Chelsea Physic Garden in London, surrounded by less strongly shaped, more rounded plants.

its close relations. Phlomises are informal in shape and blend in well with perennials, and are very easily kept in check, since they can be pruned with one's bare hands. Other candidates to give evergreen cover are rosemary, phygelius, cistus, *Olearia nummularifolia*, *Viburnum davidii*, *Convolvulus cneorum*, santolina, helianthemums and hebes. Subshrubs can also be used, such as *Salvia officinalis* (sage), *Ruta graveolens* (rue), *Iberis sempervirens* (perennial candytuft) and *Erysimum* varieties (perennial wallflowers).

Some perennials are evergreen, but perennials which are tall and also evergreen are virtually nonexistent, although

Phlomis chrysophylla makes an ideal evergreen shrub to provide evergreen cover during the winter, when planted among perennials.

A mixture of architectural plants, evergreen plants and perennials with colourful seasonal interest in a garden designed by the author.

some do have overwintering foliage which retreats to a lower stature during the winter. South American eryngiums, cardoons and kniphofias do this, while some plants retire to a mere evergreen tuft—*Acanthus mollis*, for example. But the border is obviously going to contain plants of all heights, in which case we can use plants like *Euphorbia characias*, the classic example of an evergreen perennial, of medium height but occasionally quite tall. The list of low-growing evergreen perennials is much longer and includes penstemons, *Helleborus argutifolius*, several good ferns, along with bergenias, dianthuses, epimediums, *Euphorbia myrsinites*, heucheras, liriopes and *Stachys byzantina*, which are suitable for the front row.

We now have both the architectural plants and the evergreen ones in place, which together might take up a quarter or even a third of the space in the border. The remaining areas will be available for "decorative fillers," plants which will give us a succession of colour and interest through the season. Some will be included simply because we like them, others because they flower for a long time, and some because they are good ground cover plants, to cut down on the work.

One plant providing the background to another, in this case, *Kniphofia* 'Percy's Pride' backed by *Calamagrostis ×acutiflora* 'Karl Foerster'.

Successful borders usually have a grada-
tion of heights, from tall to medium, from
short to prostrate, as we move from the back
to the front of the border. To create a border
with a sensible variation of height, it can
be useful to divide it up in one's mind, and
think of the front of the border, the back of
the border, and middle, as distinct zones,
where the plants have slightly different roles
to play. The plants at the back will form the
background to the rest of the border, and
the tall perennials in this book will obviously tend to find themselves here. If the
lower plants have distinct habit or remarkable flower shape it will show up against this

background. Ideally the plants at the back
of the border will not be uniform in height,
but offer some degree of variety. It is better
if one plant is dominant and the adjacent
plants are complementary or supportive to
it. Variations in habit can also be pleasing.
If one plant is bushy and the next has strong
verticals because of its flower spikes, and
the next has some foliage interest there is
a chance that the border will have interest
before and after the peak flowering period.

The plants in the middle of the border,
or along the front edge, will be an essential part of the ensemble, all contributing to
the effect of the whole. Particularly careful

Aster 'Little Carlow' and ornamental grasses, with a long band of *Persicaria affine* along the front of the border, in a garden designed by the author.

thought needs to be given to the front-row plants, since a mistake very easily made is to have too many different kinds. It is so tempting to fit in one of all the things we would like to try, but this creates a jumbled, restless effect. More effective is a scheme where there is a long band of one kind of plant at the front of the border, which will act as an underlining, or like a ribbon tying everything together.

In the middle of the border less restraint is needed, and one can more easily get away with a riot of shapes and colours. But if we take Gertrude Jekyll as our guide, one can see from her plans that she only used one plant on its own if it was a large architectural plant; more often she used long bands of one kind of plant, running more or less parallel with the front line of the border with maybe five or seven or more plants clustered in a long group, to create a stronger effect.

3

CULTIVATION

Perennials in the wild are usually found on grasslands and prairies or in woodland clearings, places with plenty of air and sunshine, and these are the conditions we should try to create if we want a good display of perennials. A shaded area will never be so good, as the number of interesting perennials which come from forest habitats is limited, and shade-loving plants tend to be small and retiring, with white, greenish or pale-coloured flowers. Some perennials will tolerate shade for part of the day, but it's impossible to create a riot of colour in shade.

Beds under large trees are best avoided altogether because of the additional problem of competition from tree roots. The bigger the tree, the denser the shade will be and the more demanding the tree will be, wanting first claim on the moisture and nutrients in the soil. One can get away with a border under a small sorbus or prunus, but the company of fruit trees is to be avoided, since the fruit falls into the border and is a nuisance to remove, or else the fruit rots unpleasantly.

Perennials are easy to grow, but they don't necessarily want to grow where we want to put them. The average homeowner wants a lawn in the middle of the garden with plants all around the outside, and this arrangement seems reasonable since it maximizes the amount of useable space where children can play and where the grownups can sit in the summer. It also creates an open, smooth, green area which acts as a resting place for the eye as we look out on the garden from the house. But unfortunately this arrangement is not what the perennials want. They would prefer to be brought away from the shade created by the fences, walls and trees at the boundary of the garden into the middle of the garden where there will be more light and air. In a small garden the overall layout will inevitably depend on which is most important—a place where people relax, or a place for growing plants. In a large garden, of course, you can have both.

The average perennial plant prefers soil that is not boggy or waterlogged, especially during the winter. The gardens of new houses sometimes suffer from unexpected areas of boggy ground, which occur because the building operations have disturbed the established patterns of drainage. A new system of drains may well be needed to resolve the situation. More often the underlying cause of standing water is a substrata of impervious clay. If new drains are laid in this situation one should take care that no clay soil is put back on top of the drains, as this will prevent the water reaching the drain. Some soil improvements may still be needed near the surface, to ensure that the new drains serve a wide area, and not just a small patch around the drain. It will always improve matters to cultivate the soil and introduce free-draining material.

A whole range of interesting perennials actually prefer boggy and wet soils, but even so, a bed for such plants needs careful planning. It will be no use planting moisture-loving plants in ground that seems to be boggy most of the year, but sometimes dries out in the heat of summer. Disaster will overtake the plants during those critical weeks of drought and the so-called bog garden will shrivel up and look terrible. The essential thing is to ensure that the plants are moist on a permanent basis. A bed of moisture-loving plants has to be treated almost in the same way as a pond; if you think of it as a pond filled with soil, the bog

Rudbeckias, heleniums and purple *Ricinus communis* in full sunshine at Nürtigen in Germany. These are the conditions perennials like best.

garden will be a success, and there is no reason why a plastic liner should not be used to achieve this effect.

The two most troublesome kinds of soil are clay, and very light free-draining soils. Clay needs patience, as it can take anything from three to ten years to transform it into good garden soil. Initially the ground should be roughly dug over in the autumn before any other work is done, and the heavy clods left for the frosty weather to work on. The deeper you go with the digging, the better the result will be. As much organic matter as possible should be worked in the following season. Farmyard manure or sta-

ble manure isn't pleasant to work with, but will produce good results. Almost any kind of material will be beneficial to break up the solidity of the clay—grit, ashes, manure, compost, leaf mould or mushroom compost. Even seaweed can be used, if you happen to live near the coast. One traditional solution was to grow potatoes on the ground in the first season, before attempting to make an ornamental bed—all that digging over and earthing up worked wonders.

Once this new material has been added, the entire surface should be covered in a layer of coarse grit a few centimetres thick, before the hot weather comes. The thickness

Darmera and other moisture-loving plants enjoying permanently damp conditions at Beth Chatto's garden in Essex.

of the layer may well depend on how much money you have to spare. The grit need not be worked in but can be left lying on the surface, as the worms will do the rest. The grit will greatly improve the texture and also prevent the soil from drying out or developing deep cracks in hot weather. The great consolation is that once they are improved, clay soils are very fertile and will produce good, healthy plants.

Light, free-draining or sandy soils are the opposite of clay, but the solutions have some things in common. The aim is to give the soil as much spongy, water-absorbent material as possible. Digging in organic matter is a must. Peat, or a coir-based peat-substitute, can also be usefully added as they have excellent water-retention qualities, though are low in nutrients. The next stage is to mulch the surface of the bed with pulverized bark or with mushroom or garden compost. This will need to be done as often as it takes. If it disappears, as it will, add more. Later on, it will help to plant small ground cover perennials such as *Geranium ×cantabrigiense* 'Biokovo', since the roots will help to stabilize the soil and stop it acting like the sand on a beach.

Any weeds in the border should be removed before a bed is planted up—easy to say, not always so easy to achieve. The worst are the deep-rooted perennial weeds, such as convolvulus. Ideally this operation of eradicating weeds should take some time, and if time is not an important factor one should leave the border fallow for at least a year to allow for a second or third attack at the persistent weeds. But most of us don't have this amount of time—we want results

now, and in this case the only solution is a combination of digging, spraying and diligent after-care for the first few seasons after planting.

The planting of perennials in their required positions used to be done in early autumn, allowing time for the plant to get established before the onset of winter. But in these days of containers, planting tends to be carried out at any time. Nevertheless there is no sense in reducing the chances of success by planting healthy plants in frosty weather or when the ground is extremely wet. The aim is to minimize the shock the plant receives in the planting process. It is also sensible to avoid the hottest time of the year. If plant-moving is done within a garden, the plant is best watered generously several hours before you lift it, and again once it is in its new position. If you are moving plants which are actually in flower or about to flower, it is a good idea to spray the foliage with water morning and evening to prevent the plant from flagging.

The more you prepare the place where the plant is to go, the better the results will be. Keeping plants in pots and then planting them is an artificial operation unknown to Mother Nature, so it pays to take steps to compensate for the negative impact of this operation on the plant. The hole you dig for the plant should be bigger than you might have thought. Compost should be added, along with a handful of bone meal to give the plant a boost, remembering that at first the plant won't have a root structure big enough to support all the greenery and floral display we expect of it. In dry weather the hole should be watered before putting the plant in position, and it is worth bearing in mind the particular needs of the plant being handled—for example, grit can be added under those plants which like free-draining soil.

The roots of the plant should be spread out in all directions, and any twisting or tangling found in the root system of a containerized plant should be straightened out. Some types of plants have only a weak grip on the soil that surrounds their roots, and with these every effort should be made to keep the root ball intact. After planting, the plant should be firmed in, by treading lightly on the soil. This will give the plant stability and ensure that the roots are actually in contact with the soil and not lying helplessly in an air pocket. Treading in should not be overdone if the soil is at all wet.

With tall perennials, staking is often an issue. Some plants have a tendency to sprawl or lean out awkwardly after wind or rain, and as a result look untidy and can harm adjacent plants by leaning on them. On the whole, cultivated varieties are more likely to need staking than the tough, wiry, wild ones. One should never stake a plant unless it is really necessary—sometimes it is better to accept that a few stems will have to be cut away when they start leaning out, rather than have the intrusiveness of stakes—to say nothing of all the labour involved.

If you do stake, it should be done early. Once a plant has leant out, its stems or branches become distorted when the tips try to reestablish verticality, and straightening them out afterwards is an almost impossible task. This is why one has to get ahead of the game and get the stakes in before

any trouble occurs. Some gardeners favour bamboo canes, others use twiggy branches such as are traditionally used by vegetable growers for growing peas, and are therefore called pea-sticks. The old-fashioned pea-stick, produced from coppiced hazel bushes, is now almost unobtainable, but brushwood and prunings from one's own garden can be used instead. If canes are used, it is better to have too many than too few, if the plant is to sit comfortably. Some gardeners favour horizontal metal hoops supported on two or three legs. Other practices include the use of a horizontal layer of wire mesh, which will be hidden from view later when the plants grow through it (but looks dire when it is put in). My own preference is for the pea-sticks, simply because they look the most natural. Whatever is used needs to be done in the most discreet and invisible way possible. If string is used to tie the plant in to the supports, it should never pull the stems of the plant out of vertical. The way one sees delphiniums staked in many gardens quite ruins their appearance, and from my point of view as a garden visitor rules out the chance of a decent photograph of the plant.

A feature of some tall perennials, such as rudbeckias, is the large amount of greenery visible at the lower two-thirds of the plant with the flowers all concentrated at the top. One practical way to improve this situation is to pinch out the growing tips of the section of the plant nearest the front of the border. Doing this makes the pinched-out stems develop later and also flower on shorter stems, and these shorter stems help to hide the foliage of the rest of the plant. The pinching out is best done in late May.

Obtrusive delphinium staking, which would be unacceptable in the border.

A border of perennial plants is not a natural phenomenon, even if it resembles one in some respects, so we should not imagine that the soil in the border can provide an endless resource of nutrients and goodness. Intervention is therefore necessary to maintain the fertility of the soil, so that we can maximize the floral display provided by the plants. The border will need feeding at least once a year, preferably in the spring. Fish and bone meal fertilizer is best, a natural product; alternatively, one can use some other general purpose fertilizer. The border should be watered afterwards unless rain is forecast, as the fertilizer will not be available for the plant until it is dissolved in water. Mulching the border will also help to keep weeds at bay and retain moisture during the hot weather.

Some kinds of plant will go on forever,

A few lurking stakes still showing among the delphiniums in a border at Burton Agnes in Yorkshire.

and only ask to be left alone, but there are others which benefit from being dug up and replanted every three or four years. Achilleas are an example of plants which can exhaust themselves, and such plants should be lifted and only the strongest and healthiest pieces replanted.

Deadheading should be carried out from time to time, to improve the look of the plant and to encourage the plant to produce more flowers. A plant expends a considerable amount of its resources when it produces its seeds, and there is no point in it weakening itself by running to seed if we have no use for the seeds. Deadheading should not be done mechanically, but using one's eyes to make sure the appearance of the plant is being improved rather than damaged. Cutting down perennial plants in the autumn should also be done to strengthen the plants. This is not just an aesthetic exercise to tidy up the garden. It also has a practical function in encouraging the plant to produce a new flush of basal growth which will help the plant survive through the winter.

PART II

DIRECTORY OF TALL PERENNIALS

THE PLANTS IN THIS BOOK ARE, for the most part, the giants of the perennial world: those that can reach a height of 165 cm (5½ ft). The original plan for the book was to include all perennials over 135 cm (4½ ft), but eventually it became clear that this was going to make the book far too thick. A few additional genera also had to be excluded for reasons of space, such as *Agapanthus* and *Rodgersia*, where the main body of the plant is medium or low height, but the flower spikes can reach 165 cm in one or two species or varieties.

The arrangement of the plants into the chapters of Part II is governed by the idea that the most important thing about a plant is not any temporary feature such as the colour of its flowers, but the overall effect of the plant in the garden. What is the impact of the plant as seen from the dining-room window? Is it even visible? Many a plant looks attractive when viewed in that close-focus, eyeball-to-flower manner we use when we are in plantsman mode, but it may make very little contribution to the garden picture. If our eye is on the garden as well as on the plants, we need to adopt what might be called a holistic approach when selecting plants. Does the plant do anything for the rest of the year, for instance, when not in flower? Some ornamental grasses look wonderful in September, but what about those spring and summer months when there is only a tuft of green grass lurking in the border? The foliage of some ornamental grasses is so unimpressive that it risks being pulled out, mistaken for a grass weed.

Plants with the strongest character are commonly described as "architectural." These are the ones that attract our attention, are strong on form, distinct in habit, known for their bold foliage, or are fierce and pointed, such as phormiums and yuccas. Tall plants inevitably have more impact than short ones, but size is not the whole story. Large, leafy plants, such as persicarias, echinaceas, *Campanula lactiflora* or Michaelmas daisies for instance, offer only rounded and bushy greenery, until they flower.

Page 50: Well-graduated heights and exciting colours, provided by eupatoriums at the back, ornamental grasses in the middle, with rudbeckias and *Lobelia*, and sedums at the front.

If we consider the whole personality of a plant when choosing what to grow, we find that some architectural plants are best described as "statuesque"—cardoons for example, with their heads in the sky, their tall stems like backbones and their elegant grey leaves like arms. Even more statuelike are the onopordums, which are so anthropomorphic that they would give you quite a turn on a moonlit night, should you be creeping around the garden at midnight on some illicit business. Many umbellifers (members of the cow parsley family) such as *Molopospermum*, *Conium* and *Ferula* are of statuesque proportions, but umbellifers have a chapter of their own.

Another way to attract attention, if you are a plant, is to have spikes, and these may consist of long spearlike leaves, as phormiums have, or, alternatively, prickles and thorns. Some sensitive gardeners think that having too many phormiums in the garden could be intimidating, while prickly thistle-like plants, such as *Cirsium* species or sea hollies (*Eryngium*), are liable to make the garden-visiting mothers of errant toddlers

The flowers of *Stipa gigantea* are stunning in the sunlight, but the foliage has little to offer before the plant comes into bloom.

A cluster of yuccas at Abbottsbury Gardens in Dorset, high impact plants attracting attention to themselves, surrounded by various smaller, more average plants.

Plants such as a white *Campanula lactiflora* and a veronica, with their rounded, bushy shapes, are pleasing but not strong enough in character to be called "architectural."

feel quite anxious. And, of course, such plants have an effect on the eye as well as on the hand.

The opposite of an architectural plant might be called a "social" plant or, in design terms, a "filler," since these plants are used to fill the spaces between the stronger-charactered plants. The difference between the two kinds of plants can be easily seen among the ornamental grasses. *Stipa gigantea* makes a good specimen, or architectural plant, as do *Festuca mairei*, *Carex buchananii* and many *Miscanthus* varieties. But other grasses would look ineffective planted as an isolated tuft. *Stipa calamagrostis*, for instance, *S. tenuissima*, *Calamagrostis brachytricha* and many other "average" grasses need to be planted in broad swathes, or in long bands, as if they were along the hedgerow or on the prairie.

Of course, colour can create impact just as much as size or shape, and plants grown for their flowers are to be found in the later chapters of Part II. Bright orange leaps out at you, while blue recedes. Red grabs your attention, but black flowers are almost invisible if you aren't standing right next to the plant. Bright yellow is bold and creates a "cheerful" kind of mood, but brown plants are almost undetectable on brown soil.

Foliage also has a lot to offer. Variegated foliage can brighten up a shady corner, but purple foliage is so dark that the plant may only be noticeable if you are right beside it. Sometimes the effect can be dramatic, and a question of size, as in the huge leaves of *Heracleum mantegazzianum* or *Rheum palmatum*. Alternatively, it may be the distinct leaf shape or the resultant over-all textural effect that provides the interest, as in *Macleaya*, or *Ligularia*. The foliage may be silvery, as in artemisias, blue-green as in *Melianthus*, variegated as in *Miscanthus sinensis* var. *condensatus* 'Cosmopolitan' or purple-brown as in *Ageratina altissima* 'Chocolate'. The leaves may be delicate and feathery, or coarse as in a silphium. The

The silvery white outlines of onopordums have an almost human, or vaguely skeleton-like outline, as seen here at the Old Vicarage, East Ruston, Norfolk.

A large, spiky phormium, unignorable and possibly intimidating,
by the side of the path at Hyde Hall, Essex.

plant may simply provide a large, leafy effect as in *Sambucus ebulus*, *Datisca cannabina* or one of the large perennial aralias.

Characteristic habit, or way of growing, is another feature which contributes to a plant's personality. Some are unique and instantly recognizable, such as the extraordinary *Helianthus salicifolius*. The interest of some grasses is strictly limited to their flowering heads, but one of the attractions of *Miscanthus* varieties is their habit, which in this case is the graceful way the foliage arches outwards, a characteristic which is of value long before the attractive flowerheads appear. Many ferns also have a characteristic pattern of growth which contributes to their distinctive overall shape, as in the tall royal fern, *Osmunda regalis*.

4

ARCHITECTURAL PERENNIALS

This chapter includes some of the most dramatic and architectural plants that can be grown in gardens, high impact plants, strong on form and shape. Many of these make good specimen plants, and need space and air around them to allow their outline to be clearly visible. Some of these plants have spearlike leaves, phormiums for instance; others have prickly foliage. In the case of echiums and verbascums, it is the outline of the whole plant that is remarkable.

Beschorneria

AGAVACEAE

About ten perennials from Mexico, resembling yuccas and related to agaves, preferring full sun and soil that is well drained but does not dry out. As Zone 8 or 9 plants, they need protection from cold weather in winter, except in favourable districts.

Beschorneria septentrionalis

ORIGIN: Mexico
SIZE: 150–210 × 75–105 cm; 5–7 × 2½–3½ ft
FLOWERING TIME: early summer
FLOWER COLOUR: red and green
Sun
Zone 9
Propagate by seed or division
Very high impact

DESCRIPTION: Clusters of large basal rosettes, with long, fleshy, overwintering leaves, which are pale green in colour, glossy and pointed. The long, red flower stems lean out at odd angles and bear green flowers with red bracts. Named as recently as 1987.

'Ding Dong'. Large numbers of red and green bell-shaped flowers, long flowering. Possibly a hybrid with *Beschorneria decosteriana*. Flower stalk 210 cm (7 ft) high.

Beschorneria yuccoides

ORIGIN: Mexico
SIZE: 120–180 × 120–180 cm; 4–6 × 4–6 ft
FLOWERING TIME: summer
FLOWER COLOUR: red and green
Sun
Zone 8
Propagate by seed or division

The extraordinary red flower stems of *Beschorneria yuccoides* leaning out at odd angles from the grey-green, spiky, yucca-like foliage.

Very high impact

DESCRIPTION: Irregular clusters of grey-green, overwintering rosettes, with sharply pointed, but slightly floppy, leaves, not always as neat as one might like, and tidying them up is not that easy. Well-established plants produce long red flower stems, which lean out at odd angles and bear greenish flowers with prominent pinkish red bracts.

'Quicksilver'. Leaves more silvery than usual.

Cirsium

ASTERACEAE
thistle

A genus of about 200 perennial or biennial plants, including many of the thistles grow-ing wild in temperate regions of the world. Many of them have a slightly fierce charm of their own, but are best left where they belong. The thistle *Cirsium helenioides* (syn. *C. heterophyllum*) is sometimes offered, but is not good enough for the garden. The same is true for thistles in the related genus *Carduus*, which also has some attractive species likely to cause regret if brought into the garden. *Cirsium rivulare* 'Atropurpureum' is a little too short to be included. Gardening gloves are required.

Cirsium eriophorum

woolly thistle

ORIGIN: western and central Europe, Balkans

SIZE: 90–500 × 45–90 cm; 3–16 × 1½–3 ft

FLOWERING TIME: late summer
FLOWER COLOUR: dark red
Sun
Zone 6
Interesting seed heads
Propagate by seed or root cuttings
High impact
DESCRIPTION: Clover-red flowers emerge
from huge, rounded, woolly silvery heads
up to 7 cm (2¾ in) wide. Spiny pinnate
leaves, on an upright stem, altogether
making a very sculptural plant. Wonderful seed heads occur later. Only fit for the
floral meadow, and even there it might well
become a nuisance by seeding too prolifically. A rare British native, which happens
to grow on the limestone hills a few miles
from the author's house, where it reaches
about 90 cm (3 ft). The idea of a 5 m (16 ft)
high plant, as can occur in parts of Europe,
is truly awe-inspiring.

Cirsium japonicum

ORIGIN: Japan
SIZE: 30–200 × 22–45 cm; 1–6½ × ¾–1½ ft
FLOWERING TIME: summer
FLOWER COLOUR: rose pink
Sun
Zone 6
Useful for flower arrangement
Propagate by seed or division
High impact
DESCRIPTION: Pom-poms of rose-pink to
lilac flowers forming a head up to 5 cm
(2 in) wide, on toothed or pinnate foli-
age. 'Pink Beauty' and 'Rose Beauty' tend
to be shorter. A short-lived perennial, or
biennial.

The beautiful but fiercely prickly heads
and silvery foliage of the woolly thistle,
Cirsium eriophorum, growing wild in a
nature reserve in Gloucestershire.

Cynara

ASTERACEAE
About ten thistlelike perennials from the
Mediterranean and the Canary Islands.

Cynara cardunculus

cardoon, globe artichoke
ORIGIN: southwestern Europe, Morocco
SIZE: 150–210 × 90 cm; 5–7 × 3 ft
FLOWERING TIME: summer
FLOWER COLOUR: mauve-pink
Sun
Zone 6
Useful for flower arrangement
Interesting seed heads
Propagate by seed, cuttings or root cuttings
Very high impact
DESCRIPTION: A superb foliage plant with

tall, thistlelike flowerheads. It forms a very large rosette of overwintering leaves which are long, arching, silvery grey and often spiny at the tips. The mauve-pink flowerheads are borne on tall vertical stems, which bear further, much smaller arching leaves. Long-flowering. The hard, spherical base of the flowerheads is formed from dark prickly bracts, which are more fleshy and less spiny in the *Cynara cardunculus* Scolymus Group, the edible globe artichoke. The stems need to be cut down when they are past their best. You are supposed to get better foliage if you don't allow the plant to flower, but this would seem a pity. The winter effect of the foliage is particularly valuable in the garden. Best on good, fertile soil. 'Florist

Beautiful death—the heads of a cardoon, *Cynara cardunculus*, providing interest and ornament, even though officially they are long since dead.

A magnificent clump of cardoons, *Cynara cardunculus*, with arching silvery grey foliage and thistle-topped heads, growing at Gravetye Manor, Sussex.

Cardy' has large flowers but is unlikely to exceed 150 cm (5 ft).

Scolymus Group (syn. *C. scolymus*). Generally a little shorter, though they may still reach 180 cm (6 ft). They are grown as a vegetable—the base of the flower-head and the rounded fleshy bracts are the parts used. The plant is now thought to be a form created by selection over the course of centuries, rather than a separate species. Variable from seed, and saved seeds from a particular plant will not be reliable. The named varieties of globe artichoke are too short to be included, and so is *Cynara baetica* subsp. *maroccana* (formerly *C. hystrix*).

'White Form'. White flowers.

Echinops
ASTERACEAE
globe thistle

Echinops species are characterized by their remarkable spherical flowerheads, in shades of blue, grey-blue or white, held on strong, upright stems above the foliage. The giant species *E. giganteus* reaches 3 m (10 ft) in height, but sadly this is not in cultivation. It is best to plant globe thistles in groups, so that the overall width of the group is at least twice the height of the plant. They prefer hot, sunny positions in well-drained soil. All those listed may require support. There are about 120 perennials, biennials and annuals, from Europe, the Mediterranean, western and central temperate Asia, and tropical montane Africa.

Echinops bannaticus
ORIGIN: southeastern and central Europe
SIZE: 75–150 (–210) × 60–90 cm; 2½–5 (–7) × 2–3 ft
FLOWERING TIME: summer
FLOWER COLOUR: grey-blue
Sun
Zone 5
Useful for flower arrangement
Interesting seed heads
Propagate by division or root cuttings
High impact
DESCRIPTION: A majestic plant, with spherical grey-blue flowerheads, held just above the dense foliage. The leaves are downy on the upper surface and white underneath, slightly spiny at the tips. Usually not more than 150 cm (5 ft) except in two of the varieties listed here.

'Albus'. White flowerheads.

'Taplow Blue'. Steely blue. 150–180 cm (5–6 ft).

'The Giant' is said to reach 210 cm (7 ft).

Echinops exaltatus
ORIGIN: eastern Europe, western Russia
SIZE: 75–200 × 60–100 cm; 2½–6½ × 2–3½ ft
FLOWERING TIME: mid to late summer
FLOWER COLOUR: white
Sun
Zone 3
Useful for flower arrangement
Interesting seed heads
Propagate by division or root cuttings
High impact
DESCRIPTION: White flowerheads. Leaves downy underneath, with a few slender spines.

The spherical, silvery blue heads of a globe thistle, *Echinops bannaticus*, over excellent silvery foliage, at Cambridge University Botanic Garden, England.

The metallic blue heads of *Echinops bannaticus* 'Taplow Blue' in the Weihenstephan Gardens, at the Fachhochschule near Freising, Germany.

Echinops maracandicus

ORIGIN: Turkestan
SIZE: 180–210 × 75–105 cm; 6–7 × 2½–
   3½ ft
FLOWERING TIME: mid to late summer
FLOWER COLOUR: silvery blue
Sun
Zone 4
Useful for flower arrangement
Interesting seed heads
Propagate by division or root cuttings
High impact
DESCRIPTION: Large, silvery blue heads, on
branching stems.

Echinops sphaerocephalus

ORIGIN: southern and central Europe, west-
   ern Russia
SIZE: 120–200 × 75–120 cm; 4–6½ ×
   2½–4 ft
FLOWERING TIME: summer
FLOWER COLOUR: greyish white
Sun
Zone 3
Useful for flower arrangement
Interesting seed heads
Propagate by division or root cuttings
High impact
DESCRIPTION: Greyish white flowerheads
up to 6 cm (2½ in) wide. Greyish, downy
leaves, white underneath, edged with a few
short spines. 'Arctic Glow' is shorter.

Other Echinops Varieties

'Nivalis'. White flowerheads, with silver
foliage, on a plant of slender habit. Possibly
a selection of *Echinops tournefortii*, a species
not otherwise in cultivation. 150–200 cm
(5–6½ ft).

Echium

BORAGINACEAE

Tall echiums are distinct and exotic-looking
plants, forming one or more rosettes which
tower up into a tall, narrow, pointed, vertical spire. They are on the borderline of
hardiness in temperate areas. Several other
interesting species, such as *Echium wild-
pretii*, are monocarpic or biennial. Various
named forms are offered as seed strains.
About 40 biennials, perennials and shrubs,
from southern Europe, the Canary Islands,
western Asia, and Africa.

Echium pininana

ORIGIN: Canary Islands
SIZE: 180–300 × 45–75 cm; 6–10 × 1½–
   2½ ft
FLOWERING TIME: summer
FLOWER COLOUR: blue and pink
Sun
Zone 9
Interesting seed heads
Propagate by seed
Very high impact
DESCRIPTION: A single-stemmed plant,
with small blue or rose-pink flowers, the
stem densely packed along its full height
with long, narrow, rough-textured leaves. A
short-lived perennial or biennial, it is grown
more for its statuesque outline than any-
thing else. It self-seeds in favourable areas,
and can even become a nuisance.

A startling echium, like a rocket taking off, at Tresco Abbey Gardens, Scilly Isles, Cornwall.

Eryngium

APIACEAE

sea holly, eryngo

About 240 species of perennials, annuals and biennials, worldwide except for sub-Saharan Africa. Most have spiny leaves, some with an attractive grey, metallic sheen. The flowerheads are teasel-like and surrounded by spiny bracts. South American eryngiums are distinct from the Old World species, having longer, narrower leaves, which are spiny rather than merely prickly, and the plant as a whole tends to have a more angular outline. None of the Old World species are tall enough for us. All prefer well-drained soil and full sun. Lime tolerant. It is necessary to tidy up the clumps of spiny foliage every so often, but this is not a task to be undertaken lightly—handle those spiny leaves with care.

Eryngium ebracteatum

ORIGIN: South America

SIZE: 60–200 × 45–120 cm; 2–6½ × 1½–4 ft

FLOWERING TIME: mid to late summer

FLOWER COLOUR: maroon and brown

Sun

Zone 8

Useful for flower arrangement

Interesting seed heads

Propagate by division or root cuttings

High impact

DESCRIPTION: A few tall branching stems bear clusters of many small, hard, greenish maroon-coloured flowerheads, which lack the usual accompanying bracts, held on very fine wiry stems. A clump of long narrow, blue-green, overwintering, basal leaves, up to 100 cm (3½ ft) long, spiny here and there.

Eryngium eburneum

ORIGIN: South America

SIZE: 75–200 × 60–90 cm; 2½–6½ × 2–3 ft

FLOWERING TIME: summer

FLOWER COLOUR: greenish white

Sun

Zone 8

Useful for flower arrangement

Interesting seed heads

Propagate by division or root cuttings

High impact

DESCRIPTION: Clusters of many small, round, greenish white flowerheads, almost like marbles, in branching sprays, on tall, silvery, more or less vertical stems, which arise from a basal clump of long, narrow, overwintering leaves, 100 cm (3½ ft) long, and fiercely spined along the edges. Sometimes incorrectly labelled as *Eryngium bromeliifolium*.

Eryngium pandanifolium

(syn. *E. decaisneanum*)

ORIGIN: South America

SIZE: 150–300 × 75–120 cm; 5–10 × 2½–4 ft

FLOWERING TIME: late summer

FLOWER COLOUR: maroon

Sun

Zone 8

Useful for flower arrangement

Interesting seed heads

Propagate by division or root cuttings

Very high impact

DESCRIPTION: Perhaps the most amazing of all eryngiums. Many small, hard, rounded, greenish maroon-coloured flowerheads, in airy clusters on tall stems, much-branched at the top. A large mound of arching, spiny, basal foliage, with blue-green, evergreen leaves up to 200 cm (6½ ft) long. Imagine an eryngium crossed with a pampas grass. Water generously for sumptuous results.

var. *lassauxii*. Greenish white flowerheads, with spinier foliage.

'Physic Purple'. Later flowering, maroon flowerheads, on shorter stems. May be less hardy.

The elegant flower-heads and spiny, spiky leaves of the South American sea holly, *Eryngium pandanifolium* var. *lassauxii*, at Rosemoor, North Devon.

Eryngium serra

ORIGIN: Brazil, Argentina
SIZE: 120–200 × 75–105 cm; 4–6½ × 2½–3½ ft
FLOWERING TIME: late summer
FLOWER COLOUR: greenish white
Sun
Zone 8
Useful for flower arrangement
Interesting seed heads
Propagate by division or root cuttings
High impact
DESCRIPTION: Clusters of small, rounded, greenish white flowerheads, on tall, branching stems, arising from a clump of long, narrow, evergreen leaves, up to 60 cm (2 ft) long, edged with spines. Variable, or maybe more than one species bears this name in cultivation.

Eryngium yuccifolium

rattlesnake master
ORIGIN: eastern United States
SIZE: 75–180 × 75–105 cm; 2½–6 × 2½–3½ ft
FLOWERING TIME: late summer
FLOWER COLOUR: blue-grey or greenish
Sun or shade
Zone 4
Useful for flower arrangement
Interesting seed heads
Propagate by division or root cuttings
High impact
DESCRIPTION: Variable. Clusters of grey-green, silvery blue or greenish white flowerheads, on tall stems, arising from a clump of long, narrow, blue-green foliage, edged with 5 cm (2 in) spines.

Onoportum

ASTERACEAE

giant thistle

About 40 species of thistles, from the Mediterranean and western Asia. Only one is commonly seen in cultivation. Gardening gloves are required when handling the plant.

Onopordum acanthium

Scotch thistle

ORIGIN: central and southern Europe, western Asia

SIZE: 150–300 × 60–90 cm; 5–10 × 2–3 ft

FLOWERING TIME: summer

FLOWER COLOUR: purple and white

Sun

Zone 6

Propagate by seed

Very high impact

DESCRIPTION: An archetypal architectural plant, with excellent foliage. The thistle flowers have purple florets, with a very white, prickly and rounded base to the flowerhead. The stems are white and thorny, bearing beautiful silvery white foliage, the whole forming an open, anthropomorphic, skeleton-like plant with elegant branches like arms. A biennial or short-lived perennial, it sows itself, but not enough to be a nuisance. The mature plant is tap-rooted, so if seedlings need to be moved, it should be done when they are very small—if at all. The whole plant should be cut down in September, or when it begins to look tacky. A good plant is a wonderful sight in the sunlight on a June day (the dark background of a large evergreen shrub or yew hedge is ideal) and a ghostly spectre at night, caught in a shaft of moonlight. There is also a white-flowered form.

Sometimes called the Scotch thistle, not because it is very common in Scotland, but because it is said that in the 16th century James V of Scotland chose it as his emblem. The flowerheads appear on various British coins.

The almost anthropomorphic shapes of *Onopordum acanthium*, with its silvery white limbs and thistle flowerheads.

Onopordum bracteatum

ORIGIN: eastern Mediterranean
SIZE: 150–180 × 60–75 cm; 5–6 × 2–2½ ft
FLOWERING TIME: summer
FLOWER COLOUR: purple
Sun
Zone 6
Useful for flower arrangement
Propagate by seed
Very high impact
DESCRIPTION: Similar to *Onopordum acanthium*, but a little shorter. Said to be the best onopordum, but if so, it is unaccountably very rare in cultivation.

Onopordum nervosum

(syn. *O. arabicum*)
ORIGIN: Spain, Portugal
SIZE: 180–300 × 75–120 cm; 6–10 × 2½–4 ft
FLOWERING TIME: summer
FLOWER COLOUR: pink
Sun
Zone 8
Useful for flower arrangement
Propagate by seed
Very high impact
DESCRIPTION: Similar to *Onopordum acanthium*, but not so hardy. It has smaller flowerheads but larger leaves, which are silvery green in colour.

Phormium

PHORMIACEAE
New Zealand flax
Bold foliage plants with powerful architectural impact. The clusters of evergreen, spearlike leaves are tough and full of fibres, and are grouped in fans of three or more.

They may be fiercely vertical or arch over gracefully. The flower spikes are curious and exotic and often twice the height of the foliage, but of no great floral merit or colour.

In the wild, phormiums flourish in moist soil, in locations where the air is moist. However, they don't look their best in very exposed positions, if the leaves have to take a constant battering from strong winds. The red- and purple-foliaged varieties are liable to become diseased in very humid conditions and also suffer or perish in very cold weather. On the whole, the green forms are the hardiest, the red and purple-brown the most tender, with the variegated ones in between. The foliage constantly renews itself, and the dead leaves should be cut away as soon as they become unsightly, with sharp secateurs, as near to the base as possible.

There are just two species, from New Zealand and Norfolk Island in the Pacific Ocean. A large number of varieties with coloured foliage has become available relatively recently, mostly of mixed parentage between the two species. The colours of many of the red-variegated varieties tend to fade as the plant ages. Some of the smaller varieties not listed here may well have flowers which are over 165 cm (5½ ft).

Phormium cookianum

(syn. *P. colensoi*)
ORIGIN: New Zealand
SIZE: 90–200 × 75–210 cm; 3–6½ × 2½–7 ft
FLOWERING TIME: mid to late summer
FLOWER COLOUR: brownish
Sun or shade
Zone 8
Useful for flower arrangement

Interesting seed heads
Propagate by division
Very high impact
DESCRIPTION: Mid-green spiky foliage. The height is dependent on conditions, much taller in mild and favourable areas. The flowers are dark greenish brown with yellow, orange or dark red markings, worthy of close attention, but usually only seen in silhouette. This species is distinguishable from *Phormium tenax* by its arching leaves and its pendant seed pods. The species plant is rarely grown. Unfortunately, one of the finest of all phormiums, *P. cookianum* subsp. *hookeri* 'Tricolor', is a little too short to be included here.

Phormium tenax

New Zealand flax
ORIGIN: New Zealand, Norfolk Island
SIZE: 120–180 (–300) × 90–150 cm; 4–6 (–10) × 3–5 ft
FLOWERING TIME: mid to late summer
FLOWER COLOUR: greenish brown
Sun
Zone 8
Useful for flower arrangement
Interesting seed heads
Propagate by division
Very high impact
DESCRIPTION: A splendid foliage plant of maximum impact, in fact, the strongly vertical forms are almost too aggressive-looking, and some sensitive people feel they need to be used with a degree of moderation. The wild species is green, or silvery green, often with a thin dark line along the edges of the leaves. The foliage is usually not more than 150 cm (5 ft) high in temperate gardens. The flowerheads are interesting when inspected in detail, with reddish markings on brown, but are usually too high in the air to be seen closely. Prefers moist soil, but very tolerant of average conditions.

'Guardsman'. Red variegated, with erect habit, the bronze leaves striped with red and pink. Some similarity to 'Sundowner', but the leaves are more slender and the red variegation is brighter. Slow to increase. Introduced by Dawn Nurseries of Auckland, New Zealand. 150–210 cm (5–7 ft).

'Merlot'. Spiky upright habit. Leaves are plum red to purple, with narrow black margin, and silver-grey on the reverse. Recently selected by Lyndale Nursery of Auckland, New Zealand. 150–180 cm (5–6 ft).

Purpureum Group (syns. 'Rubrum', 'Atropurpureum'). Variable. Plants with purple, wine-red, maroon or brownish green foliage. Usually strongly vertical. Most forms are among the tallest varieties. 150–270 cm (5–9 ft).

'Radiance' (syn. 'Pare Kore Tawa'). A very old variety with erect habit, with broad, yellowish leaves, with a few green stripes near the margins. 150–180 cm (5–6 ft).

'Sundowner'. An attractive red-bronze variegated form, with upright habit. After a season or two of bronze-green flashed with bright red, this variety settles down to a pleasing biscuit colour, flushed with pink and green. Newer foliage is always brighter. Introduced by Barry Porteous of Brown's Bay, New Zealand. 120–210 cm (4–7 ft).

'Variegatum'. Variable. Plants usually upright, variously striped with green and yellow. Known since the 1870s. 120–180 cm (4–6 ft).

An upright grower, *Phormium tenax* 'Sundowner' displays its curious colours: olive green, biscuit, pink and creamy yellow.

'Wildwood'. Darkest purple foliage, arching gracefully over at the tips. A wonderful, exotic phormium. Originated at Wildwood Nursery, southern California, where it was grown simply as 'Purpureum'. 120–180 cm (4–6 ft).

Other *Phormium* Varieties

'Chocolate Cookie'. Very dark bronze foliage, upright but arching over towards the top of the leaves. Tolerates part shade. Of mixed descent, recently selected in New Zealand. 150–180 cm (5–6 ft).

Verbascum

SCROPHULARIACEAE

mullein

Verbascums form tall spires, which rise from a basal rosette that is often silvery or woolly, and an attractive feature of the plant in itself. Most are biennials, others are short-lived perennials or annuals. There are about 300 species, from Europe and Turkey, all following the same basic pattern. They hybridize quite indiscriminately, and this has resulted in considerable confusion in the naming of plants in gardens and nurseries, and several well-known garden plants could well be incorrectly labelled. The English name is pronounced "mullin" and is probably derived, via Old French, from the Latin *mollis*, meaning "soft."

Full sun and well-drained soil suits them best. They are perfect for the gravel garden, if you have one. Winter wet will only shorten their already brief lives. Cutting down the plant after flowering can often promote additional later flowering. A sheltered position is needed because the foliage is easily damaged, and it also keeps the plant upright. In Great Britain, they seem to prefer the east side of the country, with its longer summer sunshine hours, rather than the wetter west. Verbascums are best grown among plants which are much shorter than themselves so that their statuesque outline can be seen to advantage.

Almost all the tall species and varieties come in shades of yellow or white—for a wider range of colours one must choose the shorter varieties. Named varieties should be propagated by root cuttings, as seeds are unlikely to come true if other species are growing nearby. Many will self-seed, especially where conditions are favourable.

Verbascum blattaria

ORIGIN: Europe, temperate Asia; introduced in the United States

SIZE: 105–180 × 45 cm; 3½–6 × 1½ ft

FLOWERING TIME: summer
FLOWER COLOUR: yellow or white
Sun
Zone 6
Interesting seed heads
Propagate by seed
High impact
DESCRIPTION: Yellow or white flowers, over a basal rosette of crinkly green leaves. Pink forms are known in cultivation, though not in the wild, and are sometimes available.

f. *albiflorum*. Pure white flowers with purple centres.

Verbascum bombyciferum

(syn. *V.* 'Broussa')
ORIGIN: Turkey
SIZE: 120–180 × 45 cm; 4–6 × 1½ ft
FLOWERING TIME: midsummer
FLOWER COLOUR: yellow
Sun
Zone 6
Interesting seed heads
Propagate by seed
High impact
DESCRIPTION: Densely packed yellow flowers in branching spikes 60–90 cm (2–3 ft) high, on silvery stems branching at the base. Silvery white foliage. Basal leaves up to 45 cm (1½ ft) long. Biennial, or very short-lived perennial.

'Polarsommer' (syn. 'Arctic Summer'). Buttercup-yellow flowers. White, felted leaves. Up to 240 cm (8 ft).

Verbascum ×hybridum

Hybrids between *Verbascum pulverulentum* and *V. sinuatum*, neither of which is likely to be seen in cultivation. Felted rosettes of greyish green, ripple-edged foliage. Summer to early autumn. Zone 6.

'Banana Custard'. Very large flowers on tall spikes. 150–180 cm (5–6 ft).

'Wega'. Large, soft yellow flowers from furry, silvery buds, on multi-branched stems. 150–180 cm (5–6 ft).

The tall, woolly white spires and silver-grey rosette of a verbascum, growing in gravel at Denmans in Sussex.

Verbascum olympicum

ORIGIN: Greece, Turkey
SIZE: 150–180 (–300) × 60 cm; 5–6 (–10) ×
  2 ft
FLOWERING TIME: summer to autumn
FLOWER COLOUR: yellow
Sun
Zone 6
Interesting seed heads
Propagate by division
High impact
DESCRIPTION: Bright golden yellow flowers
on woolly white stems, often branching into
a candelabra. Leaves woolly, greyish white,
long, narrow and pointed, forming a very
large basal rosette which can be as much as
90 cm (3 ft) wide, but usually less. Biennial
or perennial. Self-seeding. One of the best
verbascums.

Verbascum phlomoides

ORIGIN: central and southern Europe, Bal-
  kans; introduced in the United States
SIZE: 45–200 × 45 cm; 1½–6½ × 1½ ft
FLOWERING TIME: summer
FLOWER COLOUR: yellow
Sun
Zone 6

Yellow-flowered verbascums, with *Verbena bonariensis* and other drought-
tolerant plants in the Dry Garden at Hyde Hall, Essex.

Interesting seed heads
Propagate by seed
High impact
DESCRIPTION: Yellow flowers on woolly
stems, white or yellowish. Foliage downy,
white or yellowish. Basal leaves up to 45 cm
(1½ ft). Biennial or short-lived perennial.

Verbascum thapsus

Aaron's rod
ORIGIN: Europe, including Great Britain,
temperate Asia; introduced in the United
States
SIZE: 150–200 × 45 cm; 5–6½ × 1½ ft
FLOWERING TIME: early to late summer
FLOWER COLOUR: yellow
Sun

Zone 3
Interesting seed heads
Propagate by division
High impact
DESCRIPTION: Yellow flowers on
unbranched stems. Leaves and stems woolly,
white or greyish. Basal leaves to 45 cm (1½
ft) long. Biennial or short-lived perennial.

Other Verbascum Varieties

'Monster'. Pale yellow, with red stamens,
on branching flower stems. Mid-green
leaves. Vigorous. Raised by Patricia Cooper
of Mundford, Norfolk. 240 cm (8 ft).

'Spica'. Large, cream-coloured flowers.
Grey foliage. 150–200 cm (5–6½ ft).

5

FOLIAGE PLANTS AND FERNS

Flowers come and go, but foliage goes on and on right through the season. In contrast to perennials such as echinaceas which are grown for their flowers with their leaves merely tolerated, this chapter offers plants whose foliage has dramatic form, interesting texture or good habit, but whose flowers may be a mere bonus. Leaves may not be as brilliantly coloured as flowers, but nevertheless foliage can contribute a great deal to the garden, whether bold, shapely, subtle, coloured or ferny.

Ageratina
ASTERACEAE
About 40 species from Central and South America. Best known for varieties of half-hardy bedding plants, which are much shorter. The following species has been moved around from genus to genus and is now placed here.

Ageratina altissima
(syns. *Eupatorium rugosum, Ageratum altissimum*)
white snakeroot
ORIGIN: southeastern Canada, central and eastern United States
SIZE: 120–180 × 60 cm; 4–6 × 2 ft
FLOWERING TIME: mid to late summer
FLOWER COLOUR: white
Sun or light shade
Zone 4
Useful for flower arrangement
Propagate by division
Moderate impact
DESCRIPTION: Clusters of white flowers, on upright stems, branching at the top, reminiscent of *Eupatorium*, where it formerly belonged. Nettle-like leaves. Intolerant of dry soil conditions in summer. Poisonous if eaten in quantity. Cows browsing on it produce poisonous milk. Not to be confused with *Eupatorium altissimum*.

'Chocolate'. Pink buds open to off-white flowers, in large clusters, with very dark chocolate or purple-blue foliage and stems. One of the best perennials for purple foliage. Selected by Richard Lighty of the Mt. Cuba Center, Delaware. 90–150 cm (3–5 ft).

Amicia
FABACEAE
Slightly tender, leafy perennials from the Andes and Mexico.

Amicia zygomeris
ORIGIN: Mexico
SIZE: 150–210 × 120 cm; 5–7 × 4 ft
FLOWERING TIME: summer to autumn
FLOWER COLOUR: yellow
Sun
Zone 9
Propagate by seed or cuttings
Subtle impact
DESCRIPTION: An unusual foliage sub-shrub, noteworthy for its unusual bracts, and best treated as a perennial in less favourable climates. Graceful sprays bearing blue-green leaves, curiously notched at the ends, and enclosed when young by pairs of unusual but attractive, large, purple-veined appendages or bracts. The plant is randomly dotted with pale golden-yellow pea flowers, over a long period. Tender in cool areas.

Aralia
spikenard
Araliaceae
Trees, shrubs, perennials and lianas from subtropical regions of the northern hemisphere. Most have very large pinnate leaves and widely spaced clusters of spherical flowers, unobtrusively coloured, followed by small, purple or black berries. About 40 species.

The unusual foliage of *Amicia zygomeris*, a species in the pea family from Mexico.

Aralia cachemirica
Himalayan spikenard
ORIGIN: Kashmir, Nepal
SIZE: 120–300 × 90–240 cm; 4–10 × 3–8 ft
FLOWERING TIME: summer
FLOWER COLOUR: greenish white
Light shade
Zone 4
Useful for flower arrangement
Purple berries
Propagate by seed or division
High impact
DESCRIPTION: Leafy bush with woody base, giving a somewhat tropical effect. Small, rounded, ivy-like flowers, greenish or creamy white, borne in open panicles on spiny, vertical stems, just above the foliage. The leaves are huge, but made up of many separate leaflets. Maroon-black berries

in the autumn. Best in rich, moist soil, in semi-shade or woodland fringes, but accepts full sun in cooler gardens. Should be cut to the ground in winter. The roots are large but easily damaged, and therefore resent disturbance or attempts at transplanting.

Aralia californica

California spikenard, elk clover
ORIGIN: Oregon, California
SIZE: 120–180 (–300) × 120–150 (–240) cm; 4–6 (–10) × 4–5 (–8) ft
FLOWERING TIME: summer
FLOWER COLOUR: white and pink
Shade
Zone 8
Useful for flower arrangement
Purple berries
Propagate by seed or division
High impact
DESCRIPTION: Sprays of small, rounded, starry, white or pink flowers, borne in open fatsia-like panicles on deep pink stems above the leafy foliage. A large leafy bush, with huge leaves, up to 90 cm (3 ft) long, made up of many separate leaflets on stems that carry milky sap. The stems are woody at the base. The foliage turns a warm buttery yellow in the autumn, with wine-red stems. Deep purple berries. Cultivation as for *Aralia cachemirica*, but less tolerant of sun. Native to stream banks.

Aralia cordata

(syn. *A. edulis*)
udo, Japanese spikenard
ORIGIN: China, Japan
SIZE: 135–270 × 120–240 cm; 4½–9 × 4–8 ft

FLOWERING TIME: summer
FLOWER COLOUR: white and pink
Sun or light shade
Zone 4
Useful for flower arrangement
Dark purple berries
Propagate by seed or division
Subtle impact
DESCRIPTION: A fast-growing leafy bush, with white or pale pink flower spikes, followed by dark purple berries. The leaves are very large, up to 120 cm (4 ft) long, made up of many separate leaflets. The new, soft shoots in spring are used as a vegetable in China and Japan, and also medicinally. Cultivation as for *Aralia cachemirica*.

subsp. *continentalis* (Manchurian or Korean spikenard). Native to eastern Russia, northeastern China, Korea and Japan. A smaller scale, less coarse plant. Greenish or creamy white flowers. Up to 180 cm (6 ft) high.

Aralia racemosa

American spikenard
ORIGIN: central and eastern United States
SIZE: 120–180 × 120–180 cm; 4–6 × 4–6 ft
FLOWERING TIME: early to midsummer
FLOWER COLOUR: pale green
Shade
Zone 3
Useful for flower arrangement
Purple berries
Propagate by seed or division
Moderate impact
DESCRIPTION: Shrub-like in appearance, with layers of mid-green foliage, which is not quite as neat as in its Asiatic relatives. Delicate spikes of pale green flowers. Prefers rich woodland soil and situation.

Artemisia

ASTERACEAE

wormwood, sage brush

About 300 species, from temperate areas worldwide, often powerfully scented, but not always pleasantly. Usually grey, silky or hairy, with much-divided foliage and insignificant flowers. *Artemisia dracunculus* is the herb tarragon, a "useful" plant, but too weedy-looking for the ornamental garden, 100–200 cm (3½–6½ ft). *Artemisia vulgaris*, mugwort, can reach 250 cm (8 ft), but this weed (or wildflower, depending on your point of view) and its variegated garden varieties are not usually more than 120 cm (4 ft) high. *Artemisia arborescens* is a first-rate silvery subshrubby foliage plant, but slightly too short to be included.

Artemisia lactiflora

white mugwort

ORIGIN: China, India, southern Asia

SIZE: 135–180 × 75–105 cm; 4½–6 × 2½–3½ ft

FLOWERING TIME: late summer

FLOWER COLOUR: cream

Sun or light shade

Zone 4

Propagate by division

Subtle impact

DESCRIPTION: Curiously the tallest *Artemisia* species in cultivation has the greenest leaves. Plumes of tiny cream-coloured flowers on upright stems clothed in jaggedly lobed leaves. Best kept away from plants with pure white flowers. Tough, but needs rich moist soil to do well. A companion for other tough-looking guys such as *Persicaria amplexicaulis* and eupatoriums.

Guizhou Group. Variable, but the best have mahogany stems, with foliage either flushed purple, or more interestingly a deep unusual iron grey. A seed strain from a plant expedition to Guizhou in 1985. Creamy white flowers, mid to late summer. To give better reassurance to the buyer, the best of these need to be selected, renamed and propagated vegetatively.

'Jim Russell'. Similar to Guizhou Group, but with more open, arching, white flowerheads.

'Rosenschleier'. Masses of small round buds and fluffy, grey, pinkish white flowers on deep purple branching stems, in elegant, airy sprays, contrasting with the jagged-edged, dark green foliage. Late summer. The name means "rose veil." Zone 5.

Begonia

BEGONIACEAE

About 900 species, mostly from tropical and subtropical areas, mainly from the Americas. Most are Zone 10 plants, and even the hardiest are hardly worth the struggle outdoors in temperate gardens.

Begonia luxurians

palm leaf begonia

ORIGIN: Brazil

SIZE: 150–200 × 60–120 cm; 5–6½ × 2–4 ft

FLOWERING TIME: summer

FLOWER COLOUR: creamy white

Light shade

Zone 9

Useful for flower arrangement

Propagate by division

Moderate impact

DESCRIPTION: This exotic-looking species doesn't resemble the average houseplant begonia at all, but has bright green, multi-fingered foliage—imagine a fleshy-leaved cannabis. A must for those trying to create the subtropical look in favoured areas.

Colocasia

ARACEAE

coco yam, taro

Six perennial species from tropical Asia, grown for their bold and exotic-looking foliage. They require plenty of protection in temperate areas, or alternatively they can be lifted and treated like dahlias. The more you feed them, the lusher they are. The tubers are used as food in some countries, sometimes called the "potato of the tropics," but are poisonous until cooked.

Colocasia esculenta

(syn. *C. antiquorum*)

coco yam

ORIGIN: tropical East Asia, but widely naturalized in the tropics

SIZE: 90–150 (–180) × 90 cm; 3–5 (–6) × 3 ft

FLOWERING TIME: summer

FLOWER COLOUR: greenish

Light shade

Zones 8–9

Useful for flower arrangement

Propagate by division

High to very high impact

DESCRIPTION: The aroid flowers are fairly insignificant, but the leaves are very striking and tropical-looking, somewhere between arrow-shaped and heart-shaped. Indispensable for those trying to create the exotic look. Good companions for cannas, ricinuses, phormiums, banana plants, hostas and ferns. They enjoy moist soil, and respond well to being watered generously and fed regularly.

'Big Dipper'. The classic "tropical effect" plant. Slightly greyish green leaves held almost horizontal at first, later more vertical, on purple, almost black stems. The leaves can hold a small amount of rain water, dipping to let the water go when full and returning to horizontal to refill again. 180 cm (6 ft).

'Black Magic'. Stunning, dusty, ink-black leaves, up to 60 cm (2 ft) long. 100–180 cm (3½–6 ft).

The bold and exotic leaves of *Colocasia esculenta* 'Black Magic' create a distinctly tropical effect but need protection in cool areas.

'Black Runner'. Purple-black leaves, up to 60 cm (2 ft) long. Spreads benignly, on moist soil. 180 cm (6 ft).

'Chicago Harlequin'. Variegated leaves.

'Coffee Cups'. Glossy olive-green leaves on purple-black stems which form cups that hold water, bending to empty when full. Found in the wild by Gregory Hambali of Indonesia. Spreads slightly in autumn. 180 cm (6 ft).

'Fontanesii'. Green leaves, up to 90 cm (3 ft) long, purple-tinted, on dark purple stems. One of the most reliable. Yellow aroid flowers up to 30 cm (1 ft) long in favoured locations. 100–200 cm (3½–6½ ft). Zone 7.

'Nancy's Revenge'. Leaves like a typical *Colocasia esculenta* at first, but as the weather warms up, splashed with creamy white in the centre, the colour seeming to creep up the veins towards the margins. Leaves 60 cm (2 ft) wide. Spreads benignly by side stolons in moist soil. Discovered by Jerry Krantz and introduced in 2000. 180 cm (6 ft).

'Ruffles'. Slightly grey-green leaves with attractively scalloped edges, 90 cm (3 ft) long. Clumps up vigorously in moist soil, and propagates well. Found by Hayes Jackson in a garden in Alabama. Zone 7. 180 cm (6 ft).

Other *Colocasia* Varieties

'Thailand Giant Strain'. Massive plants, raised as a seed strain, possibly of *Colocasia gigantea*. Park your car under it. If the huge, mid-green leaves lack anything in elegance of shape, they make up for in size: at least 120 cm (4 ft) wide and 150 cm (5 ft) long, held on suitably chunky pale green stems.

Large, pleasantly scented, white flowers. Introduced from seeds collected in the wild by Petra Schmidt in Kachanburi Province, Thailand. Eat your heart out, *Gunnera manicata*! 270 cm (9 ft) high.

Darmera

SAXIFRAGACEAE
umbrella plant
A genus of only one species.

Darmera peltata

(syn. *Peltiphyllum peltatum*)
ORIGIN: northwestern California, southwestern Oregon, Utah
SIZE: 90–150 × 90–indefinite cm; 3–5 × 3–indefinite ft
FLOWERING TIME: late spring
FLOWER COLOUR: pale pink
Sun or light shade
Zone 5
Propagate by seed or division
Moderate impact
DESCRIPTION: A unique collection of upturned green umbrellas during the summer, perfect for the water's edge. The leaves are large, rounded, glossy and slightly jagged around the edge, and in favourable situations they can be 60 cm (2 ft) wide. Its flowering arrangement, however, is less than ideal. The flowers appear long before the leaves; they are lamppost-like and reconizably giant saxifrage flowers, but look uncomfortable over a large patch of bare (and usually untidy) ground. The leaves then follow and swamp the remains of the flowers. The foliage can die splendidly in the autumn in shades of orange, yellow and

The umbrella leaves of *Darmera peltata* growing by a pool at Oxford Botanic Garden. A few of the saxifrage-like flowers can be seen on the extreme left.

red, although such a large amount of dead foliage creates work for the gardener tidying it all up.

Darmera loves moist soil and is most often seen by lakes and ponds, but it will also tolerate good-to-average fertile soil elsewhere. Much less coarse than its larger rival, *Gunnera*. Excellent with *Osmunda regalis*, *Euphorbia palustris*, filipendulas, rodgersias and waterside irises.

Datisca
DATISCACEAE
Two large perennials, one from Asia and the other from America, only one in cultivation.

Datisca cannabina
ORIGIN: eastern Mediterranean to the Himalayas
SIZE: 165–200 × 90–150 cm; 5½–6½ × 3–5 ft
FLOWERING TIME: late summer
FLOWER COLOUR: green
Sun
Zone 6
Interesting seed heads
Propagate by seed or division
Moderate impact
DESCRIPTION: A foliage plant, which (I am told) looks like cannabis. Mid-green pinnate foliage on tall stems—moderately interesting, but not startling. The tiny flowers are of no significance. Prefers a sunny

Gunnera manicata by the lake at Cambridge University Botanic Garden. The curious ground-hugging flowers can be seen below the partially unfurled leaves.

position with soil that doesn't dry out. Good with phormiums, *Miscanthus* varieties and silphiums.

Gunnera
GUNNERACEAE

A genus of extremes—either very large plants, or very small. Rounded leaves on long stalks. Forty to fifty species from southern Africa, South America, Australasia and the Pacific region.

Gunnera manicata
ORIGIN: Brazil
SIZE: 150–250 × 150–500 cm; 5–8 × 5–16 ft

FLOWERING TIME: late spring
FLOWER COLOUR: greenish
Sun or shade
Zone 8
Propagate by division
Very high impact
DESCRIPTION: A monster plant, with giant leaves which can reach 200 cm (6½ ft) wide. Like pampas grass and *Heracleum mantegazzianum*, this is a perennial of landscape proportions. Its flowerheads nestle at ground level, like soft, elongated, upward-pointing pine cones, sometimes reaching as much as 120 cm (4 ft) in height, but the plant is not grown for its flowers. The leaves emerge from rhizomes which form large lumpy shapes above ground level, and the sight

The giant umbrella leaves of *Gunnera manicata* beginning to unfurl in spring.

of the new leaves unfurling in spring is one of the attractions of the plant.

The leaves are umbrella-like, roughly circular in shape, but jagged-edged, and held in a rhubarb-like manner on tall, coarse, prickly stalks. Permanently moist soil is required, ideally at the water's edge. At the end of the season, the leaves collapse in a mushy heap, leaving a good deal of tidying up for the gardener to do. In cooler districts, the dead leaves can be used to protect the crowns. Planted jungle-fashion, so that garden visitors can walk with the leaves arching over

their heads, this species never fails to amaze. *Gunnera tinctoria* is similar but a little shorter.

Macleaya
PAPAVERACEAE
plume poppy
A small genus of superb foliage plants. Tall, with grey-green leaves and airy plume-like flowers and not at all poppy-like in appearance. The plants are clump-forming and spread gradually on light soils, rapidly on clay or moist soils. There are just two species, which come from the Far East.

Macleaya cordata
(syn. *Bocconia cordata*)
ORIGIN: eastern China, Japan
SIZE: 150–240 × 150–210 cm; 5–8 ×
     5–7 ft
FLOWERING TIME: summer
FLOWER COLOUR: cream and buff
Sun or light shade
Zone 3
Useful for flower arrangement
Propagate by division or root cuttings
High impact
DESCRIPTION: An excellent foliage plant with tall, upright stems clad to the ground with attractive, blue-grey-green leaves, whitish underneath and white veined. This is one of the few tall perennials whose foliage is a pleasure to look at from top to bottom. Approximately spade-shaped overall, the leaves are quite irregular and curiously indented around the edges, curved and lobed like the outline of an imaginary island in Indonesia. The floral heads can be as much as 60 cm (2 ft) long or more,

creamy buff in colour, paler than in the more commonly seen *Macleaya microcarpa*, and thought by some to be more refined in appearance. But the main advantage of this species over its rival *M. microcarpa* is that it spreads less rapidly.

Macleaya ×kewensis

Hybrids between *Macleaya cordata* × *M. microcarpa*, intermediate between the two species and named at the Royal Botanic Gardens, Kew. Zone 4. 200–240 cm (6½–8 ft).

'Flamingo'. Stems and leaves grey with a pink flush. Pinkish buff flowerheads.

Macleaya microcarpa

(syn. *Bocconia microcarpa*)
ORIGIN: central and western China
SIZE: 150–200 × 120–165 (–indefinite) cm;
    5–6½ × 4–5½ (–indefinite) ft
FLOWERING TIME: summer
FLOWER COLOUR: beige and pink
Sun or light shade
Zone 5
Useful for flower arrangement
Interesting seed heads
Propagate by division or root cuttings
High impact
DESCRIPTION: Foliage is very similar to *Macleaya cordata*, and equally good. Flowerheads are beige flushed pink or bronze. Liable to spread in favourable conditions, but, alternatively, in very dry or windswept places it may not flourish at all.

'Kelway's Coral Plume'. Foliage has a pink flush. Flowerheads are deep coral pink.

'Plum Tassel'. Smoky plum-red flowerheads. Introduced by Russell Garden in Oregon.

The white-veined leaves of macleayas are large, grey-green and strangely indented, and the tall stems are topped by pale coral-coloured plumes.

'Spetchley Ruby'. Reddish tinged foliage with red-flushed flowerheads, followed by red seed heads. From Spetchley Park, Worcestershire.

Melianthus

MELIANTHACEAE

honey bush

Attractive, blue-green, evergreen foliage plants from southern Africa. Technically they are shrubs, but best treated as if they were perennials in temperate climates. They need a sunny, sheltered position, dislike winter wet and require a protective winter mulch or larger material in cool areas. Six species, but only *Melianthus major* is commonly seen, where the climate permits. Sometimes used as summer bedding.

Melianthus comosus

ORIGIN: South Africa, Namibia

SIZE: 120–200 × 90–150 cm; 4–6½ × 3–5 ft

FLOWERING TIME: summer

FLOWER COLOUR: reddish brown

Sun

Zone 7

Useful for flower arrangement

Seed capsules

Propagate by seed or division

High impact

DESCRIPTION: Arching, pinnate, blue-grey leaves give a sumptuous subtropical effect. Each leaflet is toothed along the edges. The reddish brown flowers are only likely to appear in favoured areas, but these are not important, nor the inflated fruits that follow. Regrettably the foliage has an unpleasant smell.

Melianthus major

ORIGIN: Western Cape, South Africa

SIZE: 90–240 × 75–180 cm; 3–8 × 2½–6 ft

FLOWERING TIME: late summer

FLOWER COLOUR: maroon

Sun or shade

Zone 8

Useful for flower arrangement

Propagate by seed or division

High impact

DESCRIPTION: The most beautiful blue-green foliage plant available to gardeners. Arching branches and elegant leaves, a symphony in grey-blue-green. The leaves are scented of peanut butter, and can be up to 50 cm (20 in) long, each leaflet toothed along its edges. The spikes of red-brown flowers occur on the old wood, but are not significant and only appear in warmer locations. Protect the plant with prunings from other evergreen shrubs in winter, and cut right down in spring to promote a fresh set of leaves. There is said to be a variegated form, which is not very good and best ignored. Good with cannas, colocasias and scarlet dahlias.

'Antonow's Blue'. A particularly blue form, named after the late Steve Antonow of the Seattle, Washington, area, in whose garden it was discovered.

'Purple Haze'. Deep purple stems with purple-tinged foliage. Lush.

Melianthus minor

ORIGIN: South Africa

SIZE: 90–200 × 75–180 cm; 3–6½ × 2½–6 ft

FLOWERING TIME: late spring

FLOWER COLOUR: red and orange

Sun

Zone 8

Useful for flower arrangement

Interesting seed heads

Propagate by seed or division

Subtle impact

DESCRIPTION: An untidy bush, shorter than *Melianthus major*, but of more open habit. Clusters of red, orange and green flowers, with black nectar, form after a mild winter. Grey-green foliage. Not in the same league as *M. major*.

Osmunda

OSMUNDACEAE

Larger than average ferns, from damp and waterside habitats. Among them are some of the finest ferns that can be grown in temperate regions, the tallest apart from tree ferns. There are 12 species, from temperate and tropical East Asia and the Americas, of which about six are in cultivation, but only one reaches the required height.

Osmunda regalis

royal fern
ORIGIN: Europe, including Great Britain, western Asia

SIZE: 75–180 × 75–150 cm; 2½–6 × 2½–5 ft
Shade
Zone 2
Useful for flower arrangement
Propagate by spores or division
High impact

DESCRIPTION: The best large fern that can be grown in temperate gardens. In a waterside or permanently damp position, this fern develops into a huge clump of broad, leafy fronds, dark green, arching, and luxuriant. It can be grown in more average conditions, but will be a smaller plant. The fronds unfurl in spring from curious, curled-up, beige-coloured circles like small Catherine wheels, which are then borne aloft as the fronds develop. Deciduous.

This fern has separate fertile fronds, which carry the spores needed for reproduction. These are not very prominent, but

Osmunda regalis, the royal fern, at Cambridge University Botanic Garden, left, with a phormium and *Darmera peltata*.

look like narrow brown astilbe flowerheads, and for this reason this fern has misleadingly been called the flowering fern. The basal rhizome gradually becomes very large, and can project out of the ground by 45 cm (1½ ft). The overall height of the plant is unlikely to exceed 120 cm (4 ft) in cooler temperate regions. It tolerates a sunny position, as long it is permanently wet—otherwise shade is needed. Some of the varieties are shorter.

'Purpurascens'. More delicately divided than the typical form. Fronds purple when young, turning green later.

var. *spectabilis*. Native to North America. More upright, and likely to be taller. Young fronds tinted with red.

'Undulata' (syns. 'Crispa', 'Undulatifolia'). The leafy part is wavy, but not the main stem of the frond.

Petasites
ASTERACEAE
butterbur

Wildflowers or weeds, depending on your point of view, with huge leaves like lily pads, providing ground cover of architectural proportions. They are best kept in the wild garden, and require permanently moist soil and shelter. Unfortunately, they often don't look as neat as one might hope, as the leaves get torn and battered for one reason or another. Fifteen species from northern temperate regions, of which six or seven species may be in cultivation, but only one reaches the required height.

Petasites japonicus
(syn. *P. giganteus*)
ORIGIN: Japan, China, Korea
SIZE: 165–105 (–200) × indefinite cm;
    5½–3½ (–6½) × indefinite ft
FLOWERING TIME: spring
FLOWER COLOUR: pale mauve and white
Shade
Zone 5
Propagate by division
High impact
DESCRIPTION: The typical form of this plant reaches only 100 cm (3½ ft), with leaves about 80 cm (2½ ft) wide, and it is probably not in cultivation. There is also a variegated form, 'Nishiki-buki' (syn. 'Variegatus'), spotted with creamy yellow, and a purple-leaved form, *Petasites japonicus* f. *purpureus*.

var. *giganteus* (syn. *P. giganteus*). The ginormous leaves of this plant from Japan can be as much as 150 cm (5 ft) wide, though more usually they are about 90 cm (3 ft), rounded or kidney-shaped. They are held on robust stalks up to 200 cm (6½ ft) high, often less. The pale coloured flowers are held in spikes before the leaves appear, though in comparison to the foliage, the flowers are of little significance. Allow plenty of room, as the plant spreads steadily by means of rhizomes. Not for the fainthearted.

Rheum
POLYGONACEAE
rhubarb

Rhubarb as an edible plant grown in the vegetable garden is well known, but there are also five or six ornamental species, notable for their foliage. These follow the same recognizable pattern of having large leaves supported by stout, semi-erect stalks. The flowers are on vertical stalks above the foliage, but in most cases are not particularly attractive. The large plants are better for the waterside, woodland edge or in the wild garden, rather than the traditional border where they are hard to associate with other plants. About 50 species in total, from tropical and temperate Asia and eastern Europe.

Rheum australe

(syn. *R. emodi*)

ORIGIN: Himalayas

SIZE: 120–200 × 120–180 cm; 4–6½ × 4–6 ft

FLOWERING TIME: late spring

FLOWER COLOUR: dark greenish red

Sun

Zone 6

Propagate by division

High impact

DESCRIPTION: Reddish pointed leaves with red veins, up to 60 cm (2 ft) high. Greenish red flower spikes to 200 cm (6½ ft). Happy in moderately dry shade once established.

Rheum palmatum

ORIGIN: northwestern China

SIZE: 150–240 × 150–240 cm; 5–8 × 5–8 ft

FLOWERING TIME: summer

FLOWER COLOUR: red and cream

Sun or light shade

Zone 6

Propagate by seed or division

High impact

DESCRIPTION: Stunning foliage, with leaves 50–90 cm (1½–3 ft) in diameter, lobed, jagged and pointed, supported on strong

stalks. Shelter is essential—otherwise the flimsy leaves are liable to get damaged and spoilt. Erect stems bear feathery greenish white, pinkish or cream-coloured flowers. The leaves reach about half the height of the flower spikes. There is no point in growing the wild species when the named varieties are so much better. However, some of those listed may be fairly similar.

'Atrosanguineum' (syn. 'Atropurpureum'). Variable. Young leaves deep red, fading to dark green above, red below. Flowers dark reddish pink.

Rheum palmatum in the border, with grasses, alchemilla and *Vitis coignetiae* behind.

The red flowerheads and huge tiered leaves of *Rheum palmatum*,
a species from northwestern China.

'Bowles's Crimson'. Foliage retains its red coloration longer. Darker red flowers.

'Hadspen Crimson'. Deep pink foliage when young, gradually fading. White flowers.

'Red Herald'. Good red foliage and flowerheads.

var. *rubrum*. Flowers redder than the typical species.

var. *tanguticum*. Probably a geographical variation. Deeply cut leaves, with variable flowers. Shorter flower stems, to 180 cm (6 ft).

var. *tanguticum* 'Rosa Auslese'. Huge divided leaves, reddish bronze at first, becoming dark green with purple undersides, and eventually quite red in the autumn. Dark red flowerheads. The German name means "red selection" and is pronounced "rosa owss-layza."

Sambucus
CAPRIFOLIACEAE
elder
About 25 trees, shrubs and perennials, from temperate and subtropical regions worldwide. The flowers are usually white, in umbel-like heads, followed by berries. Leaves usually pinnate.

Sambucus ebulus
danewort
ORIGIN: central, southern and eastern Europe, including Great Britain, north-western Africa, Madeira, Turkey, Middle East, Caucasus; introduced in northeastern United States
SIZE: 150 (–200) × 150 cm; 5 (–6½) × 5 ft
FLOWERING TIME: mid to late summer
FLOWER COLOUR: white
Sun or light shade
Zone 3
Black berries
Propagate by division
Moderate impact
DESCRIPTION: White, umbel-like, elder flowers, sometimes tinged pink, on a bushy, leafy plant with attractive foliage. Pinnate leaves with five to nine pointed leaflets. Black (elder) berries—but poisonous. Prefers heavy clay soil. A very aggressive spreader, best in the wild garden.

Woodwardia
BLECHNACEAE
chain fern
A small genus of ferns with large, attractive fronds. About 14 species, from Europe, Asia and North America. Like the blechnums, they prefer acid or neutral soil. *Woodwardia orientalis* is slightly too short to be included.

Woodwardia fimbriata
giant chain fern
ORIGIN: British Columbia, Canada; Arizona and the West Coast of the United States, Mexico.
SIZE: 60–180 × 60–150 cm; 2–6 × 2–5 ft
Shade or light shade
Zone 7
Propagate by spores
High impact
DESCRIPTION: A magnificent fern with large fronds, up to 3 m (10 ft) long in the wild, and up to 50 cm (1½ ft) wide. The fronds are bright green, upright and arching at the ends.

Woodwardia orientalis

ORIGIN: Himalayas, southern China, Japan
SIZE: 60–150 × 60–180 cm; 2–5 × 2–6 ft
Sun or shade
Zone 9
Propagate by division or bulbils
Moderate impact
DESCRIPTION: Large fronds, up to 100 cm (3½ ft) long, and up to 35 cm (14 in) wide. Bulbils, or adventitious plantlets, form on the upper side of the leaves—which is useful for the propagator. Creeping rhizome. Not as demanding of wet as some ferns. Sometimes mistakenly sold as *Woodwardia radicans*.

Woodwardia radicans

ORIGIN: southwestern Europe, Atlantic Islands, East Asia
SIZE: 45–210 × 60–400 cm; 1½–7 × 2–13 ft
Shade or light shade
Zone 9
Propagate by spores or division
High impact
DESCRIPTION: A large fern with huge, arching, dark green fronds, as much as 200 cm (6½ ft) long in the wild, and up to 40 cm (16 in) wide. Evergreen, but it is best to remove some of the old foliage in the spring to encourage healthy fresh new fronds. The fronds carry bulbils, or buds, towards their tip, and when these arch over and touch the ground a new plant is formed. In this way, magnificent groups of the *Woodwardia radicans* can develop in favourable situations. Not as demanding of wet as some ferns.

Woodwardia unigemmata

ORIGIN: Himalayas, southern China, Japan
SIZE: 45–210 × 60–180 cm; 1½–7 × 2–6 ft
Shade or light shade
Zone 8
Propagate by spores or division
High impact
DESCRIPTION: Similar to *Woodwardia radicans*, but a little hardier, and with the added attraction that the new fronds are a deep shade of red, later fading to green. Fairly new to cultivation.

The huge arching fronds of the fern *Woodwardia radicans*.

6

UMBELLIFERS

Plants in the umbellifer family are recognizable for the upturned-umbrella-like structure of their flowers. Many have good foliage, most are pleasing in habit and stately in form—and many of them could have been included in the "Architectural Perennials" chapter. Most have white flowers, though some are yellow; some like *Angelica* have been used as herbs since time immemorial, others such as fennel have culinary uses, while many are good plants for the wild garden.

Angelica
APIACEAE

About 50 species, of stately habit, many of which are noted for their medicinal or economic uses. Many are likely to be biennial, rather than short-lived perennials, since nearly all are monocarpic or in other words they die after setting seeds.

A few additional tall angelicas are occasionally offered by nurseries and follow a similar pattern, but are worth trying. They include *Angelica amurensis* (white, up to 2 m, far eastern Russia, China), *A. chernjaevii* (white, up to 1.5 m, northeastern Asia, doubtful name), *A. dahurica* (up to 3 m, white, northeastern Asia), *A. genuflexa* (up to 2 m, curved leaves, white or pink, Kamchatka), *A. lineariloba* (white, up to 2 m, California), *A. maximowiczii* (up to 1 m, northeastern Asia), *A. polymorpha* (white, up to 1.8 m, Japan), *A. sachalinensis* (much-divided leaves on purplish stems, up to 2.5 m, Sakhalin, Japan) and *A. venenosa* (white, up to 2 m, United States).

Angelica archangelica
ORIGIN: northern and eastern Europe to central Asia
SIZE: 200 × 150 cm; 6½ × 5 ft
FLOWERING TIME: summer
FLOWER COLOUR: greenish white
Sun
Zone 4
Useful for flower arrangement
Interesting seed heads
Propagate by seed
High impact
DESCRIPTION: The most architectural plant

to grace the herb garden, where it is grown for its culinary and medicinal uses, most commonly remembered as candied strips of green for cake decoration—rarely seen these days. But its habit is bold and attractive,

The umbellifer heads of *Angelica archangelica* at a nursery in Kent.

with domed umbellifer heads and large, bright green pinnate leaves, well deserving a place in the ornamental garden. A short-lived, monocarpic perennial or biennial, which relates well with true perennials, since it self-seeds (not enough to be a nuisance) and therefore renews itself. Plants can also be encouraged to last longer, up to four years, by preventing them from setting seed. Prefers rich, moisture-retentive soil in semi-shade.

Good with fennel, large artemisias and various tolerant, low-growing plants that will put up with the large overshadowing leaves.

Angelica atropurpurea

purple angelica, bellyache root
ORIGIN: central United States
SIZE: 200 × 120 cm; 6½ × 4 ft
FLOWERING TIME: summer
FLOWER COLOUR: greenish white
Sun
Zone 4
Useful for flower arrangement
Interesting seed heads
Propagate by seed
High impact
DESCRIPTION: Pinnate foliage, in claret and purple shades, darker in spring. Rounded umbels, sometimes up to 30 cm (12 in) wide, held well above the foliage, on purple stems. A more vertical plant than *Angelica archangelica*. The whole plant is strongly scented. Avoid getting the sap on your skin on sunny days as it can cause blistering. Prefers moist ground.

Angelica pubescens

ORIGIN: Japan
SIZE: 120–200 × 90–120 cm; 4–6½ × 3–4 ft
FLOWERING TIME: summer
FLOWER COLOUR: white
Sun or light shade
Zone 7
Interesting seed heads
Propagate by seed or division
Moderate impact
DESCRIPTION: Starry, lacy white umbellifer heads, shallowly domed, held well above the foliage.

Angelica sylvestris

wild angelica
ORIGIN: Europe
SIZE: 90–200 × 75–90 cm; 3–6½ × 2½–3 ft
FLOWERING TIME: late summer
FLOWER COLOUR: white and buff
Sun or shade
Zone 7
Interesting seed heads
Propagate by seed
High impact
DESCRIPTION: Attractive, but only suitable for the wild garden or meadow, a self-seeding biennial. It is commonly seen in the wild in Great Britain, especially Wales and western Scotland, usually in ditches or beside streams, its domed heads tinged with varying shades of pinkish buff-brown making it easily recognizable. Beware, however, of confusing it with another inhabitant of damp places, *Oenanthe crocata*, which is very poisonous.

'Vicar's Mead'. A variety with deep maroon foliage and stems, which may be shorter than the green form.

Angelica taiwaniana

ORIGIN: Taiwan
SIZE: 100–200 × 60–90 cm; 3½–6½ × 2–3 ft
FLOWERING TIME: summer
FLOWER COLOUR: creamy white
Sun or shade
Zone 6
Useful for flower arrangement
Interesting seed heads
Propagate by seed
High impact
DESCRIPTION: Very large heads on stout stems, statuesque.

Angelica ursina

bear's angelica
ORIGIN: Kamchatka and Sakhalin
SIZE: 200–350 × 100–180 cm; 6½–12 × 3½–6 ft
FLOWERING TIME: summer to late summer
FLOWER COLOUR: white
Sun or shade
Zone 4
Useful for flower arrangement
Interesting seed heads
Propagate by seed or division
Very high impact
DESCRIPTION: A giant of a plant, which can reach 3.5 m (12 ft), with strong, hollow, tree-like stems, and white umbels. Huge, much-divided leaves, forming a luxuriant mound. It often has a surprising second flush of smaller florets, curving downwards. Bears eat the roots during the freezing winters in Sakhalin. A rival for *Heracleum mantegazzianum* as the tallest and largest perennial which can be grown in temperate regions.

Conium

APIACEAE

Two, or possibly three, poisonous bienni-als, one from the northern hemisphere and another from southern Africa.

Conium maculatum

hemlock

ORIGIN: Europe (very common in Great Brit-ain) and Asia, but naturalized worldwide, in temperate and subtropical regions

SIZE: 180–250 × 90–150 cm; 6–8 × 3–5 ft

FLOWERING TIME: summer

FLOWER COLOUR: white

Sun or light shade

Zone 5

Propagate by seed

High impact

DESCRIPTION: Tall, towering, lacy and graceful, but hardly a garden plant, mainly because of being deadly poisonous—but it's certainly beautiful enough to be allowed into a meadow or wild garden. White, cow-parsley flowers on stems with purple blotches, with layers of attractive, ferny green foliage. Dies down early, leaving a skeleton of dead stems. This is the plant that produced the drug used to poison the phi-losopher Socrates. It is well worth learning how to recognize this plant in the wild, so as to avoid any problems, and then teaching your children. Its mousy smell, for example, distinguishes it from fennel.

Associate with rheums, aralias, restios and *Miscanthus ×giganteus*.

The lacy, airy heads of poisonous hemlock, *Conium maculatum*, growing wild near Dowdeswell Reservoir, Gloucestershire.

Ferula

APIACEAE

giant fennel

Umbellifers from Mediterranean, Middle East and central Asia, from areas where the summers are dry and hot. Many send out a tall flowering spike high above finely dissected foliage, and are deeply tap-rooted. They are often short-lived, but can be encouraged to persist, by providing good, deep, fertile soil, and by cutting down the flowering stalk before seed is set. Some species are said to be edible but are not to be confused with culinary fennel, which is in a different genus—*Foeniculum*.

Ferula assa-foetida

asafoetida

ORIGIN: Iran

SIZE: 75–200 × 60–105 cm; 2½–6½ × 2–3½ ft

FLOWERING TIME: summer

FLOWER COLOUR: yellow

Sun

Zone 9

Interesting seed heads

Propagate by seed

Moderate impact

DESCRIPTION: This plant is grown for a range of culinary and medicinal uses, mainly in Iran, Afghanistan and Kashmir. However, the smell of the powdered gum is so pungent and unpleasant before it is cooked that it has to be stored in air-tight containers to prevent contamination of other herbs and spices. Its alternative modern language names will give some impression—stinking gum, devil's dung, merde du diable or alternatively—ironically perhaps—food of the gods.

No such smell comes from the plant itself. It has yellow umbellifer heads over very fine and feathery, much-dissected, blue-green foliage, arising from a fleshy rootstock. Unlikely to exceed 90 cm (3 ft) in cool temperate gardens. Needs well-drained soil.

Ferula communis

giant fennel

ORIGIN: Mediterranean

SIZE: 200–300 × 120–180 cm; 6½–10 × 4–6 ft

FLOWERING TIME: summer

FLOWER COLOUR: green

Sun

Zone 7

Useful for flower arrangement

Interesting seed heads

Propagate by seed

Very high impact

DESCRIPTION: Giant fennel throws out an extraordinary tall flower spike, sometimes slightly leaning out of vertical, much-branched at the top, with clusters of green, rounded umbels. This rises out of a large mound of unusual, finely dissected, arching, green foliage. Sometimes shy to flower. The plant tends to die down early, before the summer is through, leaving a huge gap in the border, which is not very convenient. Large bedding plants, such as *Cosmos*, can be brought in to save the day.

subsp. *glauca* (syn. *F. chiliantha*). Flower spikes often mauvish red as it develops, and flowers tending to yellow or even orange, rather than yellowish green. Foliage blue-green. Sometimes behaves monocarpically (that is, it dies after setting seed).

The extraordinary heads and ferny foliage of *Ferula communis*, giant fennel, at Cambridge University Botanic Garden.

Ferula tingitana

ORIGIN: southern Spain, Portugal, north-western Africa
SIZE: 150–200 × 90–150 cm; 5–6½ × 3–5 ft
FLOWERING TIME: summer

FLOWER COLOUR: yellow
Sun
Zone 8
Useful for flower arrangement
Interesting seed heads
Propagate by seed
High impact
DESCRIPTION: Clusters of rounded, yellow umbels, on a tall flower spike, over bright green, much-divided foliage.

'Cedric Morris'. Upper surface of foliage shiny. Distributed by Beth Chatto, who got it from the artist Sir Cedric Morris.

Ferulago

APIACEAE
About 45 umbellifers from Mediterranean to central Asia. Very few are in cultivation.

Ferulago sylvatica

ORIGIN: Balkans
SIZE: 150–210 × 75–90 cm; 5–7 × 2½–3 ft
FLOWERING TIME: summer
FLOWER COLOUR: yellowish green
Sun
Zone 9
Useful for flower arrangement
Interesting seed heads
Propagate by seed or division
High impact
DESCRIPTION: A recently introduced tall umbellifer with yellowish green heads like an umbrella of little bupleurums. Followed by good yellow seed heads. A must for all lovers of green-yellow plants. Well-drained soil and full sun probably required. May die down early.

Foeniculum

APIACEAE

fennel

A monotypic genus, known and grown since ancient times as a herb, vegetable and medicinal plant. Also very decorative, if sometimes a little unkempt.

Foeniculum vulgare

(syn. *F. foeniculum*)

ORIGIN: western and southern Europe, including Great Britain, Mediterranean; naturalized in the United States, South America, India

SIZE: 120–180 (–210) × 90–indefinite cm; 4–6 (–7) × 3–indefinite ft

FLOWERING TIME: summer

FLOWER COLOUR: yellowish green

Sun

Zone 5

Useful for flower arrangement

Interesting seed heads

Propagate by seed

Moderate impact

DESCRIPTION: Many flat-topped, yellowish green umbels over a mass of beautiful, delicate foliage—"a dome of candy floss," as Jekka McVicar says—providing a unique, feathery texture. The whole plant is aromatic, and scented of aniseed. In the herb garden, it needs to be kept well away from related umbellifers such as dill and coriander, to avoid cross-pollination. It is said to keep aphids at bay, so can usefully be planted near plants which are prone to aphid attack. It prefers full sun and fertile

Fennel, *Foeniculum vulgare*, is a herb, but can also be grown for ornament, the massed heads here creating a delicate and lacy effect.

soil. Unfortunately, it can easily become a nuisance by self-seeding excessively, and although deadheading might seem a chore, it may be less time-consuming than digging up unwanted plants.

The plant is still in use for very many different purposes. The usual form of Foeniculum *vulgare* is grown as a herb for its seeds and leaves, while the plant used as a vegetable in Mediterranean countries, especially Italy, is Florence fennel or finocchio, *F. vulgare* Azoricum Group (syn. var. *azoricum*). In this form the leaf bases swell to form a broad, white, bulb-like structure. It is much shorter and usually grown as an annual. A range of named varieties is available. *Foeniculum vulgare* var. *dulce* (sweet fennel, Sicilian fennel, or carosella in Italy) is grown for its celery-like stems. Subspecies *piperitum* (Italian fennel) is used in salads and in the production of an oil. There are many variations in the way the plants are used according to local custom in different countries around the world.

'Giant Bronze'. A tall and robust form of 'Purpureum'.

'Purpureum' (syn. 'Purpurascens'). Leaves and stems flushed a bronzy brown colour, fading later. A unique plant, wonderfully brown and furry-looking as it develops in late spring. Slight variants are sometimes offered under the names 'Perfection', 'Rubrum' and 'Smoky'. All these dark-coloured forms may well be forms of *Foeniculum vulgare* var. *dulce*. Usually shorter than the green form.

Heracleum

APIACEAE

hogweed

About 60 species, from northern temperate regions and as far south as Ethiopia and southern India. Perennials and biennials, often large and usually robust. Several are common wildflowers in Great Britain and the United States. *Heracleum sphondylium*, for instance, is hogweed, native to Europe and temperate Asia, which does not have very much ornamental value, but might well be allowed in the wild meadow garden, particularly for the sake of its dead skeletons in the autumn. *Heracleum maximum* (syns. *H. lanatum*, *H. sphondylium* subsp. *lanatum*, *H. sphondylium* subsp. *montanum*), cow parsnip or pushki, from North America including Alaska, is another plant for the wild garden. It has glossier leaves and is very hardy.

Heracleum lehmannianum

ORIGIN: Turkestan

SIZE: 120–270 × 75–90 cm; 4–9 × 2½–3 ft

FLOWERING TIME: summer

FLOWER COLOUR: white

Sun

Zone 4

Useful for flower arrangement

Interesting seed heads

Propagate by seed or division

High impact

DESCRIPTION: Large flowers with creamy white or pale pink umbels, up to 45 cm (1½ ft) wide, on tall stems. Unlike *Heracleum mantegazzianum* the foliage is not harmful to the skin if handled. Like *H. sphondylium* it leaves behind a stately skeleton after flowering.

Heracleum mantegazzianum

giant hogweed

ORIGIN: Caucasus

SIZE: 240–550 × 180–300 cm; 8–18 ×
   6–10 ft

FLOWERING TIME: mid to late summer

FLOWER COLOUR: white

Sun or light shade

Zone 4

Interesting seed heads

Propagate by seed or division

Very high impact

DESCRIPTION: An amazing plant, said to be the largest perennial plant that will grow in temperate gardens. Stout, hollow stems support huge lacy umbels of white flowers, up to 50 cm (20 in) wide, which the passer-by must look up at from underneath. It can have as many as 150 rays to the umbel. Even larger leaves, pointed and pinnate, as much as 130 cm (4¼ ft) wide, which it sometimes has difficulty supporting. Very architectural. A short-lived perennial or biennial, but it seeds itself. A sheltered position is best, on deep, moist soil. This plant comes with a government health warning: it is illegal in Great Britain to allow it to escape into the countryside, because of the harm the sap can do to some people's skin and lips. Good for flower arrangements in the Royal Albert Hall, suggests Graham Stuart Thomas.

Looking up at the giant flowerheads of *Heracleum mantegazzianum*, giant hogweed, a monster of a plant, native to the Caucasus.

Heracleum sosnowskyi

ORIGIN: eastern Europe, temperate Asia,
  Sakhalin
SIZE: 240–360 × 150–240 cm; 8–12 × 5–8 ft
FLOWERING TIME: summer
FLOWER COLOUR: white
Sun or light shade
Zone 3
Interesting seed heads
Propagate by seed or division
Very high impact
DESCRIPTION: A large plant with very large
white heads on stout stems, over impressive
foliage. Like *Heracleum mantegazzianum*, it
can become a weed if allowed to escape into
the countryside.

Levisticum

APIACEAE
A genus of one species.

Levisticum officinale

lovage
ORIGIN: central and eastern Mediterranean;
  widely introduced, including Europe and
  the United States
SIZE: 120–200 × 75–100 cm; 4–6½ ×
  2½–3½ ft
FLOWERING TIME: summer
FLOWER COLOUR: greenish yellow
Sun
Zone 4
Interesting seed heads

Levisticum officinale, lovage, with its ferny foliage and yellow, umbrella-
like flowerheads, makes an attractive plant for the herb garden.

Propagate by seed or division

Subtle impact

DESCRIPTION: Sprays of domed, yellow-ish umbels of flowers, on branching upright stems. Fresh green, arching leaves to about 75 cm (2½ ft), celery-like, ferny and fragrant. It has been used for culinary and medicinal purposes since ancient times. As herbs go, it's an attractive plant—though that's not saying much. It is, or was, mainly used as an aid to digestion, or more interestingly as an aphrodisiac. It is also said to be good placed in one's shoes overnight as a refreshing deodorant. Prefers rich, moist soil which neither dries out nor becomes boggy. Not to be confused with Scots lovage, *Ligusticum scoticum*, a shorter plant.

Melanoselinum

APIACEAE

Sub-shrubby herbaceous umbellifers from Madeira and the Azores. Of the seven species, only one is occasionally seen in cultivation.

Melanoselinum decipiens

black parsley

ORIGIN: Madeira

SIZE: 150–240 × 120–210 cm; 5–8 × 4–7 ft

FLOWERING TIME: spring to summer

FLOWER COLOUR: mauve and white

Sun or light shade

Zone 8

Interesting seed heads

Propagate by seed

High impact

DESCRIPTION: Lush and bushy plant, liable to die after setting seed. Extremely large flowerheads, slightly domed, up to 90 cm (3 ft) wide in favourable situations, pale purple in bud, opening white, tinged mauve. Amazing foliage, with giant rosettes of glossy, mid-green, pinnate leaves, like an enormous celery on massive trunks. The leaves take on tints of bronzy pink in the autumn. Harmless to the touch (compare to the hogweeds). The seed heads are black—hence the common name. It needs shelter, good drainage, and a sunny position in cooler areas, some shade in hotter regions. Can be shy to flower, but the foliage is good anyway.

Molopospermum

APIACEAE

An umbelliferous genus consisting of a single species.

Molopospermum peloponnesiacum

(syn. *M. circutarium*)

coscoll, Molly the Greek

ORIGIN: Mediterranean, Pyrenees

SIZE: 150–210 × 120–180 cm; 5–7 × 4–6 ft

FLOWERING TIME: summer

FLOWER COLOUR: greenish yellow

Sun

Zone 7

Useful for flower arrangement

Interesting seed heads

Propagate by seed or division

Very high impact

DESCRIPTION: A stunning plant with tall stems bearing clusters of unusual, almost spherical, pale, greenish yellow umbels. A mound of excellent, glossy, ferny, aromatic, rich green foliage, arching, pointed and

In spite of its tongue-twisting name, *Molopospermum peloponnesiacum* has excellent dark green foliage and startling yellowy green flowerheads.

Opopanax chironium at Cambridge University Botanic Garden. An unusual umbelliferous plant with yellow heads on tall, not-very-upright stems.

several times divided. This plant may be either a short-lived perennial or monocarpic. Also liable to leave a gap in the border at the end of the season. Erratically available from nurseries. A pleasure for those who love long mellifluous and alliterative Latin names (and a pain for those who don't).

Opopanax
APIACEAE
sweet balm
A small genus of umbellifers from the Mediterranean and the Middle East. Probably short-lived as perennials, and may be best treated as biennials. The seed should be collected, as an insurance policy.

Opopanax chironium
sweet balm
ORIGIN: Mediterranean, Black Sea, Middle East
SIZE: 75–240 × 60–180 cm; 2½–8 × 2–6 ft
FLOWERING TIME: summer
FLOWER COLOUR: mustard yellow
Sun
Zone 9
Useful for flower arrangement
Interesting seed heads
Propagate by seed or division
High impact
DESCRIPTION: An interesting and rarely seen umbellifer with tall, branching flower spikes, usually leaning, and bearing clusters of mustard yellow umbels, reminiscent of

Ferula and *Molopospermum.* The terminal umbel on each branch is almost spherical. "Panax" is the masculine form of "panacea" in Latin, meaning "miraculous plant," or "heal-all." A resin, or gum, is formed from the juice in the stems and roots, and is used medicinally, and also as an ingredient of incense, and in the perfume industry.

Opopanax hispidus

ORIGIN: eastern Mediterranean, Black Sea
SIZE: 90–300 × 60–180 cm; 3–10–8 × 2–6 ft
FLOWERING TIME: summer
FLOWER COLOUR: mustard yellow
Sun
Zone 9
Useful for flower arrangement
Interesting seed heads
Propagate by seed or division
High impact
DESCRIPTION: Similar to *Opopanax chironium*, but with very rough, prickly leaves in the manner of bristly oxtongue, *Picris echioides.* Hardly ever seen in cultivation, but may well be more ornamental, since the heads give a more cloudy effect and are not so sparsely furnished with umbels as *Opopanax chironium.*

Peucedanum

APIACEAE

A genus of 170 umbellifers found in Europe, Asia and Africa; several native to Great Britain, very few worth cultivating.

Peucedanum verticillare

ORIGIN: eastern Alps, Hungary
SIZE: 75–165 (–300) × 60–150 cm; 2½–5½ (–10) × 2–5 ft
FLOWERING TIME: summer
FLOWER COLOUR: greenish yellow
Sun or light shade
Zone 7
Interesting seed heads
Propagate by seed or division
Moderate impact
DESCRIPTION: A tall and stately pinky green stem rises high above the foliage, branching Christmas-tree-fashion at the top, with layers of flat-topped, pale greenish yellow umbels. A ferny mass of waxy, deep green foliage at the base. New growth in spring flushed pink, fading to blue-green. The flower buds are cased in lumpy, pinky green bracts. Good seed heads, golden yellow. Plants usually die after setting seed, but self-seed; it is wise to save the seeds as a precaution. Good for the wild garden.

7

ORNAMENTAL GRASSES

Ornamental grasses can be divided into those which have first-class foliage, and others which offer attractive flowerheads, such as pampas grass, *Miscanthus*, *Pennisetum* and several stipas—although a few manage to have both. Among the good-quality foliage grasses, some are shapely or have good habit, such as *Miscanthus*, *Schoenoplectus*, or *Arundo*, while others offer coloured foliage, whether variegated, brownish as in *Chionochloa*, or blue as in *Elymus*.

Ampelodesmos
POACEAE
A monospecific genus—in other words, there's only one species.

Ampelodesmos mauritanica
Mauritania vine reed
ORIGIN: Mediterranean
SIZE: 150–300 × 120 cm; 5–10 × 4 ft
FLOWERING TIME: summer to autumn
FLOWER COLOUR: buff
Sun
Zone 8
Propagate by seed or division
High impact
DESCRIPTION: A specimen grass, which seems to look better growing in the wild than it does growing in temperate gardens. It forms an untidy mass of wiry evergreen leaves, with a large number of one-sided plumes above, as if it was a wispy, mini-pampas grass. Needs time to develop into a good-sized clump. On the positive side, it starts to flower early in the year, and lasts well into the winter. Best grown as a specimen, with plants which are much lower in height.

Arundo
POACEAE
giant reed
Three species of very large grasses, with tall feathery panicles of flowers, from the tropical and subtropical regions of the Old World.

Arundo donax

giant reed
ORIGIN: Mediterranean Europe
SIZE: 350–600 × 180 cm; 12–20 × 6 ft
FLOWERING TIME: autumn
FLOWER COLOUR: white and buff
Sun
Zone 7
Useful for flower arrangement
Propagate by seed or division
Very high impact
DESCRIPTION: One of the tallest perennial plants, and the tallest member of the grass family that can be grown in temperate gardens—excluding bamboos, which are woody and so not included here. I have seen great banks of it growing wild not far from the Mediterranean in Italy—it is odd how one man's wild plant becomes another man's garden plant. The upward arching stems carry large, elegant, grey-green leaves, which curve downwards and forwards. It remains evergreen in warmer areas, but in cooler districts it dies down, inevitably leaving a huge gap. In cooler areas, it often doesn't flower either. A moist situation will produce a bigger and better plant. To transplant or divide a large clump is a major operation, though the rhizomes are fairly soft and can be cut through with a spade.

In gardens it is best grown as a wild architectural statement, at least 250–350 cm (8–12 ft) wide, but not allowed to spread indefinitely. An informal swathe of it might look like a monstrous weed that is getting out of control. It should be kept away from trees, and surrounded by lawn or gravel or low-growing plants, so that it can show off its shape and habit.

Ampelodesmos mauritanica is valued for its long flowering period.

Most gardeners will feel that the variegated forms are more deserving of the garden space than the plain green one. However, they are not quite so robust.

'Golden Chain'. An impressive selection, with a broad creamy yellow stripe to the leaves. Zone 9.

'Macrophylla'. An amazing and massive variety with leaves which are wider and more glaucous than the wild species.

var. *versicolor*. Bold white- and green-

The tallest ornamental grass which can be grown in temperate regions is *Arundo donax*, the giant reed, seen here at Oxford Botanic Garden.

striped foliage. Shorter than the wild green plant.

Arundo formosana
Taiwan grass
ORIGIN: China, Taiwan
SIZE: 180–240 × 100 cm; 6–8 × 3½ ft
FLOWERING TIME: late summer
FLOWER COLOUR: pinkish brown
Sun
Zone 8
Propagate by division
Very high impact
DESCRIPTION: Upright or leaning stems of grey-green, bamboo-like foliage, narrower than in *Arundo donax*, with loose, pink-tinged flowers reminiscent of *Phragmites*. Needs plenty of warmth for a good flowering display. Performs best in moist soil.

'Golden Showers'. A yellow-variegated variety, the leaves having one central broad green band, and a wide yellow band at the edges.

Calamagrostis
POACEAE
Medium height grasses, grown for their flower spikes. Whereas most other grasses prefer sun and an open position, many *Calamagrostis* species come from wet woodlands and coastal areas, making them very versatile in the garden.

Calamagrostis ×acutiflora

SIZE: 90–180 × 75 cm; 3–6 × 2½ ft
FLOWERING TIME: late summer to autumn
FLOWER COLOUR: brown and buff
Sun
Zone 3
Useful for flower arrangement
Interesting seed heads
Propagate by division
High impact
DESCRIPTION: Hybrids between *Cala-magrostis epigejos* (a native of northern Europe, including Great Britain, and temperate Asia) and *C. arundinacea*. Rarely sets seed. Cut down in early spring, before new growth starts.

'Avalanche'. Variegated, with a good white band down the centre. A sport from 'Karl Foerster', found by Steve Schmidt of American Ornamental Perennials. Slightly more striking than 'Overdam'.

'Karl Foerster' (syn. 'Stricta'). A distinctive grass, easily recognized in late summer as the epitome of verticality, but not of any interest until then, as the foliage is unremarkable and the flowerheads at first are open, unremarkable and loosely feathery. But by late summer the flowerheads become narrow and single-mindedly upright. A fast-growing, reliable grass. Selected by Karl Foerster and named later in his honour. This is a plant for the back of the border, not a specimen grass, as only the top half of the plant with its buff flowerheads is ornamental. For a specimen plant, the shorter *Calamagrostis epigejos* would be better.

'Overdam'. A white-variegated form of 'Karl Foerster', giving a grey-green effect, although this is not sufficiently striking to

The easily recognizable vertical stems of *Calamagrostis ×acutiflora* 'Karl Foerster', with coreopsis, heliopsis and Michaelmas daisies, at Bressingham Gardens.

make it worth growing for the sake of its foliage alone.

Calamagrostis epigejos

ORIGIN: northern and central Europe, including Great Britain, temperate Asia
SIZE: 60–200 × 75 cm; 2–6½ × 2½ ft
FLOWERING TIME: late summer
FLOWER COLOUR: brown and white
Sun or shade
Zone 4

Useful for flower arrangement
Interesting seed heads
Propagate by seed or division
High impact
DESCRIPTION: Has a fatter flowerhead than
its hybrid offspring, the better known *Calamagrostis* ×*acutiflora*. Also more relaxed in
habit (in other words, more arching than
vertical). It tolerates damp, even waterlogged conditions. Liable to self-seed in
sandy soils. Unlikely to reach its maximum
height in cultivation.

Chionochloa

POACEAE
snow tussock grass
Grasses, forming dense clumps of wiry,
evergreen leaves, upright or arching. They
need an open aspect and moist soil. Unlike
most grasses, they benefit from feeding in
spring. The best specimens I have seen were
in Scotland rather than England, and they
seem to prefer a cool climate rather than a
warm one. The better known *Chionochloa
rubra* is too short to be included.

Chionochloa conspicua

hunangamoho
ORIGIN: New Zealand
SIZE: 150–210 × 60 cm; 5–7 × 2 ft
FLOWERING TIME: summer
FLOWER COLOUR: white and buff
Sun
Zone 8
Useful for flower arrangement
Propagate by seed or division
High impact
DESCRIPTION: Loose, feathery plumes,
green-white, fading to golden buff, borne
aloft on slender stems, over a tussock of
more or less tidy, more or less upright,
brownish green leaves, each with an orange
midrib. Reminiscent of *Stipa gigantea*, and
possibly better, but heads more open with
branches drooping gracefully. Prefers not to
be too dry. Good as a specimen or a drift,
among lower plants.

Chionochloa flavescens

ORIGIN: New Zealand
SIZE: 120–180 × 60 cm; 4–6 × 2 ft
FLOWERING TIME: late summer
FLOWER COLOUR: white
Sun
Zone 8
Propagate by division
Moderate impact

The feathery heads and arching bronze-
tinted foliage of *Chionochloa flavescens*,
at Rosemoor in North Devon.

DESCRIPTION: Curving white flowers heads, 30 cm (1 ft) long, fading to golden buff, on long stout stems that lean out diagonally and horizontally in all directions. Bronze-tinted leaves, forming dense, compact tussocks. Can be grown as a specimen or as a long band. Not to be confused with *Chionochloa flexuosus*, which is shorter.

Cortaderia
POACEAE
pampas grass

Pampas grass must be one of the most dramatic plants that can be grown in gardens, its 3 m (10 ft) high plumes towering over other perennials. It forms a large mound of evergreen, grassy foliage, often slightly bluish, and is not that easy to associate with other plants. However, pampas grass plants don't have to be put in isolation in an island bed—they will blend in with other plants which are appropriate in scale and impact. The options are either to hide the foliage at the back of the border, or else to bring the plant right forward to the front and have low but tough plants next to it. A position in the wild or woodland garden is also appropriate, where the mound of foliage might look more comfortable than in a suburban front garden. Why not plant half an acre with nothing but pampas grass, with wandering paths winding their way through and enjoy the thousands of amazing plumes waving above your head?

Individual plants may be female or bisexual, and the two may look quite different from each other. For this reason it's important to get a plant from a reliable source, a division from a good form, and not a seed-raised plant. As is usually the case, named varieties do not come true from seed. Division is no easy matter—a task requiring heavy tools and plenty of sweat. Cut the plant back in spring to prevent the accumulation of dead leaves which will spoil the appearance of the plant.

The genus name (from the Spanish *cortar*, "to cut") is a reference to the sharp edges of the leaves. So handle with care, and wear gardening gloves. Some gardeners believe you have to burn the foliage at the end of winter, but this is not recommended or necessary. There's the danger of smoke inhalation, the risk of the flames spreading out of control, and also the disadvantage that the black charred remains are not a pretty sight.

Cortaderia fulvida
kakaho
ORIGIN: New Zealand
SIZE: 150–240 × 150–250 cm; 5–8 × 5–8 ft
FLOWERING TIME: summer
FLOWER COLOUR: buff
Sun
Zone 8
Useful for flower arrangement
Propagate by division
Very high impact
DESCRIPTION: Shaggy, creamy brown flower plumes, aging to pale pink or creamy white. The tussock of foliage can reach 150 cm (5 ft). The plumes are arching and one-sided, and similar to *Cortaderia richardii*, but not quite so good. Earlier than *C. selloana*. Needs moist soil.

Cortaderia richardii

toe toe

ORIGIN: New Zealand

SIZE: 250–300 × 250–300 cm; 8–10 × 8–10 ft

FLOWERING TIME: midsummer to early autumn

FLOWER COLOUR: cream

Sun

Zone 8

Useful for flower arrangement

Propagate by division

Very high impact

DESCRIPTION: Opinions are divided as to whether this or *Cortaderia selloana* is the finer pampas grass. This species has the advantage of flowering earlier and for longer, and some would argue that its plumes are more elegant and graceful. Personally, I prefer the denser plumes of *C. selloana*. The flowerheads of *C. richardii* are arching and cream-coloured, on a mound of arching foliage up to 120 cm (4 ft) high. The New Zealand name is pronounced "toy-toy."

Cortaderia selloana

pampas grass

ORIGIN: Brazil, Argentina, Chile

SIZE: 150–300 × 180–350 cm; 5–10 × 6–12 ft

Cortaderia selloana 'Pumila' produces a generous array of flowerheads, as here at Cotswold Garden Flowers nursery in Worcestershire.

FLOWERING TIME: autumn
FLOWER COLOUR: white
Sun
Zone 8
Useful for flower arrangement
Propagate by division
Very high impact
DESCRIPTION: The flower stems and flower-heads of this species are usually more vertical than in the other species, and the best cultivars are a wonderful glistening white. It is well worth getting hold of reliable varieties because of the variable nature of this species. Be wary of 'Rosea' and 'White Feather', which are seed strains. I am uncertain of the value of variegated selections, considering one grows this plant for the flowers, not the leaves (which can be slightly untidy). 'Splendid Star', with the brightest variegation, is too short to be included.

'Albolineata'. Also known as 'Silver Stripe'. White striped leaves, becoming more distinctly variegated later in the season.

'Aureolineata'. Gold variegation, with some leaves almost all yellow, brighter late in the season.

'Monstrosa'. A huge mound of leaves, with very tall flower stems, 300 cm (10 ft) high.

'Pink Feather'. Large plumes with a pink flush.

'Pumila'. Attractive, reliable and hardy, 150–180 cm (5–6 ft) high. Zone 6.

'Rendatleri'. Purplish pink plumes on 250 cm (8 ft) stems. Can this be a good idea?

'Silver Fountain'. White variegated foliage mounding up to 150 cm (5 ft). Plumes to 240 cm (8 ft).

'Sunningdale Silver'. Allegedly the best variety, and possibly selected by Graham Stuart Thomas, but can be so floriferous as to look congested. 240–300 cm (8–10 ft).

Cyperus
CYPERACEAE
A large genus in the sedge family. Mostly aquatic or moisture-loving plants, often creating an umbrella effect—long slender stems topped by a "parasol" of narrow pointed stems, consisting of leaf-like bracts. Most of the ornamental species are too tender for temperate gardens.

Cyperus giganteus
Mexican papyrus
ORIGIN: tropical North and South America
SIZE: 100–450 × 75–150 cm; 3½–14 × 2½–5 ft
FLOWERING TIME: summer
FLOWER COLOUR: greenish
Sun
Zone 9
Useful for flower arrangement
Propagate by division
High impact
DESCRIPTION: Similar to the better known *Cyperus papyrus*, but more robust and upright, and slightly less elegant. *Cyperus* 'Mexico' is probably the same thing.

Cyperus involucratus
umbrella plant
ORIGIN: Madagascar
SIZE: 50–200 × 50–150 cm; 1½–6½ × 1½–5 ft
FLOWERING TIME: summer
FLOWER COLOUR: green
Sun or light shade
Zone 9

Useful for flower arrangement
Propagate by division
High impact
DESCRIPTION: Resembles *Cyperus papyrus*, but has broader, flatter green "fingers" forming the "umbrella" top to the stems. Grows in wet or boggy ground, though it tolerates drier conditions than *C. papyrus*. Can be grown in Zone 8 with protection. Containers are needed to prevent excessive spread. Very similar to, and sometimes confused with, the shorter *C. alternifolius*.

Cyperus papyrus

papyrus
ORIGIN: Egypt, Sudan
SIZE: 120–450 × 100–300 cm; 4–14 × 3½–10 ft
FLOWERING TIME: summer
FLOWER COLOUR: green
Sun or light shade
Zone 9

Semi-aquatic *Cyperus papyrus*, with its feathery umbrella heads.

Useful for flower arrangement
Propagate by division
High impact
DESCRIPTION: A clump of slender graceful stems that bend with the weight of their feathery "umbrellas" of wiry branchlets, which are between 15 and 30 cm (6 and 12 in) long. It needs shallow water, or at least permanently moist soil. Unlikely to exceed 300 cm (10 ft) in cultivation. Its eventual width is indeterminate, as it spreads rapidly when happy, and large containers are recommended in some habitats to prevent it becoming too invasive. Old stems should be removed when they become unsightly. It can be grown in Zone 8 areas, with the protection of messy mulching.

This is the plant described as "bulrushes" in the story of Moses in the Old Testament. It made a major contribution to the history of civilization, as the first paper was made by the ancient Egyptians, using the pith found in the stems of this plant.

Cyperus ustulatus

coastal cutty grass, upoko-tangata
ORIGIN: New Zealand
SIZE: 120–180 × 60–120 cm; 4–6 × 2–4 ft
FLOWERING TIME: summer
FLOWER COLOUR: greenish
Sun or light shade
Zone 7
Interesting seed heads
Propagate by division
Subtle impact
DESCRIPTION: Olive-green leaves, glossy, folded and sharp-edged. The flower stems sit a little higher than the foliage, forming an untidy tuft of upward-pointing bracts

rather than an umbrella-like structure near the flowers. Shiny, dark brown seed heads. For waterside and moist areas. Fast growing.

Elymus
POACEAE

A fairly large genus of grasses found in temperate areas, of worldwide distribution. Closely related to *Leymus*, and not all botanists agree that the two should have been separated.

Elymus californicus
(syns. *Hystrix californicus, Leymus californicus*)
California bottlebrush grass
ORIGIN: California
SIZE: 100–200 × 45–90 cm; 3½–6½ × 1½–3 ft
FLOWERING TIME: summer
FLOWER COLOUR: green and buff
Sun or shade
Zone 8
Useful for flower arrangement
Propagate by seed or division
Subtle impact
DESCRIPTION: A tall grass with arching, whiskery, barley-like heads, otherwise not very ornamental.

Elymus canadensis
Canada wildrye
ORIGIN: North America
SIZE: 75–180 × 45–100 cm; 2½–6 × 1½–3½ ft
FLOWERING TIME: late summer
FLOWER COLOUR: buff

Sun
Zone 4
Useful for flower arrangement
Propagate by seed or division
Subtle impact
DESCRIPTION: Evergreen clumps of grey-green or blue-green leaves, up to 45 cm (1½ ft) long, are of little interest. Flowerheads are whiskery, barley-like and arching in shape. A good candidate for the meadow garden. Fast growing, but often short-lived. Can self-seed annoyingly. *Elymus virginicus* (Virginia wildrye) is even less ornamental, but is a very hardy Zone 3 plant.

Juncus
JUNCACEAE
rush

Inhabitants of wet places in temperate regions. Leaves are stem-like, smooth, straight and vertical.

Juncus pallidus
wi, tussock rush
ORIGIN: Australia, New Zealand
SIZE: 120–200 × 60–120 cm; 4–6½ × 2–4 ft
FLOWERING TIME: summer
FLOWER COLOUR: pale green or brown
Sun or light shade
Zone 6
Interesting seed heads
Propagate by division
High impact
DESCRIPTION: An amazing blue-green rush, which can grow up to 200 cm (6½ ft) high, though is usually a little less, forming a dense clump of vertical or slightly leaning

stems (actually leaves) 3–8 mm (0.1–0.3 in) in diameter. The pale greenish yellow flowers turn reddish brown later, and are particularly good for a juncus (not saying a lot, I know), and appear slightly below the tip of the stems. Needs a moist or wet situation, and tolerates salinity. Fast growing, and best planted in a container to prevent excessive spread.

Leymus
POACEAE
Grasses, often blue-grey in colour, coming from temperate, northern hemisphere areas, and usually from sandy, seashore, dune or steppe habitats. Many species were formerly in the genus *Elymus*.

Leymus condensatus
(syn. *Elymus condensatus*)
ORIGIN: California
SIZE: 150–300 × 45–120 cm; 5–10 × 1½–4 ft
FLOWERING TIME: midsummer
FLOWER COLOUR: silvery green
Sun
Zone 7
Propagate by seed or division
Subtle impact
DESCRIPTION: Blue-green leaves, with upright flower spikes, 15–50 cm (6–20 in) long, standing well above the foliage. For the wild garden. Evergreen in warmer districts. 'Canyon Prince' is bluer, but only reaches 120 cm (4 ft).

Miscanthus
POACEAE
About 20 species of grasses from East Asia, South Asia and southern Africa, providing the gardener with some of the best ornamental grasses and one of the top ten tall perennials. The name, from the Greek *mischos* ("stalk") and *anthos* ("flower"), must be one of the silliest ever invented, since flowering stalks are not exactly rare in the plant world.

Some species and varieties can become a weed threat in warmer climates such as in the southeastern United States. Not all those varieties selected in Europe will be successful in the eastern United States, and vice versa.

Miscanthus floridulus
ORIGIN: Ryukyu Islands, Taiwan, Pacific Islands
SIZE: 180–250 × 120–180 cm; 6–8 × 4–6 ft
FLOWERING TIME: summer
FLOWER COLOUR: whitish
Sun
Zone 6
Useful for flower arrangement
Propagate by division
High impact
DESCRIPTION: Fairly similar to the better known *Miscanthus sinensis*, but flowering earlier. Unlikely to flower at all in areas cooler than Zone 9. It also has broader, possibly less elegant leaves, 3 cm (1¼ in) wide, matte, blue-green with a white midrib, and flowers with a stiffer central stem, usually as attractive as those of *M. sinensis*. Sometimes the plant flops untidily. *Miscanthus ×giganteus* is sometimes wrongly sold under this name.

Miscanthus ×*giganteus*

(syn. *M.* 'Giganteus')

SIZE: 180–350 × 120–180 cm; 6–12 × 4–6 ft

FLOWERING TIME: late autumn

FLOWER COLOUR: pinkish and white

Sun

Zone 4

Propagate by division

High impact

DESCRIPTION: Probably *Miscanthus sinensis* × *M. sacchariflorus*. A huge mass of foliage with broad mid-green leaves, 2.5 cm (1 in) wide, arching out from the hidden, upright main stems. Unlikely to flower in cooler districts, and in any case flowers very late in the season. There seems to be more than one plant circulating under this name, which covers both natural and garden hybrids. *Miscanthus* species do hybridize in the wild where more than one species occurs, but at least one form in circulation is a garden hybrid; further work is needed to give varietal names to these differing forms. Can be grown as a summer screen.

'Gilt Edge'. Irregularly placed bright yellow and green stripes. Introduced by Roger Grounds, who discovered it in his garden at Lymington, in Hampshire. 180–225 cm (6–7½ ft).

The *Miscanthus* beds at Bressingham Gardens; some taller, some shorter, some browner, some whiter, accompanied by helianthus, eupatorium and Michaelmas daisies.

Miscanthus sacchariflorus

Amur silver grass
ORIGIN: East Asia
SIZE: 180–240 × 90–120 cm; 6–8 × 3–4 ft
FLOWERING TIME: late summer
FLOWER COLOUR: off-white
Sun
Zone 4
Useful for flower arrangement
Propagate by seed or division
High impact
DESCRIPTION: Spreading habit, especially on light soils. Broad, arching leaves 3 cm (1¼ in) wide. The flowerheads are held well above the foliage, and are more upright and narrower than the better known *Miscanthus sinensis*. Reluctant to flower in cooler areas.

'Gotemba' (syn. 'Gotemba Gold'). A large, attractive plant. Leaves with stripes running longitudinally, strong yellow, dark green and pale lime. Unfortunately, it is a vigorous spreader. Good in a very large pot. Introduced by Koichiro Wada of Japan. 210–240 cm (7–8 ft).

Miscanthus sinensis

(syn. *Eulalia japonica*)
ORIGIN: East and Southeast Asia
SIZE: 75–250 × 75–150 cm; 2½–8 × 2½–5 ft
FLOWERING TIME: late summer to autumn
FLOWER COLOUR: off-white
Sun
Zone 6
Useful for flower arrangement
Propagate by seed or division
High impact
DESCRIPTION: One of the finest of all ornamental grasses. Forms a large clump of attractive, narrow, arching, mid-greed foliage, long, pointed and 1–2 cm (¼–¾ in) wide. The many flowerheads form elegant plumes of white, silver, or buff, sometimes even pink-tinged, depending on the variety, and usually stand well above the foliage. Most varieties need full sun. All are Zone 6 unless otherwise stated.

A small number of varieties have been available for many decades, but the majority have been introduced since 1960, some by Hans Simon of Munich, Germany, many by Ernst Pagels, of Leer, near Münster in northwestern Germany, and others by Kurt Bluemel of Maryland, United States. There is now rather an excess of varieties.

Tolerant of a wide range of conditions, but soils which are very rich in nutrients may lead to lax growth and floppy stems. No fertilizers should be added when planting. Staking is undesirable and shouldn't be necessary. The foliage should be cut back in spring. With the exception of the varieties belonging to groups, they must be propagated by division, as their seed progeny is likely to be quite unlike the parent plant. Division should be carried out in spring or early summer. Beware of twining weeds, which can bring the plant down.

'Autumn Light'. Narrow foliage, with yellow and red autumn colour, and beige flowerheads. From Kurt Bluemel in the United States. 180–240 cm (6–8 ft). Zone 5.

'Blütenwunder'. Bluish green foliage. Graceful habit. Large flowerheads. Prolific and early flowering. The German name means "bleeding wonder." 120–180 cm (4–6 ft). Zone 5.

var. *condensatus*. From Japan and Southeast Asia. Taller than the average *Miscan-*

thus sinensis variety, with robust stems, blue-green at the base. Broader leaves, blue-green on the underside. 240–300 cm (8–10 ft).

var. *condensatus* 'Cabaret'. Broad, cream-variegated leaves, 3 cm (1¼ in) wide, with a wide central strip and green edge. Can scorch in full sun. Flowers deep pink, very late. Less hardy than many but possibly the best variegated selection for warmer areas. Shy flowerer in cool districts. An old Japanese variety, introduced to the United States by Kurt Bluemel. 250 cm (8 ft). Zone 7.

var. *condensatus* 'Cosmopolitan'. A striking variegated miscanthus. Leaves with creamy white edges and central green stripe. Late flowering, but more likely to flower than 'Cabaret'. Discovered by Toyoichi Aoki of Japan, and named by Kurt Bluemel of the United States. 240 cm (8 ft). Zone 7.

var. *condensatus* 'Cosmo Revert' (syns. var. *condensatus* 'Central Park', var. *condensatus* 'Emerald Giant'). The plain green reversion of 'Cosmopolitan'. Wide, deep green leaves, 3 cm (1¼ in), arching to ground level, with large cream-coloured flowerheads. Shy to flower in cool areas. 150–200 cm (5–6½ ft).

'Dixieland'. Similar to the older 'Variegatus', but shorter, the leaves arching less, and more likely to flower in cool districts. Introduced by Kurt Bluemel. 90–160 cm (3–5½ ft).

Miscanthus sinensis in a naturalistic setting by the lake at the National Botanic Garden of Wales, near Carmarthen.

'Ferner Osten'. Slender olive-green leaves, with coppery orange tints in the autumn. Prolific flowerer, with fluffy dark red plumes with white tips, aging to silver, held all at the same height. Similar to 'China'. Introduced by Ernst Pagels in Germany. The name means "Far East." 165–200 cm (5½–6½ ft).

'Flamingo'. Narrow foliage with a white midrib, and good autumn colour. Prolific flowerer, with pendulous flowerheads with red stems, starting silvery pink, turning wine-red and fading to buff. Early flowering. Tolerates some light shade. From Ernst Pagels. 150–210 cm (5–7 ft).

'Flammenmeer'. The foliage has excellent red autumn colour, while the flower plumes are tinted pinkish red. The German name means "sea of flames." 200 cm (6½ ft).

'Gewitterwolke'. Broad, dark green leaves, with orange-tinged autumn colour, on a narrowly upright plant. Large numbers of arching flowerheads, purplish and silver, sometimes congested or concealed by the foliage. Early. Raised by Ernst Pagels. The name means "storm clouds" in German. 180–210 cm (6–7 ft).

'Ghana'. Slender, arching foliage with good reddish orange autumn colour. Feathery, russet-brown, upright flowerheads. Selected by Ernst Pagels. 150–180 cm (5–6 ft).

'Giraffe'. One of the best of the so-called zebra grasses—I've never seen a green and yellow zebra (or giraffe), but you get the idea—insofar as it has more creamy yellow than its rivals. Curiously the stripes go across the leaf instead of up and down. More interesting than beautiful. Silvery plumes. Slow to propagate. 200–250 cm (6½–8 ft).

'Goldfeder'. An attractive yellow variegated form of 'Silberfeder', with stripes running the length of the leaves. Free flowering. Rarely offered. Discovered by Hans Simon, of Germany. 180–210 cm (6–7 ft).

'Goliath'. A giant of a plant, obviously, with a mass of long, broad leaves, up to 2.5 cm (1 in) wide, with large flowerheads, tinted reddish golden brown, fading to silvery brown. Introduced by Ernst Pagels. 240 cm (8 ft).

Gracillimus Group. One of the oldest varieties, grown in Japan long before it was known in the west, and first described in the 1880s. Used as a seed strain, and therefore variable, with several differing forms in circulation. Narrow-leaved, arching foliage with a white midrib, on an upright plant, often three times as tall as it is wide. Brownish pink flowerheads, but shy to flower except in warm districts. Very late flowering, with flowers often hidden among the foliage. If all you want is foliage this is the variety for you. 210 cm (7 ft).

'Grosse Fontäne'. The name means "large fountain" in German. A tall variety, flowering early. Long arching leaves, with reddish flowerheads, held well above the foliage. Raised by Ernst Pagels of Germany. 250 cm (8 ft).

'Haiku'. Large, gracefully pendulous silvery pink flowerheads, on strong upright stems. Needs full sun. 180 cm (6 ft).

'Hercules'. Purple-pinkish brown flowerheads, and good dark red autumn colour in dry summers. 240 cm (8 ft).

'Hermann Müssel'. Broad, arching foliage with prominent white midribs. Open flowerheads, light reddish brown and ginger, fading to silvery buff, closing up with age, and held well above the foliage. From Ernst Pagels. 200 cm (6½ ft).

'Juli'. The name means "July" in German, which indicates that it is an early flowerer. The foliage is broad, 2.5 cm (1 in) wide, with narrow white midribs. Reddish brown flowerheads, fading to silvery. Another Ernst Pagels introduction.

'Kaskade'. A particularly good variety for flowerheads, with narrow upright foliage which turns coppery red, then pewter in the autumn. Long flowerheads with long drooping, "cascading" tassels in varying shades of pink and silver. Raised by Ernst Pagel of Germany. 135–195 cm (4½–6½ ft).

'Kleine Fontäne'. Narrow green foliage, not arching much, colouring to yellow, on a fairly short plant. Long flowering period, with a large number of graceful, deep pink flowerheads soon fading to fluffy beige. Introduced by Ernst Pagels of Germany. The name means "little fountain." 150–180 cm (5–6 ft).

'Kleine Silberspinne'. A neat plant, with narrow, dark green leaves providing some autumn colour. Erect, silvery flowerheads, reddish tinted at first, darker and fluffier later. Tolerant of dry soils. From Ernst Pagels of Germany. The name means "little silver spider." 120–180 cm (4–6 ft).

'Krater'. Noted for its good dark red autumn foliage. Late flowering, with pinkish silver flowerheads. 120–165 cm (4–5½ ft).

'Malepartus'. Curiously proportioned.

The tassel-like heads of *Miscanthus sinensis* 'Kaskade' are tinged with red, as seen here at Bressingham Gardens, Norfolk.

Large numbers of good flowerheads, opening purple red, turning silvery white and fading to coffee colour. But these sit just above a clump of arching green foliage, giving a squat appearance, like a person with no neck. 150–210 cm (5–7 ft). Zone 5.

'Nishidake'. Tall variety with wide leaves, up to 2.5 cm (1 in) wide, with white midribs. Flowerheads feathery, whitish, one-sided. 240 cm (8 ft).

'November Sunset'. A relative of the Gracillimus Group, with apple green leaves, selected for its clear gold-coloured autumn foliage. Very late to flower, usually late autumn, with dusky pinkish heads, turning to silvery gold. Raised by Kurt Bluemel of the United States. Up to 200 cm (6½ ft). More shade tolerant than some. Zone 5.

'Poseidon'. Very broad leaves and chunky pinkish flowerheads. Good autumn colour. 200 cm (6½ ft).

'Positano'. Broad, arching foliage, with good yellow autumn colour, especially in dry autumns. Beige-pink flowerheads on tall stems. Tolerates part shade. 180–240 cm (6–8 ft).

'Professor Richard Hansen'. Very tall variety with broad leaves and large white open flowerheads, becoming more fluffy with age. Selected by Ernst Pagels of Germany. Up to 300 cm (10 ft).

'Pünktchen'. A curious selection, whose leaves are marked with little yellow stripes in random places, too few to qualify as a zebra grass. Strongly upright clumps, with reddish flowerheads, are very vertical and Christmas-tree-like. The name means "little dot" (and so it is sometimes listed). Introduced by Ernst Pagels of Germany. 150–180 cm (5–6 ft). Zone 5.

'Roland'. A very tall variety, with broad foliage and pinkish white flowerheads, slender at first, fluffy and tousled later. From Ernst Pagels of Germany. 240–300 cm (8–10 ft). Zone 5.

'Roterpfeil' ("red arrow"). A strong grower. Foliage with excellent orange-red autumn colour. Flowerheads open with pinkish red tints. From Ernst Pagels of Germany. 180–200 cm (6–6½ ft). Zone 5.

'Rotfuchs' ("red fox"). Narrow foliage with good red autumn colour. Pink-tinged flowerheads, silvery later. 150–200 cm (5–6½ ft).

'Rotsilber' ("red-silver"). Foliage with orange-red autumn colour, narrow, erect, deep pinkish red flowerheads, aging to silvery shades. Prolific. From Ernst Pagels. Up to 180 cm (6 ft).

'Sarabande'. Related to the Gracillimus Group, but the leaves are wiry and narrower. Upright and arching form, spreading later. Free flowering, with elegant silver flowerheads, turning copper gold, aging to off-white. Raised by Kurt Bluemel of the United States. 180–200 cm (6–6½ ft).

'Septemberrot' ("September red"). Airy habit. Broad foliage with a white midrib, with good autumn colour. Large, graceful flowerheads of reddish brown on tall stems, well spaced. Late flowering. Up to 180–300 cm (6–10 ft).

'Silberfeder'. The name means "silver feather," and the cultivar is sometimes listed as such. One of the earliest varieties to be named, and still one of the best, especially for cooler climates. Large, feathery off-white flowerheads held high above the foliage, often leaning elegantly. The stems can flop if too dry or too shaded. Very hardy.

Selected by Hans Simon at the Munich Botanic Garden, Germany. 180–240 cm (6–8 ft). Zone 4.

'Silberspinne' ("silver spider"). An upright variety, with narrow green leaves, which sit at right angles to the main stem, and do not arch very much. Early flowering, silver flowerheads with pink tints. Introduced by Ernst Pagels of Germany. 150–200 cm (5–6½ ft).

'Silberturm' ("silver tower"). A very tall variety, introduced by Ernst Pagels. 270 cm (9 ft).

'Sirene'. Early flowering and prolific variety with arching foliage. Silky, crimped flowerheads held well above the foliage, opening pinkish red, aging to reddish brown, and then fluffy and silvery white.

Introduced by Ernst Pagels. 120–210 cm (4–7 ft).

'Strictus'. One of the earliest zebra grasses to be raised, with four or five yellow bands across the width of the leaf, though the overall effect is "dotty." The leaves do not arch as much as in 'Zebrinus', so that the plant as a whole has a spikier "porcupine" look. Pinkish brown flowers, late. Tolerates light shade. 165–200 cm (5½–6½ ft).

'Undine'. Some similarity to 'Graziella'. Gracefully arching leaves on upright stems, colouring orange and yellow in autumn and winter. Large, upright arching flowerheads open reddish pink, aging to silvery white. Introduced by Ernst Pagels. 150–200 cm (5–6½ ft).

'Variegatus'. An old variety, but very

The white-variegated foliage of *Miscanthus sinensis* 'Variegatus' with *Verbena bonariensis* at Bressingham Gardens.

Miscanthus sinensis 'Zebrinus', seen here at Bressingham Gardens.

showy, and one of the whitest of all herbaceous plants. Forms a wide clump. Leaves with bright white longitudinal stripes. Unlikely to flower in cool climates, and may need staking in warmer climates. 150–180 cm (5–6 ft). Zone 5.

'Zebrinus'. A zebra grass, less upright and more arching than 'Strictus'. Coppery buff-coloured flowers, but only produced in warmer districts. 165–210 cm (5½–7 ft).

'Zwergelefant'. Very broad, light green leaves, and white or pinkish flowerheads, arching and fluffy. The name, pronounced "tsvairk-ellay-fant," means "dwarf elephant." 240 cm (8 ft).

Miscanthus transmorrisonensis

Taiwan miscanthus
ORIGIN: Taiwan
SIZE: 100–210 cm × 90–150 cm; 3½–7 × 3–5 ft
FLOWERING TIME: summer
FLOWER COLOUR: off-white
Sun
Zone 6
Useful for flower arrangement
Propagate by seed or division
High impact
DESCRIPTION: Dark green leaves, with arching habit, evergreen in milder areas. Flowerheads held well above the foliage. Old foliage should be cut back in early spring.

Molinia

POACEAE

A small genus of grasses from temperate regions of Europe and Asia. A British native.

Molinia caerulea

(syn. *M. caerulea* subsp. *arundinacea*)
purple moor grass
ORIGIN: Europe, Asia
SIZE: 90–240 × 90–150 cm; 3–8 × 3–5 ft
FLOWERING TIME: midsummer
FLOWER COLOUR: buff
Sun or light shade
Zone 4
Useful for flower arrangement
Interesting seed heads
Propagate by seed or division
High impact
DESCRIPTION: As is the case with many grasses, the tufts of foliage are of no major value, although some varieties colour yellow in the autumn. But once in flower, several varieties make striking architectural specimen plants, while others are studies in airy texture. The flowerheads are usually purple-tinged and are borne on tall arching stems high above the foliage. The division of the species into two subspecies, *caerulea* and *arundinacea*, has recently been abandoned by botanical authors, since the difference was mainly one of height. All the varieties listed here were formerly in subsp. *arundinacea*.

Native to bogs, fens and moist mountainous places, it resents being too dry, but tolerates low fertility soils. In cooler districts an open sunny position is preferred. In Zone 9 areas and above, plants are likely to suffer from heat stress and refuse to flower. Named forms must be propagated by division.

'Bergfreund'. Yellow autumn foliage with shiny purple-brown flowerheads, delicate, airy and long lasting. Similar to 'Transparent' but shorter. The name means "mountain friend." 150–180 cm (5–6 ft).

'Cordoba'. Gracefully curving stems up to 180–210 cm (6–7 ft). Discovered in Spain.

'Fontäne'. Arching foliage up to 90 cm (3 ft). Large numbers of slender flowerheads, greenish, aging to purple-brown, on outward curving stems. The name means "fountain." Introduced by Kayser & Seibert's nursery near Darmstadt, Germany. 180 cm (6 ft).

'Karl Foerster'. A reliable form with airy reddish purple flowerheads aging to golden brown. 120–210 cm (4–7 ft).

'Skyracer'. Probably the tallest. Upright stems, with branching flowerheads. Good autumn colour. Selected by Kurt Bluemel of Maryland. 240 cm (8 ft).

'Transparent'. Large airy flowerheads, stems arching out in all directions. 180 cm (6 ft).

'Windsäule' ("wind column"). Upright habit with slender flowerheads. 210–240 cm (7–8 ft).

'Windspiel'. The heads move in the slightest breeze, hence the cultivar name ("wind game"). Good honey-coloured autumn foliage. 180 cm (6 ft).

'Zuneigung'. Slender stems with heavy arching flowerheads, swaying in the breeze. The name means "liking" or "affection." 180–210 cm (6–7 ft).

Panicum

POACEAE

A large genus of grasses from temperate North America and tropical regions world-wide. The name comes from the Latin for millet. *Panicum maximum* (Guinea grass), which must now be called *Urochloa maxima*, from tropical Africa, is very tall (up to 3 m), and grown throughout tropical regions of the world as a fodder plant. Very appeal-ing to birds and wildlife but not exactly ornamental.

Panicum virgatum

switch grass
ORIGIN: Central America to eastern Canada
SIZE: 120–240 × 45–150 cm; 4–8 × 1½–5 ft
FLOWERING TIME: late summer
FLOWER COLOUR: greenish
Sun
Zone 4
Propagate by division
Moderate impact
DESCRIPTION: Dense clumps of vertical or almost vertical stems, topped by a mass of frothy flowers in green, faintly tinted with purple. Their charms are subtle, but they have their devotees among grass enthusiasts. Most gardeners will think these provide just too much vertical grassiness and too little ornament. Personally, I think there are other large grasses that offer a lot more for all the space they take up. Not evergreen. Several well-known varieties are slightly too short to be included.

'Blue Tower'. One of the tallest, with blue-green foliage. Selected by Crystal Palace Perennials of Illinois, from a native population. 240 cm (8 ft).

'Cloud Nine'. Tall, very vertical, with grey-blue-green foliage. Golden autumn colour. Airy flowerheads. Introduced by Bluemount Nursery, Maryland. 150–240 cm (5–8 ft).

'Dallas Blues'. Possibly the bluest vari-ety, with wide leaves and good pink-tinged flowerheads. 150–180 cm (5–6 ft).

'Strictum'. Blue-green foliage, with autumn colour. Airy flowerheads. 150–180 cm (5–6 ft).

Pennisetum

POACEAE

fountain grass

A large genus of grasses from tropical and subtropical areas worldwide. The name comes from the Latin *penna*, meaning "feather," and *seta* which means "bristle." Most have long fluffy heads on wiry stems, over dense mounds of foliage. The best pen-nisetums are too short for us, and only one species makes it to the required height.

Pennisetum macrourum

ORIGIN: South Africa
SIZE: 135–165 × 150–200 cm; 4½–5½ × 5–6½ ft
FLOWERING TIME: late summer
FLOWER COLOUR: pale buff
Sun
Zone 6
Useful for flower arrangement
Interesting seed heads
Propagate by seed or division
Moderate impact
DESCRIPTION: Very long narrow flower-heads on arching stems. Can spread rapidly

to form large masses of green foliage, and can be difficult to eradicate once established. Flowers earlier in areas with warm summers.

Phragmites

POACEAE

reed

Four very similar, very tall grasses found worldwide in wetland habitats. The name comes from the Greek *phragma*, meaning "screen" or "fence."

Phragmites australis

(syn. *P. communis*)

common reed

ORIGIN: wetlands worldwide

SIZE: 250–400 × indefinite cm; 8–13 × indefinite ft

FLOWERING TIME: late summer to early autumn

FLOWER COLOUR: buff

Sun or light shade

Zone 4

Useful for flower arrangement

Propagate by division

High impact

DESCRIPTION: A very large and attractive grass, suitable only for wet places in the wild garden. It forms large colonies of tall stems bearing long narrow, pointed leaves, topped by large feathery flowerheads, all elegantly and picturesquely arranged, but only appropriate for the wider landscape. Flowerheads' colours range from silvery green to purple-brown. Can be highly invasive, and take over the shallow parts of poorly maintained lakes, and can even colonize water as deep as 180 cm (6 ft) deep. Commonly used for thatching in many parts of the world. The similar *Phragmites karka*, from East and South Asia, western tropical Africa and Australia, reaches 10 m (30 ft) in the wild but is not usually more than 3 m (10 ft) in cultivation, and its variegated forms 'Candy Stripe' and 'Variegatus' are even shorter, rarely exceeding 120 cm (4 ft) in height.

subsp. *australis* var. *striatopictus*. A good yellow-striped form, unlikely to exceed 2.5 m (8 ft). More ornamental than the green-leaved species, and it could be kept in check by denying it some of the moisture it needs. Flowerheads are silvery, smaller than the species.

subsp. *pseudodonax*. An absolute giant which can reach 10 m (30 ft) in the wild—possibly the record for a perennial plant—but likely to reach only a mere 7 m (23 ft) in cultivation. Usually takes four or five years to reach its full height. Native to central Europe. Zone 5.

Saccharum

POACEAE

sugar cane

About 40 grass species from warm temperate to tropical regions, usually found in moist habitats. They can be imagined as midway between a miscanthus and a cortaderia, but not as good as either ornamentally. One species is of major economic importance: *Saccharum officinarum*, or sugar cane, a Zone 10 plant which is widely cultivated in subtropical and tropical regions. The generic name comes from the Greek *sakchar* (meaning, predictably, "sugar");

Alexander the Great knew of sugar through his eastern campaigns, but it didn't challenge honey as a sweetener in western Europe until after the Crusades. This genus now includes all the species in the genus *Erianthus*.

Two other species sometimes offered have good autumn colour but are otherwise only moderately ornamental—*Saccharum baldwinii* (syn. *Erianthus strictus*) from the southern United States, and *S. brevibarbe* var. *contortum* (syn. *E. contortus*) from the eastern and southern United States.

Saccharum arundinaceum

ORIGIN: India, China to Malaysia
SIZE: 180–270 (–360) × 120–210 cm; 6–9 (–12) × 4–7 ft
FLOWERING TIME: late summer
FLOWER COLOUR: buff
Sun
Zone 6
Useful for flower arrangement
Propagate by seed or division
High impact
DESCRIPTION: Large open panicles, about 60 cm (2 ft) long, pink at first, fading to silver. Arching, substantial, grey-green leaves, 5 cm (2 in) wide, about 120–150 cm (4–5 ft) long.

Saccharum ravennae

(syn. *Erianthus ravennae*)
Ravenna grass
ORIGIN: Mediterranean
SIZE: 180–450 × 120–270 cm; 6–14 × 4–9 ft
FLOWERING TIME: late summer
FLOWER COLOUR: buff
Sun
Zone 6

Propagate by seed or division
High impact
DESCRIPTION: A feathery plume, less open (and less attractive) than those of *Miscanthus*, pinkish at first, then silvery buff and shiny, the flower stems turning pink in the autumn. A reasonably long period of summer warmth is needed for it to flower. The arching, blue-grey-green foliage forms a mound up to 120 cm (4 ft) high. Very drought tolerant; excessive moisture can cause the stems to fall forward out of their usual vertical position. Self-sows in warm regions. Can be grown in areas that are too cold for *Cortaderia*.

Schoenoplectus

CYPERACEAE
bulrush
Grass-like or reed-like plants found in aquatic or semi-aquatic habitats. They are not strictly grasses, as they are not members of the Poaceae. A cosmopolitan genus with 80 species of annuals and perennials. Note the spelling of the English name, with only one *l*. It has the same derivation as "bole," to do with trunks or stems—nothing to do with bulls.

Schoenoplectus tabernaemontani

(syns. *S. lacustris* subsp. *tabernaemontani*, *Scirpus tabernaemontani*, *S. lacustris*)
bulrush
ORIGIN: Europe, including Great Britain, Asia, Africa, North and Central America
SIZE: 90–180 (–300) × 45–240 cm; 3–6 (–10) × 1½–8 ft
FLOWERING TIME: early summer

FLOWER COLOUR: brown
Sun
Zone 4
Useful for flower arrangement
Propagate by seed or division
Moderate impact
DESCRIPTION: A study in verticality. Grown for the clean, leafless, architectural lines of its stems, which are very straight or else very slightly gracefully curved. The stems arise from a slowly spreading clump. The brownish flowers are almost insignificant, sprouting from the top or the sides of the stems. Prefers neutral to acid conditions. Can be invasive, and if so should be grown in a container within the water. Its variegated selection 'Albescens' is too short to be featured here, usually under 105 cm (3½ ft), but does make an excellent accent plant for the water's edge.

'Zebrinus'. Dark green stems with pale yellow, horizontal bands. Curious but attractive. From Japan. 150–180 cm (5–6 ft).

Stipa
POACEAE
needle grass, feather grass
Most stipas form a dense tuft of tough, narrow, foliage, and carry airy, feathery flowerheads, usually high above the foliage. They are sun lovers. There are about 300 species, mostly perennial, often from dry habitats, in temperate and warm temperate regions worldwide.

Stipa extremiorientalis
(syns. *Achnatherum extremiorientale,*
   A. pekinese)

Schoenoplectus tabernaemontani 'Albescens', seen here with candelabra primroses at Bourton House, Gloucestershire.

ORIGIN: Siberia, China, Korea, Japan
SIZE: 120–180 × 90 cm; 4–6 × 3 ft
FLOWERING TIME: late summer to early autumn
FLOWER COLOUR: green
Sun or light shade
Zone 6
Interesting seed heads
Propagate by division
High impact
DESCRIPTION: Tall, airy flower plumes,

loose, shiny green, purple-tinged and feathery, 40 cm (16 in) long. Light green, upright leaves, 1.2 cm (½ in) wide, arching over at the top. Deciduous. Pleasing, but not in the first class of grasses.

Stipa gigantea
giant oat grass
ORIGIN: central and southern Spain, Portugal, Morocco
SIZE: 150–250 × 90 cm; 5–8 × 3 ft
FLOWERING TIME: midsummer to early autumn
FLOWER COLOUR: buff
Sun
Zone 8
Useful for flower arrangement
Interesting seed heads
Propagate by seed or division
High impact
DESCRIPTION: The sight of these tall oat-like heads, caught in the sunlight on a summer's afternoon is quite stunning. Individually they are nothing much, but the overall effect is usually irresistible to the photographer. The stems rise from an unremarkable, untidy clump of narrow foliage, which is no asset to the garden. *Stipa gigantea* needs

Stipa gigantea, its airy oat-like heads catching the sunlight in a Sussex garden.

to be treated as a specimen plant—in other words, not crowded by plants of the same height but given head room. Dislikes high summer humidity.

'Gold Fontaene'. A taller form, to 250 cm (8 ft) with larger, broader, airier heads. Introduced by Ernst Pagels.

Stipa ramosissima
pillar of smoke grass
ORIGIN: Australia
SIZE: 180–225 × 90 cm; 6–7½ × 3 ft
FLOWERING TIME: spring to winter
FLOWER COLOUR: bronze and buff
Sun
Zone 8
Useful for flower arrangement
Interesting seed heads
Propagate by seed or division
High impact
DESCRIPTION: The English name gives an idea of the general effect, though I would have thought that "feathery firework" might have been equally good as a common name. Feathery, silky panicles of flowers, 15–20 cm (6–8 in) long, bronze-coloured at first, maturing to buff, on vertical or leaning stems, which are woody at the base. Evergreen and non-stop flowering in mild climates, semi-evergreen elsewhere, needing protection in cooler districts. Can be planted as a specimen, in groups or in bands. Performs best in fertile, moist, well-drained soil in full sun, and benefits from regular summer watering during dry periods. Will tolerate drought, and heavy or sandy soils. Wind tolerant, it is good for coastal gardens.

Stipa splendens
ORIGIN: central Asia, Siberia
SIZE: 120–240 × 100–120 cm; 4–8 × 3½–4 ft
FLOWERING TIME: midsummer
FLOWER COLOUR: pinkish buff
Sun
Zone 7
Useful for flower arrangement
Interesting seed heads
Propagate by division
Moderate impact
DESCRIPTION: Feathery panicles, tinged with pinkish purple, on tall, upright, slender stalks, above a mound of thin, arching, but fairly unremarkable, dark evergreen foliage. Looks best in long drifts. Coming from the steppes and semi-deserts of central Asia, it is very drought tolerant.

Typha
TYPHACEAE
reedmace, bulrush, cattail
Waterside plants with unique, velvety, cylindrical flowerheads and vertical, spearlike leaves. Not a member of the grass family (Poaceae), though similar superficially in some ways. About 12 species of a worldwide genus, the only member of the reedmace family (Typhaceae).

Typha angustifolia
lesser bulrush, narrow-leaved reedmace, narrow-leaved cattail
ORIGIN: Europe, including Great Britain, Asia, North and South America
SIZE: 120–180 × 60–indefinite cm; 4–6 × 2–indefinite ft

FLOWERING TIME: mid to late summer
FLOWER COLOUR: brown
Sun
Zone 3
Useful for flower arrangement
Interesting seed heads
Propagate by division
Moderate impact
DESCRIPTION: Similar to the better known *Typha latifolia*, but more slender and elegant. The flowers are in the form of the well-known velvety brown cylinder, rounded at the top, but narrower. The prominent part of the flowerhead consists of the female flowers—the male flowers are on the narrow, buff-coloured spike that rises out of the top of the inflorescence, separated by a short green stem. Paler, narrower leaves than *T. latifolia*, about 1.2 cm (½ in) wide.

Much less common in the wild in Great Britain than *T. latifolia*. A plant for lakes, not ponds, since it spreads rapidly.

Typha latifolia
great reedmace, false bulrush, common cattail
ORIGIN: Europe, including Great Britain, Asia, North America
SIZE: 120–180 (–270) × 90–indefinite cm; 4–6 (–9) × 3–indefinite ft
FLOWERING TIME: summer
FLOWER COLOUR: dark brown
Sun
Zone 3
Useful for flower arrangement
Interesting seed heads
Propagate by division
High impact

The great reedmace, *Typha latifolia*, growing as usual by the water's edge, seen here with *Lythrum salicaria* at Lady Farm, Somerset.

DESCRIPTION: This better known reedmace is more like a heavyweight, regal sceptre in comparison with *Typha angustifolia*. The dark chocolate column is 10–15 cm (4–6 in) long and there is no short stem separating the female parts of the flower from the fluffy golden male section above. The fruits are white and cottony. The leaves are greyish green, 2.5–3.5 cm (1–1½ in) wide, often taller than the flowering stem. Although popularly known as the bulrush in Great Britain, that name should correctly be reserved for *Schoenoplectus tabernaemontani*.

Zizania
POACEAE
wild rice
Three species of wetland grasses.

Zizania aquatica
ORIGIN: North America
SIZE: 180–270 (–360) × 180–240 (–360) cm;
  6–9 (–12) × 6–8 (–12) ft
FLOWERING TIME: summer
FLOWER COLOUR: white and buff
Sun
Zones 4 (annual) or 8 (perennial)
Useful for flower arrangement
Interesting seed heads
Propagate by seed or division
Very high impact

DESCRIPTION: Imagine a huge water-loving plant with leaves like a grassy phormium and flowers like a miscanthus, and you have *Zizania aquatica*. The broad dark green leaves often arch gracefully, and reach up to 150 cm (5 ft). A plant for shallow water at the lake edge. It is sometimes known as annual wild rice, as it tends to die in cold winters, but it is perennial in Zone 8 districts and warmer. The seeds were an important food for Native Americans. Rarely seen in cultivation for some inexplicable reason.

Zizania latifolia
Manchurian wild rice
ORIGIN: Siberia, Far East, Indochina
SIZE: 150–240 (–360) × 150–indefinite cm;
  5–8 (–12) × 5–indefinite ft
FLOWERING TIME: late summer to autumn
FLOWER COLOUR: white and buff
Sun
Zone 7
Useful for flower arrangement
Interesting seed heads
Propagate by seed or division
Very high impact
DESCRIPTION: Similar to *Zizania aquatica*, but always perennial and not quite so tall. Leaves more vertical, arching slightly, but not so much as in *Z. aquatica*. Good yellow autumn colour. For shallow water. Rare in cultivation.

8

RESTIOS AND EQUISETUMS

Restios are an unusual race of plants, mostly from southern Africa, with stiff upright stems like leafless bamboos, though some do have leafy or tassel-like appendages. They are slightly on the tender side, and offer architectural shape and form rather than colour. Equisetums have many similarities to restios visually but are not related at all botanically, being an ancient plant form, showing up in the geological records, and more closely related to ferns.

Calopsis
RESTIONACEAE
Rush-like, or bamboo-like plants, from South Africa. Male and female flowers are on separate plants; the flowers themselves are very small and insignificant—any colouring is usually produced by the bracts which surround the flowers. Although these restios need moisture-retentive soil in summer, they won't tolerate the combination of cold and winter wet, and require protection in colder areas. Prefer poor, slightly acidic soil. The fynbos habitats where these species grow are often subject to fires, and specialized smoke treatment is needed for successful seed germination. Water in well after planting. *Calopsis levynsiae* is slightly too short to be included.

Calopsis paniculata
(syns. *Restio paniculatus, Leptocarpus paniculatus*)
ORIGIN: Western Cape, South Africa
SIZE: 150–250 × 100–200 cm; 5–8 × 3½–6½ ft
FLOWERING TIME: autumn
FLOWER COLOUR: whitish
Sun
Zone 9
Useful for flower arrangement
Propagate by seed or division
High impact
DESCRIPTION: A tall fluffy, reed-like plant with bright green leaves and arching stems, arising from a densely packed cluster, the lower part of the stems being like the stems of a bamboo. Clusters of grass-like flowers

Calopsis paniculata, seen here in its native habitat in South Africa.

at the terminal ends of the stems. Female plants have small white inflorescences, the inflorescences on male plants being less showy and brownish. An architectural plant for the waterside, or bog garden.

Elegia
RESTIONACEAE
Restios from South Africa. Male and female flowers are on separate plants; male flowers drooping, female flowers upright. Cultivation requirements are similar to those of *Calopsis*. Several of these species were traditionally used for thatching in the past.

Elegia capensis
ORIGIN: Western Cape, South Africa
SIZE: 100–300 × 75–200 cm; 3½–10 × 2½–6½ ft
FLOWERING TIME: spring
FLOWER COLOUR: yellowish brown
Sun
Zone 8
Useful for flower arrangement
Propagate by seed or division
High impact
DESCRIPTION: A striking and distinctive plant, a bit like an aquarium plant that's escaped, or even a horsetail (*Equisetum*). Clumps of more or less vertical stems, with leaf-like branchlets arranged in a series of

feathery whorls at each node up each stem. Fast growing, but unlikely to exceed 200 cm (6½ ft) except in very favourable conditions. Prefers acidic soils but is not that fussy. Good beside water and prefers moist soil during the summer. Evergreen in mild areas, but cut back by frost elsewhere. Protect with a thick mulch in colder areas. Makes excellent cut foliage.

Elegia elephantinum
(syns. *Chondropetalum tectorum* f. *elephantinum, C. elephantium*)
dakriet, elephant reed
ORIGIN: Western Cape, South Africa
SIZE: 100–240 × 100–200 cm; 3½–8 × 3½–6½ ft
FLOWERING TIME: winter
FLOWER COLOUR: brown

Sun
Zone 9
Propagate by seed or division
High impact
DESCRIPTION: A clump of dark green, overwintering, rush-like stems with papery chocolate-brown bands, stiff and vertical in the centre, but radiating out in an arc around the edges of the clump, with long-lasting dark brown seed heads. *Elegia tectorum* is similar but smaller. Prefers moist but well-drained soil, low in fertility.

Elegia racemosa
rustling reed
ORIGIN: Western Cape, South Africa
SIZE: 40–180 × 100–300 cm; 1½–6 × 3½–10 ft
FLOWERING TIME: summer

The stiff, vertical reeds of the elephant reed, *Elegia elephantinum*, seen here in the wild in South Africa.

FLOWER COLOUR: pale brown
Sun
Zone 9
Interesting seed heads
Propagate by seed or division
High impact
DESCRIPTION: An accent plant, consisting of a clump of stiff, vertical, overwintering stems (another "leafless bamboo"), blue-green and bright green, topped with neat brown flowers and seed heads. Likes moist, well-drained soil. Mulching will help to retain moisture, and later will provide some frost protection.

Equisetum
EQUISETACEAE
horsetail

Horsetails are not related at all to restios, but are much more closely allied to ferns. They are included here because of their visual similarity. In terms of the development of plants through geological time, these are some of the most primitive, their allies being clearly seen in coal seams of the Carboniferous Era, about 300 million years ago. They are characterized by having clumps of vertical stems, with side branches—in some cases giving a Christmas tree effect. The visible plant consists entirely of stems—there are no true leaves, or flowers. Horsetails tend to be elegant, but rampantly invasive and hard to eradicate, and so are best confined to a large container. They are often found in damp places and even shallow water. There are about 25 species, found worldwide, except in Australia and New Zealand.

Equisetum giganteum
ORIGIN: South and Central America
SIZE: 150–300 × indefinite cm; 5–10 × indefinite ft
Sun or shade
Zone 9
Useful for flower arrangement
Propagate by division
Very high impact
DESCRIPTION: An extraordinary and highly desirable looking plant. But since it forms dense jungle-like stands in the wild, maybe one should be careful. It forms clumps of narrow, towering green stems with side branches curving slightly upwards. Few other plants are 3 m (10 ft) high but only 20 cm (8 in) wide. A good clump is needed to give the vertical stems mutual support, as they may otherwise sag under their own weight. Sadly no nurserymen are offering it at the moment.

Equisetum hyemale
Dutch rush
ORIGIN: Europe, mostly excluding the Mediterranean, Asia, North America
SIZE: 60–150 (–300) × indefinite cm; 2–5 (–10) × indefinite ft
Light shade
Zone 4
Useful for flower arrangement
Propagate by division
High impact
DESCRIPTION: Like a mini-bamboo, this horsetail has no side branches, but does have very stout, green stems with prominent joints roughly every 10 cm (4 in) up the stem, coloured buff, brown or black. Less aggressive than some other species, but still

The ornamental *Equisetum hyemale*, seen here growing in a container at Knoll Gardens, Dorset.

Ischyrolepis subverticillata

ORIGIN: Western Cape, South Africa
SIZE: 100–240 × 75–200 cm; 3½–8 × 2½–6½ ft
FLOWERING TIME: autumn
FLOWER COLOUR: greenish yellow
Sun or shade
Zone 9
Useful for flower arrangement
Interesting seed heads
Propagate by seed or division
High impact
DESCRIPTION: An extraordinary plant, and probably the restio which has been longest in cultivation—imagine a herbaceous version of a cross between a tamarisk and a Pfitzer juniper. Feathery arching sprays of mid-green overwintering foliage (in reality, loose whorls of very fine branchlets) tipped by flowers, followed by (spoilt by, some might say) silvery brown seed heads. Fast growing. Remove older outer branches as necessary when they get tatty, to encourage new growth.

not really to be trusted out of a container. The typical species is unlikely to reach a height of more than 75 cm (2½ ft) in dry or cold districts. A moist situation is much preferred.

var. *affine* (syn. var. *robustum*). Stems flushed pink when young. Can reach an astonishing 300 cm (10 ft) in the wild.

Ischyrolepis
RESTIONACEAE
Restios from South Africa. The cultivation needs are similar to those of *Calopsis*.

Restio
RESTIONACEAE
Stemmy, rush-like, or bamboo-like plants from South Africa, requiring protection in colder areas. Their cultivation needs are similar to those of *Calopsis*.

Restio brunneus

ORIGIN: Western Cape, South Africa
SIZE: 100–200 × 50–100 cm; 3½–6½ × 1½–3½ ft
FLOWERING TIME: winter
FLOWER COLOUR: brownish

Sun
Zone 9
Propagate by seed or division
High impact
DESCRIPTION: A dense clump of bright
green, vertical, overwintering, rush-like
stems, with a few persistent brown sheaths
along the stems, and dotted at the top with
bristly brownish flowerheads and seed heads.

Restio quadratus

ORIGIN: Western Cape, South Africa
SIZE: 100–200 × 100–150 cm; 3½–6½ ×
    3½–5 ft
FLOWERING TIME: midsummer
FLOWER COLOUR: white
Sun or light shade
Zone 9
Useful for flower arrangement
Propagate by seed or division
Very high impact
DESCRIPTION: A striking plant, and one
of the best restios, like a fuzzy water plant
that has emerged onto dry land. Clumps
of bright green, upright stems, with occasional brown sheaths along their length.
The stems are square in section and often
curve over with the weight of the mass of
soft, fluffy foliage (actually sterile branchlets). The females provide a more striking
show of flowers than most restios. Requires
reasonably moist soil, and won't tolerate prolonged summer drought. Old stems
(about three years old) should be cut away
down to the base as soon as they begin to
look unsightly.

Restio quadratus.

Rhodocoma

RESTIONACEAE
A small genus of restios from South Africa,
whose cultivation needs are similar to those
of *Calopsis*.

Rhodocoma arida

ORIGIN: Western Cape, South Africa
SIZE: 80–200 × 50–100 cm; 2½–6½ ×
    1½–3½ ft
FLOWERING TIME: autumn
FLOWER COLOUR: brownish
Sun
Zone 9

Rhodocoma capensis, a clump-forming restio from South Africa.

Interesting seed heads
Propagate by seed or division
High impact
DESCRIPTION: A compact clump of blue-green, overwintering, reed-like stems, vertical or slightly leaning, with large brown sheaths. Topped by brownish seed heads. Grows best in well-drained acidic soil in full sun. Tolerates dry conditions.

Rhodocoma capensis

ORIGIN: Western Cape, South Africa
SIZE: 100–200 × 100–200 cm; 3½–6½ × 3½–6½ ft
FLOWERING TIME: spring
FLOWER COLOUR: pink and brown
Sun
Zone 9
Interesting seed heads
Propagate by seed or division

Very high impact
DESCRIPTION: One of the most striking restios. Compact clumps of straight, dark green, overwintering stems, vertical or leaning out at ten degrees, occasionally arching. Whorls of leaf-like branchlets at the nodes, giving slightly equisetum-like effect.

Rhodocoma gigantea

(syns. *Thamnochortus giganteus, Restio giganteus*)
koala fern
ORIGIN: Western Cape, South Africa
SIZE: 200–300 × 100–200 cm; 6½–10 × 3½–6½ ft
FLOWERING TIME: autumn
FLOWER COLOUR: greenish and white
Sun
Zone 9
Useful for flower arrangement
Interesting seed heads
Propagate by seed
Very high impact
DESCRIPTION: One of the most attractive restios, making a good feature or background plant. Dense clumps of wiry arching stems with many whorls of fine, whiskery foliage (actually very thin branchlets) at each node. During the long flowering season, the inflorescences add considerably to the height of the plant. Male plants have small greenish yellow flowers, while the female plants have small white flowers. Fast growing, and takes about three years to reach its full height. Like many restios it is not permanently perennial, but should last at least ten years.

Grows on well-drained, slightly acid, frost-free slopes in the wild, and therefore needs protection in colder areas. Cut out old stems when they become unsightly. Difficult to divide, owing to the compactness of the clumps. Closely related to *Rhodocoma foliosus*, but distinguished by its greater height and different flowering time.

Thamnochortus
RESTIONACEAE
A small genus of restios from South Africa.

Thamnochortus cinereus
silver reed
ORIGIN: Western Cape, South Africa
SIZE: 80–400 × 50–100 cm; 2½–13 × 1½–3½ ft
FLOWERING TIME: autumn to winter
FLOWER COLOUR: greenish
Sun
Zone 9
Interesting seed heads
Propagate by seed or division
High impact
DESCRIPTION: Clumps of wiry, overwintering stems, which are velvety and almost vertical, fanning out from a small base. The stems are clad in thread-like, grey-green foliage (actually sterile branchlets), slightly reminiscent of southernwood, *Artemisia abrotanum*. The stems are topped by inflorescences of silvery or golden brown flower and seed heads, like certain grass flowers, which can be as much as 150 cm (5 ft) above the rest of the plant. Like many restios, it acts like a herbaceous plant in cold districts and re-grows in the spring. The main body of the plant is unlikely to exceed 100 cm (3½ ft) in cultivation.

Moist but well-drained soil is preferred. Like many restios it doesn't live forever, but should last for at least seven years. Remove old unattractive stems as necessary. Does well as a pot plant.

Thamnochortus insignis
Albertinia thatching reed
ORIGIN: Western Cape, South Africa
SIZE: 100–200 × 40–100 cm; 3½–6½ × 1½–3½ ft
FLOWERING TIME: autumn
FLOWER COLOUR: grey and pinkish brown
Sun
Zone 8
Interesting seed heads
Propagate by seed or division
Very high impact
DESCRIPTION: A striking accent plant. A clump of tall, straight, green stems, unbranched, vertical or leaning slightly. Pinkish brown inflorescences and seed heads. Very fast growing. Widely used for thatching in South Africa.

Thamnochortus insignis.

9

FLOWER SPIKES

The plants in this chapter could have been slotted in here and there among the plants in the "Early Perennials," "Late Perennials" and "Midseason Perennials" chapters, but have been separated out here because of their habit. They all have their flowers arranged in vertical spikes, creating a pleasing vertical effect, which contrasts effectively with leafy arching plants or others with more rounded shapes. Among the most well known are foxgloves (*Digitalis*), red hot pokers (*Kniphofia*) and delphiniums.

Acanthus
ACANTHACEAE
bear's breeches

Acanthus mollis and its forms must be among the top 20 perennials, especially for admirers of architectural plants that have bold form and stately outline. It's the kind of plant that looks good in black and white photographs. In spite of their size, acanthus plants can benefit from a position at the front of the border where the whole plant can be seen, and generally they should be treated as feature plants and as specimens. The leaves are large, in a serious shade of dark green, and the tall flower spikes range between white, mauvy white and pink. Leaves and flowers are both prickly to varying degrees. Deep rooted and drought-resistant, they are not suited to wet, cold districts. They are often hard to eradicate once planted. Sadly, the naming of varieties in gardens and nurseries is in a fairly confused state, with many wrongly labelled plants circulating.

Acanthus mollis
ORIGIN: southern Europe, northwestern Africa
SIZE: 105–200 × 120 cm; 3½–6½ × 4 ft
FLOWERING TIME: summer
FLOWER COLOUR: mauve and white
Sun or light shade
Zones 7–9
Useful for flower arrangement
Interesting seed heads
Propagate by seed, division or root cuttings
High impact
DESCRIPTION: A first-class plant, said to

have been the inspiration for the leafy carvings on Corinthian capitals on the columns of Classical architecture. It forms a large clump of large, handsome, dark green leaves, not very prickly, usually arching, and partially overwintering. Some forms have good, glossy foliage, and these are the ones to choose. The flower spikes are tall and stately, part pale mauve, part white, and surprisingly prickly. Occasionally it suffers from powdery mildew. Some plants sold as simply as *Acanthus mollis* should be labelled Latifolius Group. The varieties 'Turkish Form', 'Hollard's Gold' (syns. 'Fielding's Gold', 'New Zealand Gold') and 'Tasmanian Angel' are all shorter.

'Albus'. A white-flowered form. Beautiful, but can be shy to flower. 'Jeff Alba' or 'Jeff Albus' are probably the same, and none of them may differ much from *Acanthus mollis* (Latifolius Group) 'Rue Ledan'.

Latifolius Group. Excellent glossy foliage forms, with broad, arching, shallowly lobed leaves, and taller spikes; however, some forms have fewer flower spikes than plain *Acanthus mollis*.

(Latifolius Group) 'Oakleaf'. Larger leaves, more deeply cut, sometimes resembling the leaf of the red oak.

(Latifolius Group) 'Rue Ledan' (syn. 'Jardin en Face'). Good white and green flowers, which are scented. Floriferous, and does not self-seed, and possibly sterile. Discovered in a garden in Matignon, France.

'Niger'. The glossy leaves are a darker shade of green than typical.

'Pride of Morvan'. Leaves variegated cream and yellow. Not to everyone's taste.

The elegant foliage and flower spikes of *Acanthus mollis*.

Acanthus sennii

ORIGIN: Ethiopia
SIZE: 75–180 × 100 cm; 2½–6 × 3½ ft
FLOWERING TIME: early autumn
FLOWER COLOUR: scarlet
Sun
Zone 8
Useful for flower arrangement
Interesting seed heads
Propagate by seed, division or root cuttings
Moderate impact

DESCRIPTION: A recent introduction by Hillview Nurseries, Shropshire. Sub-shrubby, with a scrambling habit. Leaves dark green, stout, prickly and holly-like, with scarlet flowers in autumn. Needs protection in cooler areas, hardier in a well-drained situation. Deciduous.

Acanthus spinosus

ORIGIN: southern Europe
SIZE: 120–240 × 105 cm; 4–8 × 3½ ft
FLOWERING TIME: late summer
FLOWER COLOUR: mauve
Sun or light shade
Zone 7
Useful for flower arrangement
Interesting seed heads
Propagate by seed, division or root cuttings
High impact

DESCRIPTION: A study in prickliness, as the name suggests. The leaves can be up to 90 cm (3 ft) long, arching, deeply divided and armed with an array of spiny points. Tall spikes of white flowers with purple bracts. Much admired by many, but a bit too vicious for my taste. Both the white-spotted 'Lady Moore' and 'Ferguson's Form', said to be the best flowering selection, are compact growers.

'Royal Haughty'. Leaves mottled, and deeply cut, but not so spiny.

Spinosissimus Group. Narrow leaves, more spiny and finely dissected than those of *Acanthus spinosus*, with silvery white veins and spines. The flower spikes are also more spiny, but not as free flowering as normal, with slim flowers, almost white. A range of available forms means that there is no clear dividing line between this and *A. spinosus*.

Not for the fainthearted—"An established clump of this looks like a grey and green porcupine," says Graham Stuart Thomas.

Other *Acanthus* Varieties

'Morning's Candle'. A good floriferous form, thought to be *Acanthus mollis* × *A. spinosus*. 135–165 cm (4½–5½ ft).

'Summer Beauty' (syn. 'Summer Dance'). Probably *Acanthus mollis* × *A. spinosus*. Very tall flower spikes, 165 cm (5½ ft) high, with foliage to 75 cm (2½ ft), with dark, glossy green leaves more incised than is usual for *A. mollis*. More tolerant of summer heat than *A. mollis*. 'Chinese Garden' may be the same thing.

Actaea

RANUNCULACEAE

baneberry, bugbane, cohosh
Leafy, shade-loving plants, formerly in the genus *Cimicifuga*, from northern temperate regions, with ferny foliage and erect flower spikes. Now that the cimicifugas have been merged with the actaeas, we are left with no way of distinguishing between two quite distinct sets of plants, whose differences are obvious to a child—this can hardly be a convenient arrangement. The plants in the original *Actaea* group, known for their berries, are too short for inclusion. The former cimicifugas listed here offer graceful, towering panicles of sweetly scented flowers, in not-quite-straight, bottlebrush spikes, which stand well above the foliage. The conspicuous parts of the small, closely packed flowers are the stamens not the petals. These plants are versatile, but prefer

light shade and rich, moist, loamy or leafy soil. The roots are very close to the surface and so are vulnerable to drying out, and an annual mulch is advisable. They rarely need support. A great asset to the shade garden.

Actaea arizonica

(syn. *Cimicifuga arizonica*)
ORIGIN: southwestern United States
SIZE: 120–180 × 75 cm; 4–6 × 2½ ft
FLOWERING TIME: late summer
FLOWER COLOUR: whitish
Shade
Zone 4
Useful for flower arrangement
Propagate by seed or division
Moderate impact
DESCRIPTION: Forms a clump of good pale green leaves, with erect flower spikes well clear of the cut foliage. Requires moist soil.

Actaea cimicifuga

(syn. *Cimicifuga foetida*)
ORIGIN: Siberia, Mongolia, China, northern Pakistan, Bhutan, northern India, Nepal, Myanmar
SIZE: 100–240 × 75 cm; 3½–8 ft
FLOWERING TIME: late summer
FLOWER COLOUR: yellow
Sun or shade
Zones 3–7
Useful for flower arrangement
Interesting seed heads
Propagate by seed or division
High impact
DESCRIPTION: Scented greenish creamy yellow flowers on branching stems, the main stem arching gracefully well above the dark green foliage, which is attractively veined,

The irregular, white, bottlebrush flower spikes of actaeas at the back of the border at Holehird Gardens, Windermere, Cumbria.

much divided. Interesting green seed pods. The plant smells terrible, not surprising since this is the species which gave us the unappealing name "bugbane." Its foliage can be used to drive bugs from your bed, which some readers may find useful.

Actaea dahurica

(syns. *Cimicifuga dahurica, Actinospora dahurica*)
ORIGIN: eastern Russia, Siberia, Mongolia, central and northern China, Korea
SIZE: 150–270 × 90 cm; 5–9 × 3 ft
FLOWERING TIME: late summer to early autumn
FLOWER COLOUR: white
Shade or light shade
Zone 4
Useful for flower arrangement
Interesting seed heads
Propagate by seed or division
High impact
DESCRIPTION: Tall, elegant, multi-branching heads of large, fluffy, pure-white flowers. Deeply cut, aromatic foliage with many leaflets. Male and female flowers are on separate plants, the male being more floriferous. Dahuria (sometimes spelt Dauria or Davuria) is the Latin name for what is now southeastern Siberia.

Actaea podocarpa

(syns. *Cimicifuga americana, C. cordifolia, C. podocarpa*)
ORIGIN: eastern United States
SIZE: 180–240 × 75 cm; 6–8 × 2½ ft
FLOWERING TIME: late summer
FLOWER COLOUR: creamy white
Sun or light shade
Zone 7
Useful for flower arrangement
Interesting seed heads
Propagate by seed or division
Subtle impact
DESCRIPTION: Rarely cultivated, even in the United States. Fluffy white flowers on branching stems. The roots were used medicinally by Native Americans.

Actaea racemosa

(syn. *Cimicifuga racemosa*)
black cohosh
ORIGIN: eastern and north-central United States, Ontario
SIZE: 120–240 × 75 cm; 4–8 × 2½ ft
FLOWERING TIME: late summer
FLOWER COLOUR: white
Shade or light shade
Zone 4
Useful for flower arrangement
Interesting seed heads
Propagate by seed or division
High impact
DESCRIPTION: Creamy white flowers on long, irregularly curving flower spikes. Attractive fresh green foliage with very many long narrow leaflets, and a sturdy plant, earlier than other cimicifugas. Unpleasantly scented. The most closely related of the former members of *Cimicifuga* to the "original" actaeas.

Actaea simplex

(syns. *A. cimicifuga* var. *simplex, Cimicifuga simplex*)
ORIGIN: far eastern Russia, Mongolia, China, Japan, Korea, Taiwan
SIZE: 90–180 × 45–60 cm; 3–6 × 1½–2 ft
FLOWERING TIME: autumn
FLOWER COLOUR: white
Sun or light shade
Zone 4
Useful for flower arrangement
Interesting seed heads
Propagate by seed or division

Moderate impact

DESCRIPTION: Arching stems of sweetly
scented, white flowers in the autumn, the
stems unbranched (or "simple"—hence the
specific name) or sometimes with short
branches. Deeply cut and divided dark
green leaves. A species notable for the varieties it has produced.

Atropurpurea Group. A range of forms
with purplish foliage which colours well in
full sun.

(Atropurpurea Group) 'Brunette'. Scented
pinkish white flowers from purple buds,
above dark purplish brown leaves. Late
summer to early autumn.

(Atropurpurea Group) 'Hillside Black
Beauty'. Pale pink, fragrant flowers tinged
with reddish purple, opening from pink
buds, on upright or slightly arching, dark
red stems, arching at the tips. Red-flushed
purple foliage.

(Atropurpurea Group) 'James Compton'.
White, strongly scented flowers on red-
dish purple stems. Good purple-red foliage.
Raised by Piet Oudolf of the Netherlands.

(Atropurpurea Group) 'Mountain Wave'.
Dark red foliage and white flowers, not as
deep a purple as some other varieties. Very
tall flower spikes, wave-like in shape.

(Atropurpurea Group) 'Pink Spike'. Tall
pale pink spikes of scented flowers, on dark
stems, over chocolate-purple foliage.

'Prichard's Giant'. Large heads, with
long creamy white main spikes and shorter
ones below, over glossy green foliage on a
very tall plant. Good seed heads. Raised
by Maurice Prichard of Riverslea Nursery,
Hampshire. Up to 240 cm (8 ft) or even
more.

Actaea simplex (Atropurpurea Group) 'James
Compton'. Not many perennials have
purple foliage, but this is one of the best.

Actaea yunnanensis

(syn. *Cimicifuga yunnanensis*)
ORIGIN: Yunnan, Sichuan, China
SIZE: 150–210 × 75 cm; 5–7 × 2½ ft
FLOWERING TIME: summer
FLOWER COLOUR: yellow
Light shade

Zone 4
Useful for flower arrangement
Interesting seed heads
Propagate by seed or division
High impact
DESCRIPTION: Tall spikes of primrose yellow, sometimes paler.

Agastache
LAMIACEAE
giant hyssop
Sun lovers with aromatic foliage (for better or for worse), and vertical flower spikes with narrow panicles of flowers, on robust, upright stems. Most species prefer well-drained, fertile soil in full sun, and many are attractive to bees and butterflies. They tend to be short-lived as perennials, especially in Zone 7 areas and colder. The herb anise hyssop, *Agastache foeniculum*, is slightly too short for this book.

Agastache nepetoides
yellow giant hyssop
ORIGIN: southern Canada, eastern United States
SIZE: 150–180 × 120 cm; 5–6 × 4 ft
FLOWERING TIME: late summer
FLOWER COLOUR: greenish yellow
Sun
Zone 4
Interesting seed heads
Propagate by seed or cuttings
Subtle impact
DESCRIPTION: A fast-growing wildling with 12 cm (5 in) spikes densely packed with tiny, yellowish green flowers on aromatic foliage; leaves with scalloped margins.

Agastache scrophulariifolia
purple giant hyssop
ORIGIN: eastern United States, Canada
SIZE: 120–180 × 120 cm; 4–6 × 4 ft
FLOWERING TIME: summer
FLOWER COLOUR: purple
Sun or light shade
Zones 4–6
Interesting seed heads
Propagate by seed or cuttings
Moderate impact
DESCRIPTION: Pale purple spikes on a large subshrubby perennial, with jagged-edged, liquorice-scented foliage. Loved by bees and butterflies. Needs soil that doesn't dry out.

Agastache urticifolia
nettle-leaved giant hyssop
ORIGIN: western United States
SIZE: 90–180 × 75 cm; 3–6 × 2½ ft
FLOWERING TIME: late summer
FLOWER COLOUR: various
Sun
Zone 7
Interesting seed heads
Propagate by seed or cuttings
Moderate impact
DESCRIPTION: An architectural foliage plant, with spikes of flowers of green, cream, pink or violet. The nettle-like leaves are strongly fragrant.
   'Alba'. A near-white form.

Agrimonia
ROSACEAE
agrimony
All species have slender spikes of yellow flowers, rather like a verbascum without the

The elegant yellow flower spikes of *Agrimonia eupatoria* blending with the blue flowers of a short, ornamental echium.

grey foliage. The seed cases come in the form of prickly burrs, which can attach themselves to clothing and animal skins, helping to spread the plant around. Most agrimonies are wildlings, not quite smart enough for the flower border or tall enough for this book, although *Agrimonia parviflora*, from the United States, can reach 200 cm (6½ ft). Not quite as tall, *A. eupatoria*, found in the wild throughout Europe, northwest Asia and north Africa, has attractive seed heads, which makes it a good plant for lovers of the "beautiful death syndrome." Some even shorter species have long established herbal uses, but otherwise agrimonies should be reserved for the wild garden.

Chamerion
ONAGRACEAE
willow herb
About 15 herbaceous species from temperate and arctic areas of the northern hemisphere. Colourful, but mostly too invasive for the garden. Closely related to *Epilobium*, and only recently separated from that genus.

Chamerion angustifolium
(syn. *Epilobium angustifolium*)
fireweed, rosebay willowherb
ORIGIN: northern temperate areas worldwide
SIZE: 120–200 × indefinite cm; 4–6½ × indefinite ft

FLOWERING TIME: late summer
FLOWER COLOUR: deep pink
Sun or light shade
Zone 3
Interesting seed heads

The elegant white flower spikes of *Chamerion angustifolium* 'Album', with bronze fennel and *Alchemilla mollis*, in a garden in West Gloucestershire.

Propagate by division
High impact
DESCRIPTION: Introduce this into your garden at your peril. Attractive, but too invasive even for the wild garden. Elegant spires of deep, bright pink, lasting many weeks, followed by whiskery white seed heads. Quickly forms large clumps. Admire it in the hedgerows, unless you live in the harsher northern parts of the world, where you are grateful for anything.

'Album'. The white form is very tasteful and is said to be slightly less invasive—but I wouldn't be too certain about it.

'Isobel'. Paler pink.

'Stahl Rose'. A pleasanter shade of pink.

Delphinium
RANUNCULACEAE

The delphiniums seen in the gardens of the good, the great and the devotee, are almost all modern hybrids. The few species which are occasionally seen, such as *Delphinium nudicaule*, *D. requienii* or *D. tatsienense*, are all considerably shorter than the blue giants bred by man. There are about 350 species altogether, from temperate regions of the northern hemisphere, especially western China and California; a handful occur in the mountains of East Africa. They are mostly perennials, though a few are annual or biennial.

Delphinium hybrids come in every conceivable and delicious shade of blue—sky blue, china blue, gentian blue, through to violet, lilac, mauvy pink and white. Attempts have been made to raise red and yellow ones, with limited success, and considering good blue perennials are rare and special, and shades of red and yellow can easily be found in a wide range of other, easier-to-cultivate plants, this seems a fairly pointless exercise.

The flower spike consists of a closely packed mass of flowers, neatly and spirally arranged on an erect flower spike, or "bloom" as the specialists call it, the stems often branching to produce subsidiary spikes of lesser size. The brightly coloured part of the flower consists of a group of five sepals, which look as if they were petals, the true petals being small and situated in the centre of the flower, sometimes called the "bee" or the "eye." Behind each flower is the narrow spur, projecting back and containing the nectar. Regrettably the flowering period is fairly short.

The foliage rises from a woody crown and is lush and mid-green, the leaves three- to five-lobed and toothed, but this is always overshadowed but the splendour of the flowers. The new foliage is especially susceptible to attack from slugs and snails. Caterpillars too are fond of delphiniums, and there are leaf miners, spider mites and powdery mildew to contend with. Delphiniums are poisonous and should be handled with caution. As with many toxic plants they also have uses in folk medicine.

But the biggest drawback for the gardener who is looking for an easy life is the need for staking. A cage of canes is recommended, but how to do this without making the plant look as though it is wearing crutches is not easy. Devotees who grow their plants in rows and are only interested in producing magnificent flower spikes to take to flower shows won't mind if this looks dire, but this will not do for the ordinary gardener.

The classification of delphiniums seems to be in a state of confusion, with words like "group," "hybrids" and "series" floating about without much logic, partly because of the existence of seed strains. Here, following the species, they are presented in groups, which arrangement hopefully has the advantage of giving anyone unfamiliar with the varieties some idea of the plant from its name and classification.

The Pacific Coast delphiniums are just a little too short to be included.

Delphinium cardinale
scarlet larkspur
ORIGIN: southern California, Baja California, Mexico
SIZE: 45–75 (–180) × 30–60 (–90) cm; 1½–2½ (–6) × 1–2 (–3) ft
FLOWERING TIME: early summer
FLOWER COLOUR: scarlet
Sun
Zone 8
Useful for flower arrangement
Propagate by seed or cuttings
High impact
DESCRIPTION: An attractive but usually short-lived species. Flowers in loose racemes, bright red with a yellow eye and long spurs. Deeply dissected leaves. Unlikely to reach more than 75 cm (2½ ft) in its first year after planting but much taller in subsequent years—if it survives. Resents winter wet. Support required.

Delphinium elatum

ORIGIN: Pyrenees, montane, central and southern Europe, temperate central Asia
SIZE: 90–150 (–300) × 45–60 cm; 3–5 (–10) × 1½–2 ft
FLOWERING TIME: summer
FLOWER COLOUR: blue and violet
Sun or light shade
Zone 2
Useful for flower arrangement
Interesting seed heads
Propagate by seed or cuttings
High impact
DESCRIPTION: This is the species from which most of the hybrids in cultivation have been raised. The individual flowers are smallish and closely packed along a flower spike about 30 cm (1 ft) long, in variable shades of blue and violet. Less likely to require support than the hybrids. The true species is now rarely cultivated or offered for sale, though a stray second generation seedling may resemble it.

Other *Delphinium* Varieties

Delphinium Belladonna Group

This group is characterized by short spikes of single flowers, on many-branched stems, loosely spaced, thus avoiding the "fat and over-bred" look of some hybrids. The individual flowers are small and delicate, with small eyes, the colours ranging from violet, through shades of blue, to white. Almost all the varieties in this group are too short to be included—in fact, many were selected for compactness, presumably to avoid staking. High impact.

'Völkerfrieden'. Bright, gentian blue. 135–165 cm (4½–5½ ft).

Delphinium Centurion Series

A seed strain developed in the Netherlands by Sahin Zaden. Varieties with large, semi-double flowers. 150–180 cm (5–6 ft). Other colours are sometimes available.

'Centurion Sky Blue'. Pale blue.
'Centurion White Strain'. White.

Delphinium Elatum Group

A variable range of traditional garden hybrids, with large flowers, erect habit, often with flat-faced flowers, sometimes double or semi-double, flowering in midsummer. The earliest varieties were probably raised using *Delphinium elatum*, *D. formosanum* and *D. exaltatum*. Kelways of Langport, Somerset, was one of the earliest hybridizers of these plants, in the late 19th century, followed by Blackmore and Langdon of Bath, in the early 20th century. High impact.

'Blue Dawn'. Pale blue with a pink flush, with brown eyes, on a long spike. 150–240 cm (5–8 ft).

'Blue Nile'. Blue with a white eye. 120–165 cm (4–5½ ft).

'Bruce'. Violet blue with a brown eye, on long spikes. 150–180 cm (5–6 ft).

'Can-Can'. Purple-blue, double, with no eye. 140–180 cm (4½–6 ft).

'Cassius'. Deep gentian blue with a purple flush, almost black eye. 135–165 cm (4½–5½ ft).

'Emily Hawkins'. Flat, delicate, pale lavender, with a buff eye. Raised by David Bassett of Broughton, Oxfordshire. 165–200 cm (5½–6½ ft).

'Faust'. Dark blue flowers with a blue-black eye, on long spikes. 180–240 cm (6–8 ft).

'Fenella'. Small, bright gentian blue flowers, with black eye. 135–165 cm (4½–5½ ft).

'Finsteraarhorn'. Single, dark gentian blue, with black eye. Wind resistant. From Karl Foerster of Germany, 1936. 135–165 cm (4½–5½ ft).

'Gillian Dallas'. Large flowers, pale, dusky blue with a white eye. Raised by David Bassett. 150–180 cm (5–6 ft).

'Gordon Forsyth'. Amethyst blue, on long spikes, with dark grey eyes. Susceptible to mildew. 150–180 cm (5–6 ft).

'Lucia Sahin'. Dark sugar pink, with dark brown eye, on tapering stems. A breakthrough in colour. Fades with age. 200 cm (6½ ft).

'Michael Ayres'. Violet, with blue outer sepals. 180 cm (6 ft).

'Min'. Pale lavender, darker at the edges. 150–180 cm (5–6 ft).

'Olive Poppleton'. Cream, with subtle flush of lavender, with pale brown eye. 180 cm (6 ft).

'Rosemary Brock'. Deep sugar pink, flushed white, brown eye. 165 cm (5½ ft).

'Skyline'. Sky blue, double. 210 cm (7 ft).

'Susan Edmunds'. Pale lavender, double. 165 cm (5½ ft).

The subtle pink shades of *Delphinium* (Elatum Group) 'Lucia Sahin' at Rougham Hall Nurseries, Suffolk.

There is nothing quite like delphiniums for attractive shades of blue flower spikes. This one is *Delphinium* (Elatum Group) 'Skyline'.

Delphinium New Century Hybrids

Seed strains developed in the Netherlands by Sahin Zaden. Tall plants, some in a mixture of colours, separate colours sometimes offered. High impact.

'Dreaming Spires'. A mixed range of colours. 180 cm (6 ft).

Delphinium New Millennium Series

'Green Twist'. Pale lime-green flowers aging to white. Much in demand from florists as a cut flower.

'Pagan Purples'. Dark purple, dark blue or mauve, eyeless.

Delphinium New Zealand Hybrids

Allied to the Elatum Group. ORIGINally seed strains developed by Dowdeswell's of New Zealand. Tough, vigorous and bred to tolerate humid summers. High impact. 120–180 cm (4–6 ft).

'Blushing Brides'. Soft dusky pink flowers with brown or white eyes, on strong stems. Good, large foliage, and vigorous growth habit.

Dusky Maidens Group. Dusky pink, with brown eye.

Digitalis

SCROPHULARIACEAE
foxglove

Well known in the wild, for their flower spikes of pendant, wide-tubular flowers. More of a mitt than a glove—for a very small fox. About 20 short-lived perennial and biennial species from Europe, includ-

The vertical stems of white foxgloves, accompanied by white anthemis, along a narrow path.

ing Great Britain, Mediterranean, western and central Asia. Naturalized in the United States.

Digitalis purpurea

common foxglove
ORIGIN: western Europe
SIZE: 75–180 × 30–60 cm; 2½–6 × 1–2 ft
FLOWERING TIME: summer
FLOWER COLOUR: deep pink
Sun or light shade
Zone 6
Interesting seed heads
Propagate by seed
Moderate impact
DESCRIPTION: Deep pink flowers, spotted within, on vertical spires, sometimes sparsely branched. Leaves downy, pointed. Short-lived perennial or biennial. This wild plant is not without its charm.

f. *albiflora*. White flowers.

'Apricot'. A seed strain in pale apricot shades.

Gloxinioides Group. Tall spikes of wide-open, frilly edged, salmon-pink flowers. 150–180 cm (5–6 ft).

'Sutton's Apricot'. Soft peachy pink flowers. 100–200 cm (3½–6½ ft).

Other *Digitalis* Varieties

'Stewart's Form' (syn. *Digitalis stewartii* hort.). Large, dark-veined orange flowers on long thin spires. Hybrid, of uncertain origin. 120–180 cm (4–6 ft).

Eremurus

ASPHODELACEAE
foxtail lily

Eremuruses are admired for their extraordinary tall flower spikes which come seemingly from nowhere to tower over their neighbours early in the summer, and then die down before summer is over and become dormant. This is not at all a typical genus of perennials; they come from the dry, rocky steppes of central Asia, a habitat from which many bulb species come, and to cope with the drought and intense heat of the summers, they behave rather as bulbs do. In fact, they are monocots, in the same family as aloes, kniphofias and asphodeluses. Of the 40 to 50 species, only about six are in cultivation.

The flower spikes are usually about 200 cm (6½ ft) high, with a flowerhead made up of hundreds of closely packed, starry shaped flowers, the lowest flowering first, the remainder gradually coming in to flower during the course of the flowering period. The petals have a central vein or midrib, which can be darker in colour. The leaves are long and narrow, smooth-surfaced and pointed at the tips, ranging from 30–60 cm (1–2 ft) long, but they are unimportant compared with the flower spikes. The roots are thick and fleshy and radiate out from one central bud, which produces the leaves and flowering stem. Plants eventually build up a cluster of roots, and if these are divided this should be done in early autumn, with great care, as the roots are brittle and easily broken. Seeds can also be saved, and will give good results if sown fresh, but it can take seedlings five years to reach flowering stage.

Eremuruses do best in rich, fertile soil, neutral to very alkaline, but should not get too wet at any time. Clay soil is not a good idea, as the hole dug to put the plant in may well fill with water, and even on any average or heavy soil it is a good idea to rest the rootstock on a bed of free-draining material such as fine shingle or coarse sand. Full sun is preferred; protect from late spring frosts.

Eremuruses are best planted towards the back of the border, where the gap they leave will not be noticeable. Alternatively, late-developing neighbours can be planted nearby where they can help to conceal the gap, as long as the eremurus is not crowded while the foliage and flowers are present. Great care must be taken not to damage the hidden clusters of roots when the plant is dormant. Some gardeners who know the limitations of their memory put a small stake in the ground to remind them there is a good plant hiding away, and this is not a gap where yet more plants can be planted.

Other species occasionally offered include *Eremurus regelii*, up to 240 cm (8 ft) high, from central Asia, with reddish brown flowers, and *E. aitchisonii*, up to 200 cm (6½ ft), from central Asia and Afghanistan, in pink or white.

Eremurus himalaicus

ORIGIN: Afghanistan, northwestern Himalayas
SIZE: 180–240 × 45–75 cm; 6–8 × 1½–2½ ft
FLOWERING TIME: early summer
FLOWER COLOUR: white

Sun
Zone 5
Useful for flower arrangement
Interesting seed heads
Propagate by seed or division
Very high impact
DESCRIPTION: Starry, pure white flowers, over bright green leaves 50–90 cm (1½–3 ft) long. Staking may be needed, but otherwise this is one of the most tolerant species with regard to soil conditions.

Eremurus ×isabellinus

Hybrids mainly derived from *Eremurus stenophyllus* and *E. olgae*, offering a wide range of heights and colours. Most benefit from winter protection. Regrettably, the plants offered under these names sometimes differ significantly from the description, having been raised from unreliable seeds. High impact.

'Brutus'. Long spikes of pure white flowers. A selection from the Ruiter Hybrids. 180 cm (6 ft).

'Emmy Ro'. Large heads with apricot-orange flowers, paler yellow inside, with rust-red midrib. Raised by N. C. Ruiter of Assendelft, Netherlands. 150–210 cm (5–7 ft).

'Oase'. Flowers pale sugar-pink, with red-brown midrib. Raised by N. C. Ruiter. 150–180 cm (5–6 ft).

'Pinokkio'. Rich yellow flowers, from deep orange buds. 180 cm (6 ft).

'Rexona'. Bronze-yellow flowers. A Ruiter hybrid.

'Roford'. Salmon pink. 105–165 cm (3½–5½ ft).

A cluster of elegant yellow spires from *Eremurus* 'Pinokkio', in the nursery beds at Rougham Hall, Suffolk.

'Romance'. Long spikes of orange, tinted salmon pink and red, in densely packed spikes. Raised by N. C. Ruiter. 120–180 cm (4–6 ft).

Ruiter Hybrids. A mixture of pastel pinks, peach pink, pale yellows and apricots.

'Yellow Giant'. Clear, bright yellow flowers on broad spikes. 180 cm (6 ft).

Eremurus robustus

ORIGIN: Turkestan, Afghanistan
SIZE: 120–240 × 60–120 cm; 4–8 × 2–4 ft
FLOWERING TIME: early summer
FLOWER COLOUR: pink
Sun
Zone 5
Useful for flower arrangement
Interesting seed heads
Propagate by seed or division
Very high impact
DESCRIPTION: Large heads, pale apricot–peachy pink to deep pink flowers. Broad foliage, 75–120 cm (2½–4 ft) long. Tolerant of wind and some winter wet.

Kniphofia

ASPHODELACEAE
red hot poker, torch lily
The poker-shaped flowerheads of the taller kniphofias, in brilliant shades of orange, yellow or red, make a dramatic contribution to any garden. The individual flowers are small, with the lowest ones opening first,

Eremurus robustus.

the heads held on sturdy, leafless upright stems. The foliage of the taller kinds is of little value, being long, lax and often untidy. With the array of species and varieties available, one could easily have kniphofias in flower from early summer right into the winter.

There are about 70 species, all perennials, most coming from southern Africa. The name commemorates 18th-century German botanist Johannes Kniphof, and so the *k* needs to be pronounced ("knip" is one syllable and "hof" is another).

Unfortunately, the naming and identification of kniphofias is unreliable as a result of their tendency to hybridize, and even in the wild there is considerable variation. It is important for the propagation of species *Kniphofia* and the named varieties to be carried out by division, or else the plants will not be true to name. Seed is easy and rewarding, and the results may well produce excellent results—but the new plants will inevitably differ considerably from the parents.

Regrettably for gardeners in Great Britain and in the Pacific Northwest, pokers like wet summers and dry winters, and dislike poor drainage and irregular patterns of freezing and thawing. The best solution is to plant in an average position which will not become too damp in winter and be prepared to give them extra watering during dry periods in the summer.

For the best effect in the garden, the taller kniphofias should be given head room—the plants they associate with should be shorter than they are, so that the flowerheads are not crowded in, but appear to be tall. Then there is the problem of orange. This is a great colour but not always easy to handle, as it tends to kill the nearby soft pastel pinks. The deep reds of echinaceas or *Penstemon* 'Andenken an Friedrich Hahn' can be a match for these bright oranges, but it is best to keep the orange-red pokers away from roses and pink-flowering perennials.

Kniphofia ensifolia

ORIGIN: South Africa
SIZE: 105–180 × 60 cm; 3½–6 × 2 ft
FLOWERING TIME: late spring to summer
FLOWER COLOUR: whitish
Sun
Zone 6
Useful for flower arrangement
Propagate by division
High impact
DESCRIPTION: Slender, greenish white flowers opening from coral red or green buds, tapering towards the top. Early flowering. Erect, blue-green foliage, leaves up to 120 cm (4 ft) long. Hardier than average. Easy, but not as dramatic as some.

Kniphofia multiflora

ORIGIN: South Africa
SIZE: 150–200 × 75 cm; 5–6½ × 2½ ft
FLOWERING TIME: late autumn to early winter
FLOWER COLOUR: orange-red or yellow
Sun
Zone 8
Useful for flower arrangement
Propagate by division
High impact
DESCRIPTION: Very long flowerheads, up to 80 cm (32 in) high, with dark orange flowers

fading to bright yellow. Almost white forms are also found in the wild. Robust, with stiff, upright, sometimes mottled, leaves up to 75 cm (30 in). Likes moist or wet soil, as it grows in water in its native habitat. Easy and fairly vigorous in moist soil. Disease resistant.

'November Glory'. Yellow flowers opening from orange buds. Very late. Leaves up to 85 cm (34 in).

Kniphofia uvaria

red hot poker
ORIGIN: Western Cape, South Africa
SIZE: 105–150 (–400) × 75 cm; 3½–5 (–13) × 2½ ft
FLOWERING TIME: summer to late autumn
FLOWER COLOUR: orange
Sun
Zone 8
Useful for flower arrangement
Propagate by division
Very high impact
DESCRIPTION: This ranges from brilliant red to yellowy green in the wild, but in gardens is a splendid bright orange-red, yellow at the base, the flowerhead having a good shape. Sadly it also varies in commerce. However, the form offered by Cotswold Garden Flowers nursery, near Evesham, Worcestershire, must be one of the finest tall perennials that can be grown in gardens. Tall, stately and eye-catching it carries on unbelievably until January, in a good year, and this in a cool upland garden. The leaves are not significant—long, lax and an average green. Strictly speaking, this is the only kniphofia which should be called the "red hot poker."

'Nobilis' (syn. *K. ×praecox*). Similar but much taller—with pretensions to be a regional landmark, as one nursery suggests. But not nearly so long-flowering as plain *Kniphofia uvaria*. 200–400 cm (6½–13 ft).

Other *Kniphofia* Varieties

'Lord Roberts'. Hybrid, with bright coral red flowerheads, curving to a point. Late summer to autumn. 135–200 cm (4½–6½ ft).

The brilliant orange torches of *Kniphofia uvaria* at Cotswold Garden Flowers, Worcestershire.

Leonurus
LAMIACEAE

A small genus of perennials from Europe and Asia, of which only one species is commonly cultivated. Not to be confused with *Leonotis*!

Leonurus cardiaca
motherwort

ORIGIN: temperate Asia; Europe, including Great Britain; introduced to the Mediterranean

SIZE: 75–180 × 60–120 cm; 2½–6 × 2–4 ft

FLOWERING TIME: mid to late summer

FLOWER COLOUR: pink and white

Sun or light shade

Zone 3

Propagate by seed or division

Subtle impact

The medicinal herb motherwort, *Leonurus cardiaca*.

DESCRIPTION: Whorls of pale mauvy pink or white flowers on long spikes. Foliage green to dark grey-green, on tall upright stems. Leaves jaggedly toothed, the upper ones with three pointed lobes, the lower ones with five to seven. A study in muted pastel shades. Motherwort has a range of uses in herbal medicine, particularly for the heart. Not in the first class of decorative plants, but good for the herb garden. Happy in any average soil. The calyces are very prickly after flowering. Self-seeds.

Liatris
ASTERACEAE

blazing star, gayfeather

About 40 species of perennials, from the eastern half of North America, with tufty upright spikes of flowers, purple or rosy purple. They are unusual for the fact that the flowers open from the top of the spike downwards. A basal tuft of grassy leaves arises from a tuberous rootstock, while many tiers of small, narrow leaves also rise up the flowering stems. All very vertical. They dislike winter wet, and may rot in heavy soils, as a result. They can look very effective in large drifts in the wildflower garden or meadow. *Liatris spicata* is grown for the cut flower trade. The Kansas gayfeather, *L. pycnostachya*, is slightly too short to be included.

Liatris aspera
ORIGIN: eastern North America

SIZE: 105–200 × 45 cm; 3½–6½ × 1½ ft

FLOWERING TIME: summer

FLOWER COLOUR: purple

Sun
Zone 4
Useful for flower arrangement
Interesting seed heads
Propagate by seed or division
Moderate impact
DESCRIPTION: Long spikes of purple flowers, up to 45 cm (1½ ft) long. May need staking in exposed situations.

Lobelia

CAMPANULACEAE

A very diverse, worldwide genus of about 370 temperate and tropical species ranging from annuals to small trees, mostly from the Americas. The tall perennial species have erect spikes of flowers, usually brightly coloured, individually slightly penstemon-like, but narrower, consisting of a tube which flares open, with three large lobes below and two upper ones curving back.

Lobelia tupa

ORIGIN: Chile
SIZE: 150–180 × 75 cm; 5–6 × 2½ ft
FLOWERING TIME: summer to autumn
FLOWER COLOUR: coral red
Sun
Zone 8
Useful for flower arrangement
Propagate by seed, division or cuttings
High impact
DESCRIPTION: An attractive plant with orange-red or coral flowers and long narrow grey-green leaves. Clump-forming. Likes summer heat, but not too dry. Needs protection in cool areas.

The elegant orange-red spires of *Lobelia tupa*, growing with *Bidens* at Merriments Gardens, East Sussex.

Lysimachia
PRIMULACEAE
loosestrife

A genus of 180 species, nearly all perennials, mostly from China and North America. The taller species have upright flower spikes. They tend to prefer moist soil, but ordinary garden soil can be tolerated. Part shade is better if the ground is liable to get at all dry. The attractive *Lysimachia ephemerum* is slightly too short to be included.

Lysimachia vulgaris
yellow loosestrife
ORIGIN: Europe, including Great Britain, temperate Asia
SIZE: 135–165 × 45 cm; 4½–5½ × 1½ ft
FLOWERING TIME: summer
FLOWER COLOUR: yellow
Sun or shade
Zone 5
Interesting seed heads
Propagate by division
Subtle impact
DESCRIPTION: A wildling. Yellow flowers in clusters on loose, vaguely conical heads, borne on upright stems with long narrow, mid-green leaves. Cheerful, but a rapid spreader, suitable only for the meadow or wild garden.

Sidalcea
MALVACEAE
prairie mallow

Twenty species of perennials and annuals from western North America, with typical mallow flowers held on vertical stems. Most like a sunny position on soil which is not too dry in summer nor too wet in winter. Free-flowering, long-flowering and trouble-free, but often not long-lived. Easily raised from saved seed, sown fresh. The named varieties, mostly hybrids of *Sidalcea candida* and/or *S. malviflora*, are not tall enough to be listed, 'Mr Lindbergh', with deep rosy pink flowers, being about the tallest.

Sidalcea oregana
ORIGIN: Washington, Idaho, Utah, California
SIZE: 150–180 × 60 cm; 5–6 × 2 ft
FLOWERING TIME: summer
FLOWER COLOUR: pink
Sun
Zone 5
Propagate by seed or division
Moderate impact
DESCRIPTION: Pale pink or deep pink flowers on upright spikes. Lower leaves shallowly lobed, upper ones deeply.

Sinacalia
ASTERACEAE

Four perennials from China, which were formerly in the genus *Ligularia* and before that in *Senecio*. Only one species is in cultivation.

Sinacalia tangutica
(syn. *Ligularia tangutica*)
ORIGIN: central China
SIZE: 120–180 × 90–180 cm; 4–6 × 3–6 ft
FLOWERING TIME: mid to late summer
FLOWER COLOUR: yellow

Sun or light shade
Zone 5
Useful for flower arrangement
Interesting seed heads
Propagate by division
High impact
DESCRIPTION: An attractive plant with
large, loose, buddleia-shaped heads of
bright yellow flowers, lasting many weeks.
The leaves are large, mid-green, handsome
and irregularly jagged-edged, held on very
dark stems. Good feathery seed clusters follow the flowers, lasting well into the winter.
The plant is happy only on soils which never
dry out, or better still, are always quite
damp, otherwise the plant droops and looks
sad. A poolside position is ideal. A vigorous
species, liable to spread by means of creeping rootstock. Happiest in semi-shade, but
sun is acceptable as long as the soil is wet.

Veronicastrum

SCROPHULARIACEAE
Culver's root
A genus of about 20 species of plants, formerly in the genus *Veronica*. Clusters of very
long, narrow, veronica-like flower spikes, at
the top of tall erect stems. The leaves are in
whorls of up to seven long, narrow, pointed
leaflets, very slightly toothed, clothing the
stems all the way up, giving a very vertical, tiered effect. The foliage is neat, but
there is a lot of it. All the species are quite
similar—in fact, some botanists think all
20 species should be "lumped" into two
species. Veronicastrums prefer rich, moist
soil, in sun or very slight shade. Attractive

Sinacalia tangutica, with fluffy yellow
flowerheads and jagged, dark green foliage, likes
a permanently damp situation in the garden.

to bees and butterflies. Two other species
are worthwhile and occasionally offered:
Veronicastrum japonicum, from Japan, with
lilac-white flowers, and *V. sachalinense*, from
Sakhalin, with long, blue flower spikes.

Veronicastrum sibiricum

(syn. *Veronica sibirica*)
ORIGIN: eastern Russia, northeastern China,
    Japan, Korea
SIZE: 90–180 × 60–90 cm; 3–6 × 2–3 ft
FLOWERING TIME: summer
FLOWER COLOUR: purple
Sun
Zone 4
Useful for flower arrangement
Interesting seed heads
Propagate by division
High impact

DESCRIPTION: Flowers purple, blue or lavender, sometimes red-tinged, erect or curving. Broader spikes than in *Veronicastrum virginicum*.

'Spring Dew'. Silvery white.

Veronicastrum virginicum

(syn. *Veronica virginica*)
ORIGIN: northeastern North America
SIZE: 90–180 × 75 cm; 3–6 × 2½ ft
FLOWERING TIME: summer
FLOWER COLOUR: blue, mauve or white
Sun
Zone 3
Useful for flower arrangement
Interesting seed heads
Propagate by division
High impact

DESCRIPTION: Flowers blue, purple, mauve, white, usually with plenty of side spikes. A good winter silhouette, for those who like to leave their half-dead plants in place.

'Alboroseum'. Palest pink. 90–165 cm (3–5½ ft).

'Album'. White flowers, side flower spikes quite upright. 165–200 cm (5½–6½ ft) high.

'Fascination'. Lilac buds open to lilac-rose flower spikes, bending and curving in a wayward fashion. Tends to become top-heavy and flop. 150–165 cm (5–5½ ft).

'Lavandelturm'. Lavender mauve flowers. Sturdy. 120–200 cm (4–6½ ft).

'Temptation'. Pale lilac-blue flowers, with side flower spikes pointing out sideways. Tends to lean in all directions. Early flowering.

The narrow, pale lilac-blue flower spikes of *Veronicastrum virginicum* 'Temptation', at Scampston, in Yorkshire.

10

DAISY FLOWERS

Most plants in this chapter are sun lovers with a cheerful and extrovert air to them, and all belong botanically to the daisy family, Asteraceae (formerly Compositae). The most unusual colours can be found among the heleniums; some are brownish yellow, others are red-mahogany shades. But apart from *Leucanthemella* and *Leucanthemum* which are white with yellow centres, all the other plants in this chapter can be expected to provide a bright splash of yellow and not much subtlety.

Helenium
ASTERACEAE

Heleniums come in a range of dark red, orange, yellow and coppery brown colours, and have distinctive, knobbly spherical centres, with drooping petals which usually hang at an angle of about 45 degrees, often having a graceful flare to them. The flowers photograph well—the combination of various shades of orange and yellow, contrasting with the dark green, always seems to make a good picture.

Heleniums have a long flowering period during late summer and early autumn. They are easy-going, but prefer rich, fertile soil which must not be too dry. Deadheading them increases continuity of flowering. They are best divided every two or three years, to maintain vigour. The foliage is dark green and unremarkable, and there can be too much of it. To counter this, some gardeners pinch out the growing tips of a section of the plant at the front in late May, so that those stems develop later and flower on shorter stems—this helps to hide the foliage of the rest of the plant. Sometimes there can be loss of foliage at the base of the stems, giving the "leggy" look. People who suffer from skin allergies should wear gloves when handling heleniums, and they are also poisonous if eaten.

There are about 40 species of perennials, annuals and biennials, all from North and Central America, but only four in cultivation. The named varieties are derived from *Helenium autumnale*, *H. bigelovii* and *H. flexuosum*, all three of which are rarely seen as species in gardens. The majority of cultivars are slightly too short to be included; those listed here may well need staking. The genus name is derived from a legend about Helen of Troy, but this must relate to *Inula helenium*, since heleniums as we know them today are from America.

Helenium autumnale

ORIGIN: North America
SIZE: 75–165 × 60–75 cm; 2½–5½ × 2–2½ ft
FLOWERING TIME: late summer to autumn
FLOWER COLOUR: yellow
Sun
Zone 3
Useful for flower arrangement
Interesting seed heads
Propagate by seed or division
Moderate impact

DESCRIPTION: Tall and yellow, but later flowering than many of the cultivars derived from it.

Other *Helenium* Varieties

'Gartensonne'. Frilly, pale scrambled-egg yellow petals contrasting well with the warm chocolate brown cone. Late summer flowering. The name means "garden sun." 150–200 cm (5–6½ ft).

'Goldrausch' (syns. 'Gold Intoxication', 'Gold Rustle', 'Septembergold', 'Zimbel-stern'). Reddish brown overlaid on clear bright yellow, with slightly frilly edge. Yellow-green centre. Very free-flowering. 120–165 cm (4–5½).

'Summer Circle'. One of the tallest, with large flowers on long, branching stems, and

Helenium 'Goldrausch', showing the distinctive knobbly centres and flared petals of a helenium.

clusters of smaller subsidiary flowers. Bright yellow petals, with a brown centre. Selected and named by Inez Arnold of the Netherlands. 135–200 cm (4½–6½ ft).

Helianthus
ASTERACEAE
sunflower

The most famous member of this genus is the annual common sunflower, *Helianthus annuus*, widely grown commercially as a source of vegetable oil. Often seen in ornamental gardens, but usually looking gangly and out of scale with the plants around it. There are about 70 species of perennials and annuals, all from North or South America, almost all of which have brightly coloured flowers, with a yellow or brown central disc surrounded by yellow petals. The flowers are borne on tall, erect stems, in late summer and autumn, over coarse, dark green foliage. Full sun is preferred, and fertile soil which is not too damp; the taller kinds often needing to be staked.

Sunflowers are easy to cultivate; the main problem is usually to restrain the more aggressive ones. Even so, they benefit from being divided every two or three years, either to maintain vigour, or to keep them in check. The seeds are appreciated by birds, but leaving the dead seed heads can lead to self-seeding, which, in the case of named forms, will lead to poorer plants, not true to name. Regrettably there is considerable confusion in nurseries and gardens over the naming of several of the perennial varieties.

Helianthus angustifolius
swamp sunflower
ORIGIN: eastern and southern United States
SIZE: 165–200 × 60–90 cm; 5½–6½ × 2–3 ft
FLOWERING TIME: early autumn
FLOWER COLOUR: yellow
Sun
Zone 6
Useful for flower arrangement
Interesting seed heads
Propagate by seed or division
High impact
DESCRIPTION: Yellow petals surrounding a purple-red or yellow disc, flowers 5 cm (2 in) wide. Tolerates damp conditions. Often short-lived.

'Gold Lace'. Shorter than the species, and earlier-flowering. Selected by North Creek Nurseries, Pennsylvania. 150–180 cm (5–6 ft).

'Matanzas Creek'. Pale yellow flowers cover the upper third of the plant, early to late autumn. It was discovered at Matanzas Creek Winery in northern California, and distributed by Digging Dog Nursery. They grow it with other late-flowering plants such as *Salvia corrugata* and *Miscanthus* 'Adagio'.

Helianthus atrorubens
dark-eyed sunflower
ORIGIN: southeastern United States
SIZE: 150–180 × 60 cm; 5–6 × 2 ft
FLOWERING TIME: late summer to early autumn
FLOWER COLOUR: yellow
Sun or light shade

Zone 7
Useful for flower arrangement
Propagate by seed or division
High impact
DESCRIPTION: Yellow or orange-yellow petals around a purple-red disc, flowers 5 cm (2 in) wide, with large leaves. A spreader, but suitable for meadow gardens.

Helianthus decapetalus

ORIGIN: central and southeastern United States
SIZE: 150 (–200) × 60 cm; 5 (–6½) × 2 ft
FLOWERING TIME: summer to early autumn
FLOWER COLOUR: pale yellow
Sun
Zone 5
Useful for flower arrangement
Interesting seed heads
Propagate by seed or division
High impact
DESCRIPTION: Pale yellow petals, with yellow disc, sparsely petalled, on foliage with bushy growth. Attractive, but a strong spreader, especially on moist soil. Suitable for naturalizing, or for meadow gardens. For the varieties sometimes listed under this name, see *Helianthus ×multiflorus*.

Helianthus giganteus

giant sunflower
ORIGIN: central and southeastern United States, Canada
SIZE: 180–300 (–400) × 120 cm; 6–10 (–13) × 4 ft
FLOWERING TIME: summer to autumn
FLOWER COLOUR: yellow
Sun
Zone 4

Useful for flower arrangement
Interesting seed heads
Propagate by seed or division
Very high impact
DESCRIPTION: Can be very tall in the wild. Pale yellow petals, with a darker disc, and a lot of foliage. Prefers moist soil. A spreader. For the wild garden.

'Sheila's Sunshine'. Soft, pastel-yellow petals. Introduced by Niche Gardens nursery of North Carolina. 240–300 cm (8–10 ft).

Helianthus ×kellermanii

A wild hybrid between *Helianthus grosseserratus* and *H. salicifolius*. Yellow flowers, 6 cm (3 in) wide. Not very floriferous, but appreciated for the effect of its long, grey-green foliage—reminiscent of *H. salicifolius*, but not so delicate.

Helianthus ×laetiflorus

A wild hybrid, *Helianthus pauciflorus × H. tuberosus*. North and central United States. Well-spaced bright yellow petals, with a small brown disc, flower up to 10 cm (4 in) wide. Comes true from seed. Invasive. 120–200 cm (4–6½ ft).

Helianthus maximiliani

ORIGIN: central United States, southern Canada
SIZE: 120–300 × 90 cm; 4–10 × 3 ft
FLOWERING TIME: autumn
FLOWER COLOUR: yellow
Sun
Zone 4
Useful for flower arrangement
Interesting seed heads

Propagate by seed or division
Very high impact

DESCRIPTION: Another giant, with yellow petals and small brown centres. It flowers up the stem fairly well—rather than having all the flowers being at the top. The taller it gets the more it is likely to lean in odd directions. Self-sows, and spreads, so best relegated to the wild garden, if you have one.

Helianthus microcephalus

ORIGIN: central and southeastern United States
SIZE: 150–300 (–400) × 90 cm; 5–10 (–13) × 3 ft
FLOWERING TIME: summer to autumn
FLOWER COLOUR: pale yellow
Sun
Zone 4
Useful for flower arrangement
Interesting seed heads
Propagate by seed or division
Very high impact

DESCRIPTION: Pale yellow petals with small matching centre, flowers 7.5 cm (3 in) wide. Long-flowering. Prefers soil which is not too dry, but tolerates clay.

Helianthus ×multiflorus

Helianthus annuus × *H. decapetalus*. An old hybrid, probably originating in Spain in the 16th century. Not unduly vigorous. The naming of these varieties in nurseries and gardens is often unreliable.

'Capenoch Star'. Light yellow petals, notched at the tip, with dark yellow disc, and flowers 15 cm (6 in) wide or even more. Late summer to autumn. Slightly unstable. 150 cm (5 ft). Zone 4.

'Flore Pleno' (syns. *Helianthus decapetalus* 'Flore Pleno', 'Grandiflorus', 'Maximus'). A range of double-flowered plants are sold under these names. A good plant called 'Duplex' may also belong here.

'Hazel's Gold'. A variegated form.

'Loddon Gold'. Deep yellow with a hint of green, fully double flowers with no disc, 7.5–12.5 cm (3–5 in) wide. Not invasive. Has a tendency to face the sun, rather than the garden. May need staking. Introduced in the 1920s by Thomas Carlile's nursery in Berkshire.

'Major'. Large, golden yellow petals, pointed at the tips. Flowers tend to face the sun. 120–150 cm (4–5 ft).

'Meteor'. Deep yellow petals, on an anemone-centred flower, up to 10 cm (4 in) wide. A 19th-century variety which arose as

Helianthus ×multiflorus 'Capenoch Star'.

Helianthus ×*multiflorus* 'Meteor' at Nürtigen, Germany.

a sport of 'Soleil d'Or'. *Helianthus* ×*multi-florus* 'Anemoneflorus Flore Pleno' may well be the same thing.

'Soleil d'Or'. Dark yellow, double, 10 cm (4 in) wide.

Helianthus nuttallii

ORIGIN: Rocky Mountains
SIZE: 150–240 (–400) × 90 cm; 5–8 (–13) × 3 ft
FLOWERING TIME: autumn
FLOWER COLOUR: yellow
Sun
Zone 5
Useful for flower arrangement
Propagate by seed or division

High impact
DESCRIPTION: Deep yellow, single flowers, deep yellow disc with orange ring around it, held over plumes of long, narrow leaves.

Helianthus occidentalis

fewleaf sunflower
ORIGIN: central United States, Texas, Florida
SIZE: 120–200 × 75 cm; 4–6½ × 2½ ft
FLOWERING TIME: summer to early autumn
FLOWER COLOUR: yellow
Sun
Zone 4
Useful for flower arrangement
Propagate by seed or division
High impact

DESCRIPTION: Small, deep yellow petals, with yellow disc, 6 cm (2½ in) wide. Free-flowering, on slender, branching heads.

Helianthus salicifolius
willowleaf sunflower
ORIGIN: south-central United States
SIZE: 210–300 × 90 cm; 7–10 × 3 ft
FLOWERING TIME: autumn
FLOWER COLOUR: yellow
Sun
Zone 4
Useful for flower arrangement
Propagate by seed or division
High impact
DESCRIPTION: The attraction of this species is the unique and slightly exotic effect of its foliage, created by the columns of long narrow leaves, curling and arching over each other in tiers. Discreet staking will be necessary in exposed positions. The flowers are slightly chocolate-scented, though small—5 cm (2 in) wide. Some shorter varieties have been developed in New Zealand. Looks best with a carpet of much shorter plants in front of it, and other good foliage plants such as rheums, *Miscanthus* or *Macleaya* on each side of it.

'Bitter Chocolate'. Larger flowers, 7.5 cm (3 in) wide, more strongly scented of chocolate and appearing earlier, on a shorter plant, 200 cm (6½ ft) maximum. Leaves a little broader.

Helianthus strumosus
ORIGIN: North America
SIZE: 180–200 × 90 cm; 6–6½ × 3 ft
FLOWERING TIME: summer to early autumn

FLOWER COLOUR: yellow
Sun
Zone
Useful for flower arrangement
Propagate by seed or division
High impact
DESCRIPTION: Yellow petals and disc, 10 cm (4 in) wide. Some forms are a relatively pale yellow.

Helianthus tuberosus
Jerusalem artichoke
ORIGIN: south-central and southeastern
   Canada, southeastern United States
SIZE: 210–300 × 120 cm; 7–10 × 4 ft
FLOWERING TIME: autumn
FLOWER COLOUR: yellow
Sun
Zone 4
Propagate by seed or division
Moderate impact
DESCRIPTION: This is grown as a vegetable, for its knobbly, edible tubers, although it does have the usual helianthus flowers. Very easy to grow. There is no connection with artichokes, though when it was first introduced it was thought to taste similar. Nor is there any connection with Jerusalem—this comes from the similarity of the sound of the Italian word for sunflower (*girasole*) with the word "Jerusalem."

Other *Helianthus* Varieties
'Gullick's Variety'. Flowers up to 12 cm (5 in) wide, with several rows of petals. Fairly vigorous. 150 cm (5 ft). There is sometimes confusion in nurseries between this and 'Miss Mellish', which, like it, is a

hybrid of uncertain parentage, most likely involving *Helianthus atrorubens*.

'Lemon Queen'. A recent, pale-yellow-flowered variety which seems set to oust all other *Helianthus* cultivars from gardens—everyone is growing 'Lemon Queen', it seems, probably because its pale colour appeals to those with sensitive taste. However, it flowers prolifically, and its sturdy habit appeals to all sensible people who try to avoid staking whenever they can. Probably a natural hybrid; however, its parentage (and therefore its name) is contested. The parents claimed for it include *H. microcephalus*, *H. pauciflorus* and *H. tuberosus*. Single flowers, 7.5 cm (3 in) wide. Late summer to autumn. 180–210 cm (6–7 ft).

'Miss Mellish'. Yellow petals, in-rolled at first, semi-double, flowers up to 12.5 cm (5 in) wide. Needs support. 200 cm (6½ ft). Zone 4.

'Monarch' (syn. 'The Monarch'). Hybrid, formerly thought to be a selection of its known parent, *Helianthus atrorubens*. Large flowers with yellow petals, semi-double, with dark red disc, 15 cm (6 in) wide or more. Staking required. Very tall and not for the fainthearted. 240–300 cm (8–10 ft). Zone 7.

Heliopsis

ASTERACEAE

Sun-loving plants with bright yellow daisy flowers, which deserve to be seen in gardens more often. There are 13 species from North America, but only one is in cultivation.

Heliopsis helianthoides

ORIGIN: Canada, eastern United States, Mexico

SIZE: 90–150 (–165) × 60 cm; 3–5 (–5½) × 2 ft

FLOWERING TIME: late summer

FLOWER COLOUR: yellow

Sun

Zone 4

Useful for flower arrangement

Propagate by seed, division or cuttings

Moderate impact

DESCRIPTION: Yellow petals with a yellow central disc, flowerheads 5–7.5 cm (2–3 in) wide, held on upright stems, with the flowers horizontal, looking up at the sky. Unexciting though harmless mid-green foliage, with long narrow, pointed leaves. Full sun is preferred, and fertile soil which is not too wet in winter. Plants should be divided every three or four years to maintain vigour. Early growth needs to be protected from slugs and snails. An excellent plant, but currently out of fashion for some reason, and as a result several named varieties are at risk of being lost. Most varieties are just too short for this book.

var. *helianthoides*. Smooth stems and leaves.

var. *scabra*. Downy stems and leaves. Staking may be required.

var. *scabra* 'Benzinggold'. Warm orange-yellow petals, with a deep orange disc, semi-double flowers up to 12.5 cm (5 in) wide, in airy sprays. 150–180 cm (5–6 ft).

var. *scabra* 'Prairie Sunset'. A wild form found by Neil Diboll in Wisconsin. Orange-yellow petals aging attractively to white at the edges, with a wine-red-brown central disc, the flowers held on purple-brown stems. Free-flowering, fast-growing and with a long flowering period. Deep green, purple-veined leaves on dark stems. 165–180 cm (5½–6 ft).

Inula
ASTERACEAE

Bold, upright plants with yellow daisy flowers, closely related to *Telekia*. The petals are narrow, each one separate from the other, giving a whiskery or spidery appearance. The central disc is slightly raised and a darker yellow. The tall species are tough, slightly coarse plants, clump-forming, with large, bold, simple leaves. They prefer full sun, but will tolerate a little shade, and prefer deep, rich, moisture-retentive soil. Nearly 100 species from temperate and warm temperate regions of Europe, Asia and Africa.

The botanical name probably comes from the Latin *hinnulus*, meaning a young mule. The herb elecampane, *Inula helenium*, was formerly used to cure horses and mules, as well as humans—in fact, horseheal is one of the many local English names for that species.

Inula helenium
elecampane
ORIGIN: western and central Asia, introduced in Europe (including Great Britain) and the United States
SIZE: 105–200 (–300) × 120 cm; 3½–6½ (–10) × 4 ft
FLOWERING TIME: summer to late summer
FLOWER COLOUR: yellow
Sun or light shade
Zone 5
Useful for flower arrangement
Propagate by division
High impact
DESCRIPTION: Yellow flowers up to 9 cm (3½ in) wide, on downy, leafy stems. The leaves are large, sometimes as much as 75 cm (2½ ft) long, elliptical, wrinkled above, downy and white below. They clasp the main stem and undulate slightly along their edges. The rhizomes of elecampane are aromatic and have antiseptic properties, the plant having been used medicinally in the past for coughs, respiratory complaints and skin diseases, and has also been valued for its culinary uses. The English name is a corruption of the Latin *Inula campana*, meaning "inula of the fields." The specific name *helenium* commemorates Helen of Troy, who, according to legend, was gathering the herb in the fields when she was abducted by Paris. Or, as others claim, the plant sprang up where her tears fell.

Inula magnifica
ORIGIN: eastern Caucasus
SIZE: 200 × 90 cm; 6½ × 3 ft
FLOWERING TIME: summer
FLOWER COLOUR: yellow
Sun or light shade
Zone 6
Useful for flower arrangement
Propagate by seed or division
High impact
DESCRIPTION: Not necessarily any more

magnificent than *Inula helenium*, although it has larger yellow flowers, up to 15 cm (6 in) wide, and the leaves are shorter and narrower. The leaves are downy and up to 25 cm (10 in) long. It likes moist soil, and is happy by the waterside.

'Sonnenstrahl'. A more free-flowering form, raised by Ernst Pagels. The name means "sunbeam."

Inula racemosa
ORIGIN: western Himalayas
SIZE: 200–250 × 90 cm; 6½–8 × 3 ft
FLOWERING TIME: late summer

FLOWER COLOUR: yellow
Sun
Zone 7
Useful for flower arrangement
Propagate by seed or division
High impact
DESCRIPTION: Bright yellow flowers, up to 6 cm (2½ in) wide, held close to the main, erect stems, in spire-like heads, the stems purple-flushed and leafy. Lower leaves up to 30 cm (12 in) long.

'Sonnenspeer'. An even taller form, up to 300 cm (10 ft).

The bright flowers of *Inula racemosa* reach for the sky at Dyffryn Fernant Garden in West Wales.

The classic white daisy flowers of *Leucanthemella serotina* like to turn and face the sun, seen here at Bressingham Gardens.

Leucanthemella

ASTERACEAE

Two perennial species, with classic daisy flowers—white petals and greenish yellow centres. They have had various botanical names over the years, but now have a genus of their own.

Leucanthemella serotina

(syns. *Chrysanthemum serotinum,*
    C. uliginosum)
ORIGIN: southeastern Europe, Far East Asia
SIZE: 120–165 (–200) × 75 cm; 4–5½ (–6½)
    × 2½ ft
FLOWERING TIME: late summer to autumn
FLOWER COLOUR: white
Sun or light shade
Zone 8
Useful for flower arrangement
Propagate by seed, division or cuttings
Moderate impact
DESCRIPTION: Archetypal white daisies up to 7.5 cm (3 in) wide, at the top of unremarkable pale green foliage, carried on very upright stems, branching at the top. The taller it gets, the more it is likely to need staking. The flowerheads turn to face the sun—which has to be borne in mind when planting. Tolerates clay soil. The emerging shoots are vulnerable to slug attack in spring.

Leucanthemum

ASTERACEAE

dog daisy, marguerite, shasta daisy
White, yellow-centred daisies, formerly in the genus *Chrysanthemum*. Twenty-five species, from Europe and northern Asia, of which three are in cultivation, and only a few hybrid varieties are tall enough. They prefer full sun and fertile soil which doesn't get too wet. The taller varieties usually need staking.

Leucanthemum ×superbum

(syn. *Chrysanthemum superbum*)
shasta daisy, Esther Reid
DESCRIPTION: Large white daisies, up to 10 cm (4 in) wide, sometimes double or semi-double, with substantial dark green leaves. Early summer-flowering, old-fashioned stalwarts of the herbaceous border, many dating from the early 1900s, but still well worth growing. More than 50 varieties have been named over the years, many of which are still currently available. But many have been selected for their dwarf or medium height, so that only one variety is tall enough for us. Moderate impact.

'Manhattan'. Single, 165 cm (5½ ft) high.

Rudbeckia

ASTERACEAE

Brilliant yellow daisies with a raised black centre, and petals which usually droop at an angle slightly below horizontal. The cone-shaped central disc is usually black, but can be green or yellowish. Most species are very free-flowering, the flowers borne in clusters on upright stems, over unremarkable green foliage. The name commemorates Swedish botanists Olof Rudbeck and his son of the same name, one-time teacher of Linnaeus. There are about 15 species, all from North

America. Some are quite short, some very tall—not many are in between.

A position in full sun is best, on fertile soil that doesn't dry out. The early growth may need protection from slug damage. They should be divided and replanted every four or five years. All are robust enough for naturalizing, but in the border the tallest ones benefit from staking. The taller species do have a large amount of greenery, but this can be countered by pinching out the stems at the front of the plant in late May. In addition to those listed, *Rudbeckia californica*, from California, is occasionally offered. It reaches 200 cm (6½ ft), has large yellow flowers with a greenish yellow conical disc, and long, narrow leaves.

Rudbeckia laciniata 'Juligold'.

Rudbeckia laciniata

ORIGIN: Quebec, Canada; eastern and central United States
SIZE: 150–210 (–270) × 90 cm; 5–7 (–9) × 3 ft
FLOWERING TIME: summer to autumn
FLOWER COLOUR: yellow
Sun or shade
Zone 3
Useful for flower arrangement
Interesting seed heads
Propagate by seed, division or cuttings
High impact
DESCRIPTION: Bright yellow petals, curving slightly and held at about 45 degrees below horizontal, with a prominent greenish central cone, the flowers held on erect, leafy stems, the lower leaves divided, upper ones less so. Tolerates damp soil. Spreads well.

'Goldkugel'. Double flowers, in a neat dome shape; the name means "golden sphere." 135–165 cm (4½–5½ ft).

'Herbstsonne'. Flowers in late summer, followed by long green seed heads. The name, which means "autumn sun," is frequently misspelt in listings. 180–240 cm (6–8 ft).

'Juligold'. Summer flowering (the name means "July gold"), earlier than 'Herbstsonne'. Single flowers have knobbly greenish yellow centres and yellow tutu-petals, and are mostly clustered at the top of the plant. 240 cm (8 ft).

Rudbeckia maxima

ORIGIN: central and southern United States
SIZE: 150–240 × 90 cm; 5–8 × 3 ft
FLOWERING TIME: summer to early autumn
FLOWER COLOUR: yellow

Sun
Zone 9
Useful for flower arrangement
Interesting seed heads
Propagate by seed or division
High impact
DESCRIPTION: A curious species with a dis-proportionately elongated cone, resembling a headless ballet-dancer with a drooping tutu. Yellow petals with a dark brown cone, the flowers on erect stems arising from a basal rosette. Large, attractive, ribbed, blu-ish green leaves. Prefers a moist situation, but tolerates a more average one. Not as hardy as some species.

Rudbeckia nitida

ORIGIN: North America
SIZE: 165–200 × 90 cm; 5½–6½ × 3 ft
FLOWERING TIME: late summer to early autumn
FLOWER COLOUR: yellow
Sun
Zone 3
Useful for flower arrangement
Interesting seed heads
Propagate by seed or division
High impact
DESCRIPTION: Yellow petals with a raised green disc. 'Herbstsonne' and 'Juligold' are considered by some to be selections of this species, so it is not altogether certain that the plants offered under this label are in fact *Rudbeckia nitida*.

Rudbeckia occidentalis

ORIGIN: western North America
SIZE: 60–200 × 60 cm; 2–6½ × 2 ft
FLOWERING TIME: summer

FLOWER COLOUR: black and green
Sun
Zone 7
Useful for flower arrangement
Interesting seed heads
Propagate by seed or division
Moderate impact
DESCRIPTION: A curiosity. The flowers con-sist of a prominent black, or dark brown central cone surrounded by small, stiff, green petals, 7.5–12.5 cm (3–5 in) wide in all. Flowers borne on leafy upright stems, with few side branches. Good as a cut flower. The species is rarely offered, and its two named varieties 'Black Beauty' and 'Green Wizard', which seem to be nearly identical, are usually not more than 150 cm (5 ft).

Senecio

ASTERACEAE
A very large genus, with about 1250 species worldwide, including trees, shrubs and lia-nas as well as perennials. Many are weeds. Among those which are cultivated, the tall perennials are not really the best. The flow-ers are usually yellow, but occasionally white or mauve.

Senecio paludosus

fen ragwort
ORIGIN: Europe (extremely rare in Great Britain), western temperate Asia
SIZE: 150–180 × 75 cm; 5–6 × 2½ ft
FLOWERING TIME: early to late summer
FLOWER COLOUR: yellow
Sun or light shade
Zone 5

Propagate by division
Subtle impact
DESCRIPTION: A plant for the wild garden. Clusters of starry yellow daisies at the top of upright stems, clad with long, narrow, solidago-like leaves. Clump-forming. Likes moist soil and even tolerates winter flooding.

Silphium

ASTERACEAE
prairie dock

Bold, tough and upright perennials, usually with yellow petals, spaced out as in *Inula*, but with a smaller central disc than *Inula* or *Telekia*. Most species form strong, leafy plants with upright stems bearing coarse but handsome foliage. They are happy on almost any soil. Sun or part shade is acceptable, though shade may lead to plants which are willowy and therefore need staking. All are tough enough for the wild garden. There are 20 species, from North America, several of which were used medicinally by Native Americans. In addition to the three featured here, *Silphium terebinthinaceum*, the prairie dock, from eastern Canada to southeastern United States, is sometimes offered. It can reach 3 m (10 ft), and has widely spaced clusters of flowers with yellow petals and black-dotted yellow centres. The large, blue-green basal leaves can reach 90 cm (3 ft), and are quite dock-like. The plant is spindly and leafless above, making it look as though it has bolted. Very drought-resistant. The most commonly seen of the four species in cultivation is *S. perfoliatum*.

Silphium integrifolium

ORIGIN: central and eastern United States
SIZE: 60–150 (–240) × 90 cm; 2–5 (–8) × 3 ft
FLOWERING TIME: summer
FLOWER COLOUR: yellow
Sun or light shade
Zone 5
Useful for flower arrangement
Propagate by seed or division
High impact
DESCRIPTION: Well-spaced yellow petals and loose, whiskery, yellowy green discs, up to 7.5 cm (3 in) wide in all. The flowers are in terminal clusters, opening from prominent, knobbly, pale green, rosette-like buds. Long-flowering. The leaves are stemless, large, long and pointed. Tolerates clay soil.

Silphium laciniatum

compass plant
ORIGIN: central United States
SIZE: 150–210 (–300) × 90 cm; 5–7 (–10) × 3 ft
FLOWERING TIME: late summer to early autumn
FLOWER COLOUR: yellow
Sun or light shade
Zone 4
Useful for flower arrangement
Propagate by seed or division
High impact
DESCRIPTION: The common name of the plant refers to the fact that leaves turn their surfaces west or east, apparently to minimize the effect of the heat of the sun, and end up pointing north or south. Quite closely packed, yellow petals, notched at the tips, with a yellowy green central disc

fading to yellowy brown. The flowers are about 10 cm (4 in) wide, held near the stems, hollyhock fashion, rather than in broad clusters. Deeply lobed and pointed leaves, on erect white-hairy stems. An extremely deep tap-root, up to 4 m (13 ft) long, helps the plant cope with summer drought.

Silphium perfoliatum

cup plant
ORIGIN: southern Canada, eastern United States
SIZE: 150–240 × 90 cm; 5–8 × 3 ft
FLOWERING TIME: summer to early autumn
FLOWER COLOUR: yellow
Sun or light shade

Zone 4
Useful for flower arrangement
Propagate by seed or division
High impact

DESCRIPTION: Flowers in terminal clusters, with bright yellow, starry petals and a yellow central disc. Robust, slightly coarse dark foliage; the large blue-green leaves cling to the upright stems, forming a cup around the stem.

Telekia

ASTERACEAE
Two species of yellow daisies, closely allied to *Inula*.

Silphium perfoliatum.

Telekia speciosa

(syn. *Buphthalmum speciosum*)

ORIGIN: central Europe, Balkans, central and southern Russia, Caucasus

SIZE: 120–165 (–200) × 60 cm; 4–5½ (–6½) × 2 ft

FLOWERING TIME: summer

FLOWER COLOUR: yellow

Light shade

Zone 6

Useful for flower arrangement

Interesting seed heads

Propagate by seed or division

High impact

DESCRIPTION: The flowers of this species have widely spaced petals, like *Inula*, which give it a spidery look, though the petals droop more than with *Inula*, progressively as the flower ages. The broad central disc is raised like a shallow dome, at first yellow, soon fading to brown, finally black, if left on long enough. The flowers are borne singly or in clusters, above large, coarse but handsome leaves, which are pointed at the tips. A clump-forming plant, liking soil that doesn't dry out, even a streamside position. Dislikes full sun and strong winds, both of which can damage the foliage. Tough enough for naturalizing.

Verbesina

ASTERACEAE

crown beard

One hundred and fifty species of perennials, shrubs and trees, with yellow or white daisy flowers. From temperate and subtropical Americas.

Verbesina alternifolia

(syn. *Coreopsis alternifolia*)

wingstem

ORIGIN: eastern Canada, eastern United States

SIZE: 180–210 × 75 cm; 6–7 × 2½ ft

FLOWERING TIME: late summer to early autumn

FLOWER COLOUR: yellow

Sun

Zone 5

Useful for flower arrangement

Propagate by seed or division

Moderate impact

DESCRIPTION: Widely spaced clusters of bright yellow daisy flowers—imagine a less densely petalled version of a rudbeckia or helianthus, on graceful but sturdy stems. Long narrow, rough-textured leaves on branching stems. Tolerant of a wide range of conditions.

Telekia speciosa.

11

EARLY PERENNIALS

The plants in this chapter are a fairly diverse group with little in common apart from the time of year they flower—the months of May and June. It can take quite a few weeks for the typical tall perennial plant to reach its full height and flowering size. This explains why (even with the inclusion, for convenience, of a few mid and even late summer flowering species, for example *Euphorbia sikkimensis*, whose genus for the most part flowers early) there are fewer plants in this chapter than in the "Mid-season Perennials" and "Late Perennials" chapters.

Aruncus
ROSACEAE
goatsbeard
Four species of perennials, related to spireas. All have feathery flower spikes and prefer moist, shady situations.

Aruncus dioicus
(syns. *A. sylvester, Spiraea aruncus*)
ORIGIN: western and central Europe, western Russia, Caucasus
SIZE: 120–200 × 90–150 cm; 4–6½ × 3–5 ft
FLOWERING TIME: early summer
FLOWER COLOUR: cream and greenish white
Sun or shade
Zone 3
Propagate by seed or division
Moderate impact

DESCRIPTION: A leafy clump of greenery, with upright, astilbe-like flowerheads. Separate male and female plants, creamy white and greenish white respectively. A useful plant for shade, coming fairly early in the year, but leaving behind rather a large mass of foliage. Can self-seed annoyingly in the conditions it likes. Tolerates full sun if the soil remains reliably moist. The varieties 'Glasnevin' and 'Zweiweltenkind' are shorter.

Baptisia
FABACEAE
wild indigo
About 17 perennial species, usually with upright spikes of lupin-like flowers and

The white flowers of *Aruncus dioicus*, with delphiniums and shasta daisies, in front of the flame creeper, *Tropaeolum speciosum*, at Burton Agnes in Yorkshire.

grey-green, trifoliate leaves. Flowering earlier than the average perennial, this makes a useful contribution to the border, best planted towards the back of the border, not just because it is tall, but to prevent the foliage hiding later flowers. *Baptisia tinctoria* is grown commercially as a source of dyes, but is not decorative enough for the garden. Baptisias prefer deep, moist, slightly acidic soils, but are fairly tolerant of others.

Baptisia alba

ORIGIN: eastern United States
SIZE: 120–180 × 75–120 cm; 4–6 × 2½–4 ft
FLOWERING TIME: early summer
FLOWER COLOUR: white and pale mauve
Sun or light shade

Zone 4
Interesting seed heads
Propagate by seed or division
Moderate impact
DESCRIPTION: Thirty centimeter (1 ft) spikes of white flowers, often with purple blotches, followed by yellowish brown seed pods. No staking required.

var. *macrophylla*. Taller than average, with larger leaves.

Crambe

BRASSICACEAE
Twenty perennial or annual species, often woody at the base, from central Europe, western and central Asia and tropical

Crambe cordifolia, seen here with cranesbill geraniums at Cambridge University Botanic Garden.

Africa. The British native species is the low-growing sea kale, *Crambe maritima*.

Crambe cordifolia

ORIGIN: Caucasus
SIZE: 200 × 150–180 cm; 6½ × 5–6 ft
FLOWERING TIME: early summer
FLOWER COLOUR: white
Sun or light shade
Zone 5
Useful for flower arrangement
Interesting seed heads
Propagate by seed, division or root cuttings
High impact
DESCRIPTION: A massive airy cloud of tiny, delicate, white, scented flowers on wiry green stems, sitting above a mound of coarse, inappropriately dock-like leaves, which are dark green, wrinkled and slightly bristly, up to 60 cm (2 ft) long. Visually this is a unique plant. It likes deep fertile soil, or it may not perform. Unfortunately, it dies down early, leaving a massive gap—so it needs careful placing. The flowerheads need shelter from strong winds.

Euphorbia

EUPHORBIACEAE
spurge
A large, cosmopolitan genus of about 2000 species, many of which are succulents from the tropics. The floral heads of the hardy herbaceous species are usually greenish

yellow and consist of specialized, brightly coloured leaves rather than petals. They are found from the Atlantic Islands, across the Mediterranean region and the Middle East to the Himalayas, China and Japan. All species carry a white latex which appears when any part of the plant is broken. This is harmful to the skin and could be poisonous in large doses. Several species are of particular value in the garden because of their excellent overwintering foliage. The unusual-looking caper spurge, *Euphorbia lathyris*, sometimes reaches the required height, but is strictly biennial, and can become a nuisance.

The excellent bold foliage of *Euphorbia mellifera*, a curious plant which grows as a tree in its native Madeira but as a perennial in cooler areas.

Euphorbia mellifera

honey spurge

ORIGIN: Canary Islands
SIZE: 150–240 × 90–150 cm; 5–8 × 3–5 ft
FLOWERING TIME: early summer
FLOWER COLOUR: honey
Sun
Zone 9
Propagate by seed or cuttings
High impact

DESCRIPTION: A first-rate foliage plant for mild areas. Oddly, it grows as large tree on its native mountains in Madeira and Funchal, with long bare trunks and leaves borne on the ends of the branches, like a fatsia. In cooler temperate areas, plants don't get enough warmth to harden the stems and make them woody, and they behave as perennials instead. Specimens as tall as 6 m (20 ft) can be seen in sheltered gardens in southern and south-western parts of the British Isles.

It has large honey-coloured flowerheads, about 15–20 cm (6–8 in) wide, above and among large, elegant, pale green leaves, 20 cm (8 in) long, with a prominent white midrib. In temperate areas, it is a good idea for it to be planted against a wall for protection. Can be cut to the ground in cold weather, but if the frost is not too severe, the plant will shoot again.

Euphorbia sikkimensis

ORIGIN: Nepal, Tibet, Sikkim, Bhutan, southern China, North Vietnam
SIZE: 105–180 × 120–165 cm; 3½–6 × 4–5½ ft

FLOWERING TIME: late summer
FLOWER COLOUR: lime yellow
Sun
Zone 7
Propagate by seed or division
Moderate impact
DESCRIPTION: Bright yellow flowerheads
12.5–20 cm (5–8 in) wide, topping a mass
of greenery. Deciduous. It flowers much
later than most other garden euphorbias,
but it does have interest in spring when the
new shoots emerge, an attractive pinky red
colour, which later fades to green. Some
support may be needed.

Euphorbia stygiana

ORIGIN: Azores
SIZE: 105–150 (–1000) × 150 cm; 3½–5
   (–30) × 5 ft
FLOWERING TIME: early summer
FLOWER COLOUR: yellowish
Sun
Zone 7
Useful for flower arrangement
Propagate by seed or division
Moderate impact
DESCRIPTION: Technically a shrub, but
behaves like a perennial in temperate
regions, as the stems don't get enough heat
to harden and become woody. Pale greenish
yellow floral heads, over bold foliage. The
leaves are leathery, bluish green, oblong, up
to 13.5 cm (5½ in) long, turning brilliant red
in the autumn.

Iris
IRIDACEAE

A well-known genus with distinctive flowers, usually bearing three upper, upward-
curving petals (standards) and three lower,
arching petals (falls). The foliage is spearlike
and usually held vertically. About 300 species, and at least 2500 varieties currently
commercially available.

Iris virginica
blue flag

ORIGIN: eastern United States
SIZE: 45–90 (–180) × 45–indefinite cm;
   1½–3 (–6) × 1½–indefinite ft
FLOWERING TIME: early summer
FLOWER COLOUR: pale blue and yellow
Sun
Zone 5
Useful for flower arrangement
Propagate by seed or division
Subtle impact
DESCRIPTION: Pale blue falls with pale
yellow centres, in groups of one to four,
on unbranched stems. Native to wet and
swampy ground. Mildly toxic.

'Contraband Girl'. Robust clumps with
larger than normal, purple-blue flowers.
Very vigorous and soon forms clumps 180
cm (6 ft) wide on moist sites, but also happy
on normal soils.

Iris wattii

ORIGIN: India, western China, Tibet
SIZE: 90–180 × 45–90 cm; 3–6 × 1½–3 ft
FLOWERING TIME: late spring
FLOWER COLOUR: lilac and white
Sun or light shade

Zone 7
Useful for flower arrangement
Propagate by seed or division
Subtle impact
DESCRIPTION: Large flowers, lavender blue with a white centre spotted with yellow and mauve, feathery crest, orange or white spotted with yellow, up to 7.5 cm (3 in) wide, nearly flat, and grouped in twos or threes. Stems are slightly reminiscent of bamboo canes, but much-branched at the top.

Meconopsis
PAPAVERACEAE
A genus famous for its blue poppies, although there are exceptions which have red, yellow or orange flowers. The blue poppies are the cause of much swooning among gardeners, though the truth is they are not that much more beautiful than the common red ones that grow in cornfields—they just happen to be more upright and stately, and the petals a little more substantial. For most people they are quite difficult to grow, to the extent that success gives you the kind of kudos usually reserved for getting rare alpines to flower.

The Asiatic species are accustomed to high summer rainfall in the wild, and therefore are most likely to succeed in northwestern Europe, such as western Scotland and Ireland, and in the Pacific Northwest. They need rich, fertile, acidic soil, moist but not boggy, and not too wet in winter, in semi-shade. The tall species also need shelter from winds. The named varieties in the various hybrid groups are all shorter than the two species included here. They look good grouped with candelabra primroses and ferns, and are usually seen in the kind of aristocratic woodland that also houses a collection of rhododendrons and azaleas.

There are about 50 species of perennials, annuals and biennials, many of which die after flowering, though taking several years to do so. They are all are from the Himalayas, Tibet and western China, except for the Welsh poppy, *Meconopsis cambrica*, which is from western Europe. The genus *Meconopsis* is closely related to the genus *Papaver*.

Meconopsis betonicifolia
(syn. *M. baileyi*)
Himalayan blue poppy
ORIGIN: Yunnan, China; southeastern Tibet, northern Myanmar
SIZE: 105–165 × 30 cm; 3½–5½ × 1 ft
FLOWERING TIME: early summer
FLOWER COLOUR: blue
Shade
Zone 7
Propagate by seed or division
Subtle impact
DESCRIPTION: Classic blue poppies, nodding or held at 45 degrees, sky-blue to lavender with pleasantly contrasting orange-yellow stamens, the flowers 7.5–10 cm (3–4 in) wide and held in groups of up to ten on tall, bristly, upright stems. Long, pointed, downy, mid-green leaves, of no importance. The stems die down to a small overwintering crown in the autumn. Likely to be biennial if not happy with its situation, but comparatively easy from seed. Removal of seed pods before the seeds ripen may encourage the plant to stay with you.

Meconopsis napaulensis

satin poppy

ORIGIN: Nepal

SIZE: 150–240 × 30–45 cm; 5–8 × 1–1½ ft

FLOWERING TIME: summer

FLOWER COLOUR: pink and red

Shade

Zone 7

Propagate by seed

Subtle impact

DESCRIPTION: Cerise pink, deep red or purply blue poppy flowers, with orange-yellow stamens, the flowers 6.5–7.5 cm (2½–3 in) wide, in branching heads. Long leaves, slightly lobed, with orange or buff hairs, borne on upright stems, which rise from a large, attractive, evergreen rosette up to 60 cm (2 ft) wide. Monocarpic—in other words, it dies after flowering.

'Alba'. White.

Polygonatum

CONVALLARIACEAE

Solomon's seal

Elegant woodland plants with arching vertical stems, neat leaves and small, usually white, bell-like flowers. The emergence of the stems in early spring is one of the attractions of these plants. Good companions for ferns. About 30 species in Europe, Asia and the northern United States.

Polygonatums are susceptible to sawfly attack which can reduce plants to skeletons within a few days. The pests can be picked off by hand (tedious!) or one can use an insecticide. Slugs and snails are also keen on Solomon's seals, and will return night after night. Divide in very early spring, just before the plant appears above ground. Cool, moist, humus-rich soil is preferred.

Polygonatum biflorum

ORIGIN: eastern United States, southern Canada

SIZE: 90–210 × 45–60 cm; 3–7 × 1½–2 ft

FLOWERING TIME: late spring

FLOWER COLOUR: white

Shade or light shade

Zone 3

Useful for flower arrangement

Propagate by seed or division

Subtle impact

DESCRIPTION: White flowers, tipped with green, solitary or in clusters of between two and four, pendant. Upright, arching stems with lance-shaped or elliptical leaves. Variable in height.

Polygonatum verticillatum

ORIGIN: Europe, temperate Asia, Afghanistan

SIZE: 90–200 × 60 cm; 3–6½ × 2 ft

FLOWERING TIME: midsummer

FLOWER COLOUR: purple and pink

Light shade

Zone 5

Useful for flower arrangement

Propagate by seed or division

Moderate impact

DESCRIPTION: Rich deep pink flowers, which hang in a ring in the leaf axils below the whorls of narrow pointed leaves, on tall stems. The new shoots are pink as they emerge in spring. The upper parts act as tendrils and are liable to clasp adjoining plants for support.

12

MIDSEASON PERENNIALS

To create a succession of interest in the garden, with plants flowering one after another, is one of the pleasures of gardening, and by July the garden should be in full swing. The tall perennials that flower at this time offer a wide range of delights from the silky pure white flowers of romneyas and pale blue flowers of campanulas to cheerful yellow coreopsises and bright red salvias, with forms as diverse as the spindly and delicate dieramas to the dense and tough-looking polygonums.

Achillea
ASTERACEAE
yarrow

Distinctive plants with flat, vaguely circular, tabletop-like flowerheads, which hold themselves up towards the sunlight. The inflorescence may look like an umbel to the uninitiated, but is actually a corymb of tiny, closely packed daisy flowers. The ferny, grey-green foliage contrasts pleasantly with the flowers. Achilleas used to be either yellow or white until quite recently. However, the plants featuring the new colours such as salmon pink and dusky orange are all too short for this book. Some of these new colours fade unpleasantly into dreary cardboard-beige colours. However, if you actually like biscuit-coloured flowers, there is always 'McVities' (up to 100 cm, 3½ ft).

Achilleas are often long-flowering, but prompt deadheading will extend their flowering period. They tolerate soils which are either poor and dry or fertile, but dislike heavy soils. After a few years they tend to grow weary and fade away, and for this reason, the plants should be lifted every three or four years, and replanted, with the spent parts removed. Propagate by division or cuttings in spring.

Achillea chrysocoma
(syn. *A. aurea*)
ORIGIN: Albania, Macedonia
SIZE: 150–180 × 120 cm; 5–6 ft × 4 ft
FLOWERING TIME: midsummer
FLOWER COLOUR: white
Sun
Zone 6

Useful for flower arrangement
Interesting seed heads
Propagate by division
Moderate impact
DESCRIPTION: White flowerheads, over light green finely divided foliage, leaves up to 25 cm (10 in) long.

'Grandiflora'. Much taller than the species, a stately plant, the tallest of all achilleas, with large white flowerheads, 13 cm (5 in) wide on long stems. There seems to me some doubt whether this is the correct name for this plant.

Achillea filipendulina

(syn. *A. eupatorium*)
ORIGIN: Caucasus, Iran, central Asia
SIZE: 60–165 × 135 cm; 2–5½ × 4½ ft
FLOWERING TIME: midsummer to early
    autumn

FLOWER COLOUR: yellow
Sun
Zone 6
Useful for flower arrangement
Interesting seed heads
Propagate by seed, division or cuttings
Moderate impact
DESCRIPTION: A handsome overwintering plant, with good green feathery foliage, holding its heads up well. The plant as a whole usually requires support. The flowerheads can be as much as 15 cm (6 in) wide, between primary and mustard yellow in colour, while their shape gives the whole plant an architectural quality. The flowers are best picked before they fade, if they are to be used for dried flower arrangements.

'Cloth of Gold'. The tallest of the varieties, floral heads 10 cm (4 in) wide in deep yellow-gold. 125–170 cm (4–5½ ft).

The yellow, flat-topped, sun-worshipping heads of *Achillea filipendulina*, seen here at Cambridge University Botanic Garden.

Achillea macrophylla

ORIGIN: central Europe
SIZE: 180 × 120 cm; 6 × 4 ft
FLOWERING TIME: midsummer
FLOWER COLOUR: white
Sun or light shade
Zone 6
Interesting seed heads
Propagate by seed or division
High impact
DESCRIPTION: A wilding, native to Europe, rarely grown in gardens, with off-white heads and jagged, green foliage which is musky and aromatic. Not a spreader, and said to be deer-resistant.

Aconitum

RANUNCULACEAE
monkshood, wolf's bane, aconite
Aconites come in shades of deepest blue, mid-blue, pale yellow or white, but their strange hooded shape is what makes them instantly recognizable. The foliage is usually dark, glossy and ferny, and is borne on sturdy, erect stems. The plants come early into growth, and although most are quite robust, the taller ones benefit from staking. The seed heads are moderately good, but not outstanding. Aconites are tolerant of a wide range of situations in light shade or sun, and are easily grown, but nevertheless prefer rich, moist, fertile soils whenever possible, and like to be given a mulch in the spring.

All parts of the plant are poisonous, and once you know this it can make them seem slightly sinister. The roots contain the strongest concentration of poison, but this poisonous characteristic should not prevent aconites from being grown in any garden uninhabited by children. To get the best results, the clumps should be dug up every few years (in late autumn) and the strongest tuberous roots replanted, but this is when care needs to be taken, in view of the plant's toxicity. At least the poisonous nature of these plants makes them deer- and rabbit-resistant.

The naming of aconites is complicated by the intergradation of one species into the next. It seems that the concept "species" is a human invention, not fully understood by nature. The parentage of the many cultivars is also fairly doubtful, which is why many varieties "float free" rather than sitting conveniently under a species name.

Aconitum ×cammarum

(syn. *A. ×bicolor*)
Hybrids between *Aconitum napellus* and *A. variegatum*.
'Doppelgänger'. A strong, branching plant, with dark blue flowers. Raised by Partsch in 1981. 165 cm (5½ ft).

Aconitum carmichaelii

(syn. *A. fischeri*)
ORIGIN: central and western China, North America
SIZE: 90–200 × 90 cm; 3–6½ × 3 ft
FLOWERING TIME: late summer to autumn
FLOWER COLOUR: blue
Sun or light shade
Zone 3
Propagate by seed or division
Moderate impact
DESCRIPTION: Good foliage, and a range of flower colour. Very late flowering.

'Blue Bishop'. Violet blue. 120–180 cm (4–6 ft).

Wilsonii Group. Lavender blue to purple-blue. Vigorous. Midsummer to early autumn. 150–210 cm (5–7 ft).

(Wilsonii Group) 'Barker's Variety'. Deep amethyst blue. Staking is advisable. Raised by a Mr. Barker of Ipswich, Suffolk. 135–200 cm (4½–6½ ft).

(Wilsonii Group) 'Kelmscott'. Violet blue. Long inflorescence. Glossy green foliage. Long flowering period. Up to 180 cm (6 ft).

(Wilsonii Group) 'Spätlese'. Pale, powdery violet blue, almost white in bud. Early summer to early autumn. 120–210 cm (4–7 ft).

(Wilsonii Group) 'The Grim Reaper'. Large, very dark blue flowers on clustered heads. 180 cm (6 ft).

Aconitum ferox

ORIGIN: Himalayas
SIZE: 90–200 × 90 cm; 3–6½ ft × 3 ft
FLOWERING TIME: late summer
FLOWER COLOUR: mid-blue
Sun or light shade
Zone 6
Propagate by seed or division
Moderate impact
DESCRIPTION: Best grown from a reliable source, as seed-grown plants of this rarity may vary, and poorer examples are variously described as a dingy or dirty blue. Finely divided foliage. Threatened in the wild, due to over-collection for medicinal purposes.

Other Aconitum Varieties

'Blue Sceptre'. White with a purple-blue edge, on strong upright plants. Some sup-

The hooded, purple-blue flowerheads of *Aconitum carmichaellii* Wilsonii Group, with the contrasting white plumes of pampas grass behind.

port needed. Raised by Alan Bloom. Up to 210 cm (7 ft), but often very much less.

'Spark's Variety'. Large, deep dusky blue flowers on strong, broadly branching stems, with finely cut foliage. Mid to late summer. Usually needs support, but can be slightly scandent. Sometimes listed under *Aconitum henryi*. Raised in England by Prichard's nursery about 1898. 150–180 cm (5–6 ft).

'Unikum'. A tall, upright variety with dark violet blue flowers, flowering in mid to late summer. A sport from 'Bressingham Spire' discovered in 1993 by Otto Markworth of the Berggarten, Hannover, Germany. First published as *Aconitum napellus* 'Unicum', a seemingly invalid Latin varietal name. 200 cm (6½ ft).

Alcea

MALVACEAE

hollyhock

Tall biennials or short-lived perennials, with erect stems and flowers in upright panicles. The stately hollyhock, *Alcea rosea*, is a well-known cottage garden plant, but there are several other worthwhile species. Some will self-sow, but otherwise the short-lived kinds should be propagated every other year from saved seeds. They do best in rich, heavy soils. They require a sheltered position, or staking, and watering in dry weather.

Alcea ficifolia

(syn. *Althaea ficifolia*)
Antwerp hollyhock
ORIGIN: Siberia

SIZE: 150–225 × 60 cm; 5–7½ × 2 ft
FLOWERING TIME: summer
FLOWER COLOUR: yellow and orange
Sun
Zone 3
Interesting seed heads
Propagate by seed
High impact
DESCRIPTION: Good seven-lobed, fig-like foliage, much more rust-resistant than the usual hollyhock. Double flowers, and other colours, from seed merchants. Hybridizes with other hollyhocks.

'Happy Lights' is seed mix offering mixed colours and single flowers.

Alcea pallida

(syn. *Althaea pallida*)
eastern hollyhock
ORIGIN: southeastern and central Europe, Turkey
SIZE: 180–200 × 60 cm; 6–6½ × 2 ft
FLOWERING TIME: late spring to early autumn
FLOWER COLOUR: rose pink
Sun
Zone 4
Interesting seed heads
Propagate by seed
High impact
DESCRIPTION: Well-shaped, lilac-rose-pink flowers, often with greenish yellow centres. Greyish, woolly, downy leaves. Differs botanically from *Alcea rosea* only in slight particulars. Usually biennial, but persistent. Rust resistant.

Alcea rosea

hollyhock
ORIGIN: Asia
SIZE: 150–300 × 60 cm; 5–10 × 2 ft
FLOWERING TIME: early summer to mid
   autumn
FLOWER COLOUR: various
Sun
Zone 4
Interesting seed heads
Propagate by seed
High impact
DESCRIPTION: Biennial or short-lived
perennial. Hollyhocks were originally pink,
but now come in a vast array of colours,
including almost-black but excluding blue,
and regrettably are also available with congested double flowers. The leaves are light
green and rough-textured, and unfortunately very prone to rust disease. The plants
should therefore be sprayed with fungicide
in May, with repeated treatment later in the
season.

Alcea rugosa

ORIGIN: Ukraine, Caucasus
SIZE: 180–240 × 60 cm; 6–8 × 2 ft
FLOWERING TIME: summer
FLOWER COLOUR: yellow
Sun
Zone 4
Interesting seed heads
Propagate by seed
High impact
DESCRIPTION: A very hardy species, with
spikes of well-shaped, pale sulphur-yellow
flowers. Rust resistant.

Althaea

MALVACEAE
marshmallow
Bushy perennials resembling *Lavatera*,
often with open habit, sometimes woody at
the base and tap-rooted, with typical mallow flowers. Worth growing for their long
flowering period. Usually short-lived, but
easily raised from seed. Plants now in the
genus *Alcea* were at one time placed here.

Althaea cannabina

ORIGIN: southern and central Europe,
   southern Russia, Caucasus, northwestern
   Iran, Turkestan
SIZE: 100–200 × 75 cm; 3½–6½ × 2½ ft
FLOWERING TIME: midsummer to early
   autumn
FLOWER COLOUR: pale pink
Sun
Zone 4
Propagate by seed or cuttings
Subtle impact
DESCRIPTION: Leaves three- to five-lobed,
divided to the base, on erect stems, allegedly
cannabis-like.

Althaea officinalis

marshmallow
ORIGIN: central and southern Europe,
   including Great Britain, northern Africa;
   introduced in North America
SIZE: 100–200 × 90 cm; 3½–6½ × 3 ft
FLOWERING TIME: midsummer to early
   autumn
FLOWER COLOUR: pink and pale pink
Sun
Zone 3

Propagate by seed or cuttings
Subtle impact
DESCRIPTION: Clusters of delicate flowers with dark centres, on erect stems and soft, downy foliage. Flowers are delicious on close inspection, but the plant as a whole is hardly a riot. Drought-resistant. Can self-seed a bit too much.

'Alba'. A white-flowered form.

'Marshmallow'. Silky white flowers. Soft, hairy grey leaves. A varietal name which is the same as the common English name for the species as found in Great Britain seems inadvisable. Early to late summer. 150 cm (5 ft).

'Romney Marsh'. Presumably as collected from the Romney Marshes in Kent. Whether, or to what extent, this plant differs from the species as found in Great Britain is unclear. Soft pink flowers. Grey-green foliage. Mid to late summer. 90–120 cm (3–4 ft).

Campanula

CAMPANULACEAE

A large genus characterized by bell-shaped flowers, usually blue in colour. There are about 300 perennials, biennials, alpines and annuals from temperate regions of the northern hemisphere, but only two species are tall enough for us.

Campanula lactiflora

ORIGIN: Caucasus
SIZE: 120–165 × 60 cm; 4–5½ × 2 ft
FLOWERING TIME: summer to early autumn
FLOWER COLOUR: blue and lilac
Sun or light shade
Zone 5
Interesting seed heads
Propagate by seed or division
Moderate impact
DESCRIPTION: Large domed heads of bell-flowers, typically blue, wide-open, with

Campanula lactiflora, seen here at Rosemoor in North Devon.

pointed, curving petals, each 2.5 cm (1 in) wide. Erect stems with thin, light green, oval, toothed leaves. Requires soil that is not too dry, in full sun or light shade. It can self-sow, but not annoyingly. Tough enough to grow in rough grass, as long as the competition is not too fierce. Staking needed in exposed positions.

'Alba'. Pure white.

'Loddon Anna'. Pale, slightly murky pink, 90–210 cm (3–7 ft). Raised by Thomas Carlile's nursery in Berkshire, about 1950.

Campanula pyramidalis
chimney bellflower, steeple bells
ORIGIN: southern Europe
SIZE: 135–210 × 60 cm; 4½–7 × 2 ft
FLOWERING TIME: summer
FLOWER COLOUR: blue
Sun
Zone 8
Interesting seed heads
Propagate by seed
High impact
DESCRIPTION: Tall spires of bell-flowers, 2.5–3.5 cm (1–1½ in), on long stems with heart-shaped leaves. Tends to perform badly after the second year, so best treated as a biennial. Also does well in pots. A lavender blue form is so far unnamed, and there is also (regrettably) a variegated form.

'Alba'. A white form.

Centaurea
ASTERACEAE
knapweed, hardhead, cornflower
The flowerheads are reminiscent of thistle flowers, with the petals springing from what

is initially a dense, hard bud, later forming the rounded, dark-coloured base of the flower. About 450 species worldwide, the majority coming from the Mediterranean. The impressive yellow *Centaurea macro-cephala* is slightly too short for us, as are the crimson *C. benoistii*, the mauve-pink *C. jacea*, and the pale yellow *C. ruthenica*. *Centaurea scabiosa* is a European wildflower, not ornamental enough for the cultivated garden, but attractive in the wild garden or meadow.

Centaurea atropurpurea
ORIGIN: central Balkans, Romania
SIZE: 150–200 × 75 cm; 5–6½ × 2½ ft
FLOWERING TIME: summer
FLOWER COLOUR: dark purple
Sun
Zone 6
Useful for flower arrangement
Interesting seed heads
Propagate by seed or division
High impact
DESCRIPTION: Large, dark purple flowers. Leaves deeply, pinnately lobed. Forms with yellow flowers are occasionally found in the wild.

Cephalaria
DIPSACACEAE
giant scabious
About 65 perennials and annuals, from Europe and the Mediterranean Africa to central Asia, closely related to *Scabiosa*. Those listed here are best planted in a group at the back of the border, since most of them are sparsely branched and have a lanky and vertical outline. Long flowering period.

Cephalaria dipsacoides

ORIGIN: eastern Mediterranean
SIZE: 180 × 45 cm; 6 × 1½ ft
FLOWERING TIME: summer
FLOWER COLOUR: creamy yellow
Sun
Zone 4
Useful for flower arrangement
Interesting seed heads
Propagate by seed or division
Moderate impact
DESCRIPTION: Large flowers, 2 cm (¾ in) wide, creamy, dotted with deep mauve stamens, on tall stems and dark green basal foliage.

Cephalaria gigantea

(syns. *C. tatarica* hort., *Scabiosa gigantea*)
ORIGIN: Caucasus, Siberia
SIZE: 180–200 × 45–60 cm; 6–6½ × 1½–2 ft
FLOWERING TIME: summer
FLOWER COLOUR: pale yellow
Sun
Zone 3
Useful for flower arrangement
Propagate by seed or division
Moderate impact
DESCRIPTION: The most commonly seen cephalaria. Primrose yellow flowers up to 5 cm (2 in) wide, on tall vertical stems and light green basal foliage. Long-flowering. Well-drained soil preferred. Can self-seed annoyingly in gravel or bare soil.

Cephalaria leucantha

ORIGIN: Mediterranean
SIZE: 105–200 × 45–60 cm; 3½–6½ × 1½–2 ft

A good-sized clump of *Cephalaria gigantea* at Burton Agnes in Yorkshire.

FLOWERING TIME: summer
FLOWER COLOUR: white and yellow
Sun
Zone 4
Useful for flower arrangement
Propagate by seed or division
Moderate impact
DESCRIPTION: Creamy white scabious flowers, on wiry stems. Long flowering period. Prefers well-drained soil.

Coreopsis
ASTERACEAE
A genus of about 110 perennials or annuals, mainly from Mexico and the southern United States. Most species have very bright yellow daisy flowers, usually free-flowering and long-flowering. The *Coreopsis* species most commonly seen are the shorter species, and their varieties.

Coreopsis tripteris
ORIGIN: central and southeastern United States
SIZE: 200–300 × 90–150 cm; 6½–10 × 3–5 ft
FLOWERING TIME: late summer to early autumn
FLOWER COLOUR: pale yellow
Light shade
Zone 4
Useful for flower arrangement
Propagate by division
High impact
DESCRIPTION: Pale yellow, daisy flowers, sometimes fading to purple, in corymb-like clusters, on green foliage with tripartite leaves. Long-lived and easily grown. Good with *Aster turbinellus* and panicums.

Dierama
IRIDACEAE
angel's fishing rod, wand flower
Clusters of pink or magenta bell-like flowers, which dangle precariously from delicate and gracefully arching stems. The grassy, evergreen foliage grows from clusters of corms, forming tufts of tough, grey-green leaves. The flower stems are usually about three times the height of the foliage. Because of their unusual habit dieramas don't mix well in the border, but look better among lower-growing plants, or beside a pool. They need moist, fertile soil in summer, but will not tolerate excessive winter wet—the opposite of what they are liable to get in Great Britain or the Pacific Northwest. The corms should not be lifted as if they were bulbs, since they will dry out and

The towering stems and yellow heads of *Coreopsis tripteris*.

perish. They need protection in cooler areas, as they are Zone 7–9 plants. There are about 45 species, from Ethiopia, East Africa and South Africa.

Genera which end in the letter -*a* are normally assumed to be feminine and have specific names with an adjectival -*a* to match. However, the name *Dierama* comes from the Greek, and is masculine, and, therefore, the second name also has to be masculine—so it usually ends in -*um*.

Dierama latifolium

ORIGIN: KwaZulu-Natal
SIZE: 120–270 × 30–indefinite cm; 4–9 × 1–indefinite ft
FLOWERING TIME: summer
FLOWER COLOUR: pink and red
Sun
Zone 8
Useful for flower arrangement
Interesting seed heads
Propagate by seed or division
Subtle impact
DESCRIPTION: Flowers vary from pink to wine-red, open in shape, held at the far ends of the stems. Foliage reaches 120–150 cm (4–5 ft). Plants in the wild form very large clumps.

Dierama pendulum

fairy bells
ORIGIN: Western Cape, South Africa
SIZE: 105–200 × 45 cm at base; 3½–6½ × 1½ ft at base
FLOWERING TIME: summer
FLOWER COLOUR: purple and pink
Sun

Zone 8
Useful for flower arrangement
Interesting seed heads
Propagate by seed or division
Subtle impact
DESCRIPTION: Tall flowering stems over low-growing foliage up to 75 cm (2½ ft). Flowers mauvy pink, flaring out elegantly, like the hem of a skirt.

Dierama pulcherrimum

ORIGIN: South Africa
SIZE: 90–180 × 45 cm at base; 3–6 × 1½ ft at base
FLOWERING TIME: summer
FLOWER COLOUR: pink and purple
Sun
Zone 7
Useful for flower arrangement
Interesting seed heads
Propagate by seed or division
Subtle impact
DESCRIPTION: Very narrow flowers, variable in colour from pale mauvy pink to deep purple or white. Leaves to 60–90 cm (2–3 ft).

Dierama reynoldsii

ORIGIN: Eastern Cape, KwaZulu-Natal
SIZE: 105–200 × 30 cm at base; 3½–6½ × 1 ft at base
FLOWERING TIME: summer
FLOWER COLOUR: deep red
Sun
Zone 8
Useful for flower arrangement
Interesting seed heads
Propagate by seed or division
Subtle impact

DESCRIPTION: Clusters of about 12 deep mauvy red flowers, each about 2.5 cm (1 in) long, with a silvery, papery bract at the base. Foliage consists of rather a sparse tuft of leaves.

Dierama robustum

ORIGIN: Free State, Lesotho, Western Cape
SIZE: 75–200 × 30 cm at base; 2½–6½ × 1 ft at base
FLOWERING TIME: summer
FLOWER COLOUR: pink and white
Sun
Zone 8
Useful for flower arrangement
Interesting seed heads
Propagate by seed or division
Subtle impact
DESCRIPTION: Clusters of large flowers, 2.5–3.5 cm (1–1½ in), flared at the mouth, variable in colour from almost white to pale pink to pale mauve. Leaves 45–120 cm (1½–4 ft) high.

Filipendula

ROSACEAE
meadowsweet, dropwort
Clump-forming perennials with fluffy topped flowerheads, consisting of irregular clusters of tiny pink or white flowers. They have better than average foliage, carried on erect stems, with large leaves, either maple-leaf-like or consisting of several leaflets. Filipendulas prefer moist to average soil, in full sun or part shade. There are about ten perennial species, from northern temperate regions. Related to *Spiraea*.

Filipendula camtschatica

ORIGIN: Kamchatka, Russia; northern China, Korea, Japan
SIZE: 180–240 (–300) × 105 cm; 6–8 (–10) × 3½ ft
FLOWERING TIME: midsummer
FLOWER COLOUR: white and pale pink
Sun or light shade
Zone 3
Interesting seed heads
Propagate by division
High impact
DESCRIPTION: White flowers, sometimes flushed pink, in large clusters, 30 cm (12 in) wide, on a huge, tough plant with bold foliage. Large, three- or five pointed leaves, up to 25 cm (10 in) wide. Cut down after flowering to promote new growth. Requires soil that doesn't dry out. Full sun and dry conditions will lead to leaf scorch.
'Rosea'. Pink-flowered form.

Filipendula rubra

queen of the prairie
ORIGIN: northeastern and central United States
SIZE: 150–240 × 120 cm; 5–8 × 4 ft
FLOWERING TIME: summer
FLOWER COLOUR: pink
Sun or light shade
Zone 3
Interesting seed heads
Propagate by division
High impact
DESCRIPTION: Large, fluffy candy-floss-pink flowers, flowerheads 30 cm (12 in) wide, on a massive plant with presence and bold foliage. Jagged, acer-like leaves, up to

The fluffy pink heads of *Filipendula rubra* 'Venusta', a selected form of queen of the prairie.

20 cm (8 in) wide. A rapid spreader. For wild, woodland and poolside gardens.

'Venusta' (syns. 'Magnifica', *F. palmata* 'Rubra'). A good shade of soft salmon pink. Raised in 1853. Shorter on dry soils. Very good winter silhouette, if left to stand. Staking not normally required. Can be invasive. 135–200 cm (4½–6½ ft).

Hemerocallis

HEMEROCALLIDACEAE

day lily, daylily

Lily-shaped flowers (predictably, given the common name) over clumps of arching green foliage. Each flower lasts one day, which seems an extraordinary waste of effort on the part of the plant. But rest assured, a mature plant can be expected to produce a constant succession of flowers over the course of several weeks. One important piece of information about any particular variety is always hard to come by—do the flowers die neatly by falling off, or do they die messily leaving half-dead petals lingering on the plant? This seems rarely to be recorded.

There are about 20 wild species from China, Japan and Korea, and amazingly there are more than 100,000 named varieties, which is sheer madness. You could raise your own nice varieties quite easily (I have), and register them (though I haven't). Only one species and a handful of hybrids reach the required height.

Hemerocallis altissima

ORIGIN: China
SIZE: 180–210 × 75 cm; 6–7 × 2½ ft
FLOWERING TIME: late summer
FLOWER COLOUR: yellow
Sun
Zone 6
Propagate by seed or division
Subtle impact
DESCRIPTION: Small, sweetly scented yellow flowers, 7.5 cm (3 in) wide. Flowers open very late in the day. Late flowering in the season.

Other Hemerocallis Varieties

'Autumn Minaret'. Single, peach yellow flowers with a yellow band. Midsummer. Good performer. Foliage winter-dormant. Raised by Arlow Stout in 1951. 165 cm (5½ ft).

'Banana Smoothie'. Very large single flowers, 25 cm (10 in) wide, yellow self with green throat. Midsummer, reflowering. Foliage semi-evergreen. Raised in 2006 by T. George. 150–165 cm (5–5½ ft).

'Berlin Tallboy'. Fairly large single flowers, orange-yellow, dusted with brown, with orange throat. Midsummer, foliage winter-dormant. Raised by Tomas Tamberg of Berlin in 1989. 180 cm (6 ft).

'Challenger'. Clusters of rich red flowers with a yellow centre and central line to each petal. Raised by Arlow Stout before 1956. 180 cm (6 ft).

'Jolly Red Giant'. Fairly large, single flowers, red with yellow-green throat. Midsummer, repeat flowering, with evergreen foliage. Raised by Patrick Stamile in 1999. 150–165 cm (5–5½ ft).

'Notify Ground Crew'. Single yellow flowers. Midsummer. Foliage winter-dormant. Raised by Curt Hanson in 2000. 180 cm (6 ft).

'Rognvaldur'. Quite large, single flowers, smoky violet with a purple chevron band, with a creamy lemon to lime-green throat. Foliage winter-dormant. Raised by Brian Mahieu in 2003. 165 cm (5½ ft).

'Sears Tower'. Yellow multi flowers. Midsummer, foliage winter-dormant. Raised by Alfred Goldner in 2000. 180 cm (6 ft).

Impatiens

BALSAMINACEAE
balsam, busy lizzie

The average *Impatiens* species is a Zone 10 plant—too tender for temperate gardens. The commonly seen varieties of busy lizzie are actually perennials, varieties of *I. walleriana*, but are treated as houseplants, annuals or bedding plants. *Impatiens* is a large genus with about 1000 annuals, perennials or subshrubs from the tropical and subtropical regions of Europe, Asia, Africa and North America.

Impatiens glandulifera, or Himalayan balsam, has become naturalized in many countries including Great Britain and might look like a candidate for the wild wet garden. It is tall enough for us, reaching 200 cm (6½ ft)—but is an annual species.

Impatiens tinctoria

ORIGIN: Sudan, Ethiopia, East Africa
SIZE: 90–180 × 60–90 cm; 3–6 × 2–3 ft
FLOWERING TIME: midsummer to autumn
FLOWER COLOUR: white
Light shade
Zone 8
Useful for flower arrangement
Propagate by cuttings
High impact
DESCRIPTION: Large, sweetly fragrant flowers, which can be up to 12.5 cm (5 in) long and 7.5 cm (3 in) wide, in clusters, held well clear of the foliage. The flowers are white with a purple or deep pink throat spreading out into the two large lower petals. Leaves up to 25 cm (10 in) long, slightly toothed at the edges, on stout, fleshy, erect stems, which are reddish or purplish. Moist soil, in full sun is preferred. A thick mulch is needed for winter protection in cool temperate areas.

Kitaibelia

MALVACEAE
poppy mallow
A genus of two large, leafy perennials from the Balkans and the eastern Mediterranean. Named after Hungarian botanist Paul Kitaibel (1757–1817). *Kitaibela* is an orthographic variant.

Kitaibelia vitifolia

ORIGIN: Slovenia, Croatia, Serbia, Macedonia
SIZE: 150–300 × 90–240 cm; 5–10 × 3–8 ft
FLOWERING TIME: mid to late summer
FLOWER COLOUR: white

Sun
Zone 4
Propagate by seed or cuttings
Subtle impact
DESCRIPTION: Forms a large leafy bush dotted with white, or sometimes pale pink, mallow flowers with yellow stamens. The five petals are like isosceles triangles curved at the corners, each petal distinctly separated from the next by a continuous, more or less parallel gap. The seed heads are surrounded by prominent leafy bracts. The leaves are large, elegant, multi-pointed, acer-like, and up to 17.5 cm (7 in) long. A fairly short-lived perennial, but fast-growing and likely to flower in the first year of planting. Propagate from seeds, or from basal cuttings, as the crown of the plant is woody and hard to divide. A fertile, sunny spot is preferred—in dry places it will be shorter.

Lavatera

MALVACEAE
tree mallow
Fast-growing and prolific but sometimes short-lived, lavateras are covered in typical mallow flowers, like mini-hollyhocks. Often woody at the base, it is hard to decide whether some are shrubs or perennials. They prefer full sun and well-drained soil. Cut back by half in autumn, and to the ground in early spring. Protect from cold winds. Twenty-five species of shrubs, perennials, biennials and annuals, from Mediterranean Europe to the Himalayas, central Asia and Siberia; Australia; California; northwestern Mexico.

Lavatera cachemiriana

ORIGIN: Kashmir, western Himalayas
SIZE: 200–240 × 180 cm; 6½–8 × 6 ft
FLOWERING TIME: mid to late summer
FLOWER COLOUR: pink
Sun
Zone 8
Useful for flower arrangement
Propagate by cuttings
High impact
DESCRIPTION: Pale pink flowers, white at the base, 5–7.5 cm (2–3 in) wide, borne prolifically for many weeks, on upright stems, woody at the base. Downy, three- or five-lobed leaves. Dislikes winter wet. Vigorous but short-lived.

Ligularia

ASTERACEAE

Good foliage plants, often stately in form, with bright yellow-flowers, best in a moist situation or at least a rich fertile bed which is never allowed to dry out. The more they are exposed to the sun the more moisture they need. Shelter from the wind is also needed, to prevent damage to the foliage, and protection from slugs and snails. Ligularias come from montane situations in Europe and East Asia, about 180 species in all. They associate well with other lovers of moist ground or the pond side—aruncuses, astilbes, rodgersias, filipendulas and darmeras.

Ligularia fischeri

ORIGIN: Himalayas, China, Far East
SIZE: 165–200 × 60 cm; 5½–6½ × 2 ft
FLOWERING TIME: summer to autumn
FLOWER COLOUR: yellow
Light shade
Zone 4
Interesting seed heads
Propagate by seed or division
Moderate impact
DESCRIPTION: Starry yellow flowers, 5 cm (2 in) wide, in short broad spikes about 7.5 cm (3 in) high, on upright stems. Large rounded leaves, kidney-shaped, up to 40 cm (16 in) wide, with toothed edges. Similar to *Ligularia veitchiana* and *L. wilsoniana*.

Ligularia macrophylla

ORIGIN: Siberia, Russia; Xinjiang, China; Kazakhstan, Kyrgyzstan
SIZE: 150–180 × 75 cm; 5–6 × 2½ ft
FLOWERING TIME: mid to late summer
FLOWER COLOUR: yellow
Sun or light shade
Zone 4
Useful for flower arrangement
Interesting seed heads
Propagate by division
Moderate impact
DESCRIPTION: Many bright yellow flowers in a dense panicle, up to 30 cm (12 in) wide. Blue-grey-green foliage, with large leaves, slightly toothed, the basal ones up to 60 cm (24 in) long. Not so demanding of damp conditions as the other species. Easily mistaken for a senecio.

Ligularia przewalskii

ORIGIN: northwestern China
SIZE: 180 × 90 cm; 6 × 3 ft
FLOWERING TIME: late summer
FLOWER COLOUR: yellow
Light shade

Ligularia przewalskii, with good foliage and interesting flower spikes.

Zone 4
Interesting seed heads
Propagate by seed or division
High impact
DESCRIPTION: Tall, narrow, flower spikes, up to 50 cm (20 in) long, made up of many small yellow flowers, 2.5 cm (1 in) wide, each with only a very few petals, the flower spikes standing proud of the foliage and held on dark purple, almost black stems. Clump-forming, with excellent foliage, the leaves almost palm-like, jagged and toothed, 30 cm (12 in) wide.

'Light Fingered' has foliage which is even more deeply divided.

Ligularia stenocephala

ORIGIN: China, Taiwan, Japan
SIZE: 120–180 × 60 cm; 4–6 × 2 ft
FLOWERING TIME: late summer
FLOWER COLOUR: yellow
Light shade
Zone 4
Interesting seed heads
Propagate by seed or division
High impact
DESCRIPTION: Tall, narrow flower spikes, with small yellow flowers, each only having a small number of petals, the flower spikes and foliage held on dark purple stems. A clump-forming plant, with pointed, deeply jagged and toothed leaves, up to 20 cm (8 in) wide. Similar to *Ligularia przewalskii* but shorter and flowering earlier.

Ligularia veitchiana

ORIGIN: western China
SIZE: 150–180 × 75 cm; 5–6 × 2½ ft
FLOWERING TIME: late summer

FLOWER COLOUR: yellow
Light shade
Zone 4
Interesting seed heads
Propagate by seed or division
High impact
DESCRIPTION: Tall, narrow flower spikes, up to 75 cm (30 in) high, made up of bright yellow flowers, 5 cm (2 in) wide, with brown eyes and many petals. Large, rounded, toothed, kidney-shaped leaves, up to 45 cm (18 in) wide, on long stalks. Similar to *Ligularia stenocephala*, but broader flower spikes.

Ligularia wilsoniana

ORIGIN: China
SIZE: 165–200 × 75 cm; 5½–6½ × 2½ ft
FLOWERING TIME: late summer to early autumn
FLOWER COLOUR: yellow
Light shade
Zone 4
Interesting seed heads
Propagate by seed or division
High impact
DESCRIPTION: Long, branching spikes of yellow flowers. Similar to *Ligularia veitchiana*, but with smaller individual flowers, and later flowering. Large rounded leaves, up to 50 cm (20 in) wide, with toothed edges.

Other *Ligularia* Varieties

'Gregynog Gold'. *Ligularia dentata* × *L. veitchiana*. Chunky pointed candles, with clusters of bright orange-yellow flowers up to 10 cm (4 in) wide, with irregular petals. Good foliage, with large rounded leaves, toothed at the margins, with the flower

Ligularia 'Hessei' at Bressingham Gardens, Norfolk.

spikes on long stems held well above the foliage. Performs well. Originated at a garden of this name in Wales. A major statement. Summer to early autumn. Zone 4. 165–200 cm (5½–6½ ft).

'Hessei' (syn. *L.* ×*hessei*). A hybrid, probably between *Ligularia dentata* and *L. wilsoniana*. Similar to 'Gregynog Gold', but slightly paler in flower colour and a little earlier flowering. Zone 4. 165–200 cm (5½–6½ ft).

'The Rocket'. *Ligularia przewalskii* × *L. stenocephala*. Tall flower spikes up to 45 cm (18 in) high, made up of many small yellow flowers on a dark purple stem. Large, jagged, more or less triangular leaves, on long stalks. A magnificent plant. Zone 4. 180 cm (6 ft).

'Zepter'. An excellent hybrid, with *Ligularia veitchiana* as one parent, and maybe *L.* 'The Rocket' as the other, or possibly *L. przewalskii*. Tall spikes of orange-yellow flowers held on very dark stems, well above the foliage. Clump-forming, with large, rounded leaves up to 30 cm (12 in), on long stalks. Raised in Germany. 180 cm (6 ft).

Phytolacca
PHYTOLACCACEAE
About 35 perennials, shrubs and trees worldwide, remarkable for their spikes of fleshy fruits.

Phytolacca americana, one of the few perennials grown for its fruits.

Phytolacca americana

Virginian pokeberry

ORIGIN: eastern Canada, United States

SIZE: 120–165 × 120 cm; 4–5½ × 4 ft

FLOWERING TIME: midsummer to early autumn

FLOWER COLOUR: whitish

Sun or light shade

Zone 4

Red and black fruits

Propagate by seed or division

Moderate impact

DESCRIPTION: A sinister-looking plant, with the leaves of a weed and child-tempting fruits. It forms a large bush, at least as wide as it is tall, with unremarkable whitish flower spikes and broad, uninteresting, poisonous leaves. But the fruits are very distinctive, red and black, like evil mulberries, borne in elongated clusters. Rich, fertile soil is preferred. It can seed itself annoyingly. *Phytolacca acinosa* is slightly shorter.

'Melody'. Foliage with a fairly subtle variegation—a creamy yellow base dusted with green specks and flecks. Not as bright as 'Silberstein', but more consistent. Slow growing compared with the species.

'Silberstein'. Foliage speckled creamy white, especially around the edges of the leaves. The distribution of colour across the leaf is quite variable, and also the proportion of green and cream overall. Leaves on pinkish stems. Slow growing.

Polygonum
POLYGONACEAE
knotweed
Tough, leafy plants, fairly ornamental but
sometimes invasive or coarse, from northern
temperate regions. Plants in this genus have
been moved about by botanists to a range of
other genera, including *Bistorta*, *Fallopia*,
Persicaria and *Tovara*.

Polygonum polymorphum, seen here at
Waterperry Gardens near Oxford.

Polygonum polymorphum
ORIGIN: Himalayas
SIZE: 165–200 × 180 cm; 5½–6½ × 6 ft
FLOWERING TIME: summer to autumn
FLOWER COLOUR: cream
Sun or light shade
Zone 5
Interesting seed heads
Propagate by seed or division
High impact
DESCRIPTION: A feathery mass of tiny,
creamy white flowers, on large, airy,
branching heads about 15 cm (6 in) high. A
tough, massive clump of stout stems, with
very large leaves, the largest at the base of
the stem, up to 45 cm (18 in) long. A stunning, though not refined, plant, the flowerheads turning pinky brown in the autumn,
then red brown in seed. Suitable for wild
and meadow gardens and borders, it prefers moist soil but is tolerant of some summer dryness once established. Not invasive. It looks good with late grasses such as
Miscanthus.

Romneya
PAPAVERACEAE
California tree poppy
A genus with only one species, which has
white poppy flowers and attractive blue-
grey foliage. A sunny, sheltered position is
preferred, with deep rich soil. The roots are
liable to sucker, especially on light soils, but
the plant is nevertheless difficult to divide
and resents disturbance. The stems may
overwinter in mild areas, but should be cut
away in favour of new growth in the spring.

Romneya coulteri

ORIGIN: California, northwestern Mexico
SIZE: 150–240 (–300) × 120 cm; 5–8 (–10) × 4 ft
FLOWERING TIME: summer to autumn
FLOWER COLOUR: white
Sun
Zone 7
Useful for flower arrangement
Propagate by root cuttings
High impact
DESCRIPTION: Large, sweetly scented poppy flowers, white and tissue-y, 10–12.5 cm (4–5 in) wide, with a dense central rosette of bright yellow stamens and five or six petals. Substantial, grey-blue-green foliage, deeply and irregularly lobed and divided, on upright stems, woody at the base. Long flowering. Sometimes hard to establish.

subsp. *trichocalyx*. Foliage more finely divided, on a narrower plant. Flowers in clusters instead of solitary. More likely to sucker widely.

subsp. *trichocalyx* 'White Cloud'. A large-flowered form.

Salvia

LAMIACEAE

Salvias are recognizable by their aromatic foliage and their distinctive flower shape. The individual flowers of salvias have petals that have fused to form an upper hooded lip and a lower down-turned lip, and these occur clustered in circular groups, or whorls, along a vertical flower spike, sometimes on branching stems. The flowers are attractive to bees. The leaves are often thick, rough-textured or downy, held on square-angled stems. *Salvia officinalis* is the Latin name of sage, the subshrubby herb with its distinctive smell.

The most ornamental species tend to be on the borderline of hardiness in temperate areas (Zones 6–8), the combination of cold and wet being the difficulty in Great Britain and the Pacific Northwest. The more tender species will not perform well unless they get enough sunshine hours in summer, and a mild but cloudy climate will produce disappointing results. Some species have overwintering foliage, and it is a good idea in this case to leave some of the foliage in position until spring, to protect the plant. However, in very favourable areas some species will keep flowering indefinitely. In temperate areas, they enjoy full sun, though in warmer climates, many will accept or enjoy semi-shade. Very easy from cuttings.

A delicate, whiter than white poppy flower with yellow centre from *Romneya coulteri*, a native of California and Mexico.

Salvia atrocyanea

ORIGIN: Bolivia
SIZE: 175–300 × 75–100 cm; 5¾–10 ×
    2½–3½ ft
FLOWERING TIME: summer to autumn
FLOWER COLOUR: blue
Sun
Zone 7
Propagate by seed or cuttings
Moderate impact
DESCRIPTION: Good display of rich, bright
blue flowers, with prominent green bracts,
on graceful, drooping or horizontal spikes
30–50 cm (12–20 in) long. Heart-shaped
foliage borne on thick stems, arising from
tuberous roots. Winter dormant. May
spread too much, in warm districts, by
tubers or seeds.

Salvia azurea

blue sage
ORIGIN: central and southeastern United
    States
SIZE: 105–180 × 75 cm; 3½–6 × 2½ ft
FLOWERING TIME: late summer to mid
    autumn
FLOWER COLOUR: blue
Sun
Zone 8
Propagate by seed, division or cuttings
Subtle impact
DESCRIPTION: Clear delphinium-blue flow-
ers with a white marking on the lower lip,
on slender, willowy spikes, flowering pro-
fusely in favourable districts. Downy grey-
green foliage, subshrubby at the base. Fast
growing, with narrow leaves and lax, arch-
ing habit, benefiting from pinching back, as
it can get leggy. Flowers tend to be sparse in

temperate areas. Susceptible to winter wet.
    var. *grandiflora* (syn. subsp. *pitcheri*).
Larger, paler flowers, more closely packed
together. Mexico. 150–200 cm (5–6½ ft).

Salvia barrelieri

ORIGIN: southern Spain, northwestern
    Africa
SIZE: 180 × 120 cm; 6 × 4 ft
FLOWERING TIME: midsummer
FLOWER COLOUR: blue
Sun
Zone 8
Propagate by seed
Subtle impact
DESCRIPTION: Very large sky-blue flowers,
on long stems, up to 180 cm (6 ft) long, over
bluish grey foliage. A short-lived perennial,
or biennial, which will flower from seed
sown the previous year. Fairly short flow-
ering season, for a salvia. Requires good
drainage.

Salvia concolor

ORIGIN: Mexico
SIZE: 180–600 × 60–90 cm; 6–20 × 2–3 ft
FLOWERING TIME: late summer to autumn
FLOWER COLOUR: blue
Sun or light shade
Zone 8
Propagate by cuttings
Moderate impact
DESCRIPTION: A rival for *Heracleum man-
tegazzianum*, as the largest perennial that
can be grown in Great Britain, or the
Pacific Northwest; however, it is unlikely to
reach its maximum height in such temperate
areas. Bright indigo blue flowers, with slate-
coloured calyces on 30–50 cm (12–20 in)

spikes. Downy, toothed leaves, on vigorous stems, woody at the base, from large tuberous roots. Prone to spider mite infestations in some districts. A plant with green calyces, sometimes offered under this name, is actually a form of *Salvia guaranitica*, similar to *S. g.* 'Black and Blue'.

Salvia darcyi

(syn. *S. oresbia*)
ORIGIN: northeastern Mexico
SIZE: 100–180 × 60–90 cm; 3½–6 × 2–3 ft
FLOWERING TIME: midsummer to late autumn
FLOWER COLOUR: scarlet
Sun
Zone 8
Propagate by seed, division or cuttings
Moderate impact
DESCRIPTION: Bright scarlet flowers, in widely spaced whorls, on flower spikes up to 15–30 cm (6–12 in) long. The dark green foliage is heart-shaped, sticky and pleasantly scented, on semi-woody stems, from tuberous roots. Protect the roots from winter wet, and new shoots from frost.

Salvia elegans

(syn. *S. incarnata*)
tangerine sage
ORIGIN: Mexico, Guatemala
SIZE: 60–200 × 60–100 cm; 2–6½ × 2–3½ ft
FLOWERING TIME: midsummer to late autumn
FLOWER COLOUR: scarlet
Sun
Zone 8
Propagate by division or cuttings
Moderate impact

DESCRIPTION: Large sprays of small cerise flowers. Tolerates humidity on warm areas. Unlikely to reach more than 120 cm (4 ft) in areas cooler than Zone 9.

Salvia guaranitica

(syns. *S. ambigens, S. coerulea, S. ianthina*)
ORIGIN: Argentina, Brazil, Uruguay
SIZE: 125–240 × 75–90 cm; 4–8 × 2½–3 ft
FLOWERING TIME: late summer to mid autumn
FLOWER COLOUR: blue
Sun or shade
Zone 8

A form of *Salvia guaranitica* growing at Sue Templeton's nursery in Australia.

Propagate by seed, cuttings or root cuttings
Moderate impact
DESCRIPTION: Named after the Guarani people, native to the subtropical regions of South America where this plant occurs. The flowers are beautiful shades of violet blue or gentian blue, with a black or blue-tinged calyx, 2.5–5 cm (1–2 in) long, on a flower spike 25 cm (10 in) long, produced over a long period until the frosts come. Mid-green, aromatic foliage on an erect, freely branching bush, arising from a spreading rootstock. In some forms the flowers are so dark that they don't show up very much against the foliage. Some support may be needed. Winter dormant. Protect in winter, or take cuttings, in colder areas. Spreads rampantly in hot districts.

'Argentine Skies'. Light blue, with a deeper slate-mauve tint. Liable to spread. Selected by Charles Cresson of Philadel-phia. 100–170 cm (3½–5½ ft).

'Blue Enigma'. Deep blue with a green calyx. Pale green, shiny foliage. 120–170 cm (4–5½ ft). The hardiest selection.

'Kergunyah'. Formerly simply known as 'Large Flowered'. Distributed by Sue Templeton, the salvia specialist in Australia. Large, royal blue flowers. Long flowering. Requires full sun. This may not correctly belong under *Salvia guaranitica*. 200 cm (6½ ft).

'Omaha Gold'. Blue flowers with black calyces and variegated foliage. Long flower-ing. Needs support. Overwintering foliage, weather permitting. 150–180 cm (5–6 ft). Zone 7.

Salvia involucrata

ORIGIN: Mexico
SIZE: 90–180 × 60–90 cm; 3–6 × 2–3 ft
FLOWERING TIME: midsummer to late autumn
FLOWER COLOUR: pink and purple
Sun
Zone 8
Propagate by cuttings
High impact
DESCRIPTION: Vivid pink flowers in open spikes, on a fast-growing, sometimes sprawling subshrubby plant, with aromatic foliage. There sometimes seems to be too few flowers to justify such a lot of green-ery. Overwinters in Zone 9 areas and above. There is some confusion about the names of some of the following varieties.

'Boutin'. Purplish red flowers with white bracts, on longer spikes than 'Bethellii'. Fast growing to 90–180 × 180 cm (3–6 × 6 ft), from midsummer to the frosts. Protect from wind damage.

'Hadspen'. Purplish red, possibly the same as 'Boutin'.

var. *puberula* (syn. *S. puberula*). Bright pink flowers on a bushier plant, later, with short flowering period. Winter dormant.

Salvia madrensis

forsythia sage
ORIGIN: Mexico
SIZE: 90–300 × 120–200 cm; 3–10 × 4–6½ ft
FLOWERING TIME: early to late autumn
FLOWER COLOUR: yellow
Sun
Zone 9

Propagate by cuttings
High impact
DESCRIPTION: Canary yellow flowers, on 30 cm (12 in) spikes. Large, heart shaped leaves, textured and bright green, up to 15 cm (6 in) long. Forms a large, robust, spreading subshrubby perennial, though in frost-prone areas it is only likely to reach 90–150 cm (3–5 ft) high. Tolerates shade in warmer areas.

'Dunham'. Said to be hardier, possibly Zone 8.

'Red Neck Girl'. Butter-yellow flowers in large panicles, dark red-violet stems. Large fuzzy, silvery green leaves. Flowers a little earlier than the species. From Tony Avent's Plant Delights Nursery, North Carolina.

Salvia recognita

ORIGIN: Turkey
SIZE: 40–200 × 60–100 cm; 1½–6½ × 2–3½ ft
FLOWERING TIME: early summer to early autumn
FLOWER COLOUR: pink
Sun
Zone 7
Propagate by division or cuttings
Moderate impact
DESCRIPTION: A subshrubby perennial, with low pinnate foliage and tall spikes of dusky pink, widely spaced flowers. Short lived but may self-seed. Unlikely to exceed 100 cm (3½ ft) in temperate areas (Zones 6–8). Deadhead, to try and prevent sudden death syndrome.

Salvia uliginosa

bog sage
ORIGIN: Argentina, Brazil, Uruguay
SIZE: 90–210 × 60 cm; 3–7 × 2 ft
FLOWERING TIME: midsummer to late autumn
FLOWER COLOUR: blue
Sun
Zone 7
Propagate by seed, division or cuttings
High impact
DESCRIPTION: Delicate, sky blue flowers in spikes up to 12 cm (5 in) long, on odd-angled, graceful stems. Narrow dark green leaves, with slightly jagged edges. Prefers moisture-retentive soil. Discreet staking is desirable as the plant tends to lean awkwardly in unpredictable directions. Needs watering in summer, but dislikes excessive winter wet. Protect or take cuttings in cold areas. A good companion for asters, or for the buff shades of late grasses.

Other Salvia Varieties

'Phyllis' Fancy'. A subshrubby hybrid, possibly between *Salvia leucantha* and *S. chiapensis*. Small, pale lavender flowers, each with a purple and green calyx, on 30 cm (12 in) long purple spikes. The tall clumps are narrow at the base, but can have a 210 cm (7 ft) spread at the top. Discovered at the University of California, Santa Cruz Arboretum, and named for Phyllis Norris. Early to late autumn. Up to 210 cm (7 ft) high. High impact. Zone 8.

'Purple Majesty'. Probably *Salvia guaranitica* × *S. gesneriiflora*. Impressive purple flowers. A subshrubby plant, with foliage

The less-than-upright flowerheads of *Salvia uliginosa*, seen here at Old Court Nursery, Colwall, Worcestershire.

similar to that of *S. guaranitica*. Prefers full sun. Take cuttings in temperate areas in case of winter loss. 100–180 cm (3½–6 ft). Zone 8.

Sanguisorba

ROSACEAE

The charms of sanguisorbas are fairly subtle—they would hardly bowl you over. Their flowers are unusual, like small fluffy bottlebrushes held on tall wiry stems, but don't really offer a lot. The plants as a whole are bushy, with much-divided pinnate foliage, which could be described as above average. Sanguisorbas fit well into any garden, especially the wild garden, and blend particularly well with tall grasses such as *Panicum*. Many of them need support. They prefer moist soil, but nevertheless are fairly tolerant. Some self-seed generously. There are about 18 species, from temperate northern regions.

Sanguisorba canadensis

Canadian burnet

ORIGIN: eastern Canada, northern United States and Alaska

SIZE: 120–200 × 75 cm; 4–6½ × 2½ ft

FLOWERING TIME: summer

FLOWER COLOUR: white

Sun or light shade

Zone 3
Useful for flower arrangement
Interesting seed heads
Propagate by division
Moderate impact
DESCRIPTION: Clusters of long, greenish white, upright (slightly plantain-like) flower spikes, up to 12.5 cm (5 in) long, on long stalks. Grey-green pinnate leaves made up of seven to fifteen leaflets.

Sanguisorba officinalis

great burnet
ORIGIN: Europe, temperate Asia, Canada, United States
SIZE: 60–120 (–200) × 45–75 cm; 2–4 (–6½) × 1½–2½ ft
FLOWERING TIME: mid to late summer
FLOWER COLOUR: dark red
Sun or light shade
Zone 4
Useful for flower arrangement
Interesting seed heads
Propagate by division
Subtle impact
DESCRIPTION: Hard, rounded, knobbly, dark red heads, in large numbers, on wiry stems that rarely stand up straight. Pinnate leaves with seven to fifteen leaflets. Several cultivars have been selected to be shorter; these need less support than the species.

'Arnhem'. Up to 90–200 cm (3–6½ ft). Flops a lot and has to be supported.

'Martin's Mulberry'. Reliably self-supporting. Found in a Norfolk garden, England, and distributed by West Acre Gardens. 180 cm (6 ft).

Sanguisorba tenuifolia

ORIGIN: China, Japan, Korea, far eastern Russia
SIZE: 90–150 (–200) × 75 cm; 3–5 (–6½) × 2½ ft
FLOWERING TIME: summer
FLOWER COLOUR: pink, white and red
Sun or light shade

A tall, white sanguisorba backed by a tall yew hedge at Arley Hall, Cheshire.

Zone 4
Useful for flower arrangement
Interesting seed heads
Propagate by division
Moderate impact
DESCRIPTION: The flower spikes are held on long slender stems, arch over like catkins and become increasingly fluffy with age. The flower colour is quite variable: pink, red or white. Ferny, cucumber-scented foliage, the pinnate leaves having 15 to 19 leaflets, slightly toothed at the edges.

'Alba'. A good white form. 150–200 cm (5–6½ ft).

'Pink Elephant'. Long pinkish red spikes. 120–180 cm (4–6 ft).

Sida

MALVACEAE
There are about 150 species, mainly from the Americas, but only one or two in cultivation.

Sida hermaphrodita

Virginia mallow
ORIGIN: northeastern United States
SIZE: 150–180 (–300) × 90 cm; 5–6 (–10)–3 ft
FLOWERING TIME: mid to late summer
FLOWER COLOUR: white
Sun
Zone 4
Propagate by seed or cuttings
Subtle impact
DESCRIPTION: Clusters of white mallow flowers, the petals widely separated from each other, and the reproductive parts of the flower on a prominent central stalk. Pale

green leaves, without much substance, acer-like in shape, on a bushy plant. Tolerates poor soils.

Tanacetum

ASTERACEAE
tansy
About 150 perennials, annuals and sub-shrubs, mostly from northern temperate areas of the Old World, but a few come from the New. Many have deeply divided, aromatic foliage, harmful to the skin in some cases, and all have daisy-like flowers.

Tanacetum macrophyllum

(syn. *Achillea grandifolia* hort.)
ORIGIN: southeastern Europe, southwest-ern Asia, Caucasus
SIZE: 105–165 × 75 cm; 3½–5½ × 2½ ft
FLOWERING TIME: summer
FLOWER COLOUR: off-white
Sun or light shade
Zone 6
Propagate by division
Subtle impact
DESCRIPTION: Shallowly domed heads rem-iniscent of an achillea, the flowers varying in colour and quality—from beige or dingy white to off-white and cream-coloured. It's best to go for a selected form, such as the one listed here. A clump-forming plant, with pleasing grey-green, ferny foliage and large, deeply divided leaves up to 20 cm (8 in) long, which clothe the upright, unbranched stems. Tolerant of a wide range of situations and soils.

'Cream Klenza'. Cream-coloured flowers. A good plant offered by Bob Brown of

Cotswold Garden Flowers, Worcestershire. I hope you like the name.

Thalictrum

RANUNCULACEAE
meadow rue

Thalictrums have unusual flowerheads, forming clouds of smallish flowers in shades of purple, lavender cream or white. The foliage is attractive and much-divided, altogether creating a delicate effect. There are about 130 species from northern temperate regions. In some cases one plant is narrow on its own, and several need to be planted together to create a better effect. New growth appears late in the spring. Deadheading is often necessary to prevent excessive self-seeding. Alternatively, the seed heads can be quite good, though not in the first class. Division of the taller species is possible but not easy as they tend to be woody and hard at the base.

Thalictrum lucidum

ORIGIN: eastern Europe, Turkey
SIZE: 105–180 × 60 cm; 3½–6 × 2 ft
FLOWERING TIME: summer
FLOWER COLOUR: yellow-green
Sun
Zone 4
Useful for flower arrangement
Propagate by seed or division
Moderate impact
DESCRIPTION: Frothy creamy yellow flowers, over shiny green, much-divided foliage. Dislikes dry conditions.

Thalictrum pubescens

(syn. *T. polygamum*)
ORIGIN: central and eastern United States
SIZE: 150–180 (–300) × 60 cm; 5–6 (–10) × 2 ft
Flowering season: early to midsummer
FLOWER COLOUR: purple or cream
Sun
Zone 4
Useful for flower arrangement
Propagate by seed or division
Subtle impact
DESCRIPTION: Airy heads of elderflower white, although purple flowers are also found in the wild. Much-divided foliage on

Thalictrum pubescens, an unusual species from central and eastern United States.

sturdy upright stems. Dislikes dry soils. For the border or wildflower garden.

Thalictrum rochebruneanum

ORIGIN: Honshu, Japan
SIZE: 105–210 × 60 cm; 3½–7 × 2 ft
FLOWERING TIME: mid to late summer
FLOWER COLOUR: lavender or white
Sun
Zone 5

The delicate flowerheads of *Thalictrum rochebruneanum*, a Japanese species.

Useful for flower arrangement
Interesting seed heads
Propagate by seed or division
Moderate impact
DESCRIPTION: Heads of tiny lavender or white flower with yellow stamens, on red-brown stems, over much-divided blue-green foliage. Sometimes requires staking. Dislikes soil which dries out in summer.

'Lavender Mist'. A good coloured form.

Thalictrum uchiyamae

ORIGIN: Korea
SIZE: 150–180 × 60 cm; 5–6 × 2 ft
FLOWERING TIME: summer
FLOWER COLOUR: mauve
Sun or light shade
Zone 4
Useful for flower arrangement
Propagate by seed or division
Moderate impact
DESCRIPTION: Large, light purple or pinkish flowers over divided foliage with rounded leaflets. Dislikes dry conditions.

Other *Thalictrum* Varieties

'Elin'. *Thalictrum flavum* subsp. *glaucum* × *T. rochebruneanum*. Large numbers of tiny lavender-mauve flowers with soft yellow stamens in open sprays. Good foliage, almost black when it first appears, later blue-grey-green flushed purple, on purple-tinted stems. Vigorous and sturdy. Plant several together for best effect. Late summer. Raised by Rune Bengtsson of Sweden. Zone 4. 180–300 cm (6–10 ft).

Clouds of tiny flowers from *Thalictrum* 'Elin'.

Valeriana

VALERIANACEAE

valerian

Two hundred perennials, shrubs and annuals from every continent except Australia, but only a handful are in cultivation. The one tall perennial has been grown as a herb since Roman times.

Valeriana officinalis

valerian

ORIGIN: Europe, including Great Britain, western Asia; introduced in the United States

SIZE: 120–150 (–200) × 90 cm; 4–5 (–6½) × 3 ft

FLOWERING TIME: mid to late summer

FLOWER COLOUR: pale pink and white

Sun or light shade

Zone 4

Useful for flower arrangement

Propagate by seed or division

Moderate impact

DESCRIPTION: Pale pink or white flowers in umbel-like heads, with smaller heads on side branches. Clump-forming and leafy, with attractive elder-like foliage. The young foliage is pink-tinted. Usually grown as a herb, but also has possibilities for the wild garden, meadow or border. It prefers a moist or waterside situation. Can spread too fast for comfort, both at the root and by self-seeding. The roots are used as a calmative or sedative, and also in the perfume industry. Small animals are attracted to the smell of the plant. There is said to be a variegated form.

subsp. *sambucifolia*. Similar flowers, but with slightly differing, slightly better foliage.

Valeriana officinalis, a medicinal herb and a good plant for the wild garden.

13

LATE PERENNIALS

Late summer is peak time for tall perennials—bearing in mind that many of the plants in the chapters "Ornamental Grasses" and "Daisy Flowers" also flower at the end of the season. Rich and deep colours tend to be a feature of flowers at this time of year, whether the mauves and purples of *Aster* species, the rich yellows of solidagos, the dusky pinkish reds of eupatoriums or the brilliant scarlets and oranges of hedychiums and cannas.

Aster

ASTERACEAE

Michaelmas daisy

The rich and subtle colours of the genus *Aster* bring the year to a splendid close in shades of purple, misty blue and deepest red. The richest colours and largest flowers of the genus are found among varieties of the Michaelmas daisy itself, a name which should be reserved for *A. novi-belgii*. However, these cultivars demand a fair degree of dedication from the gardener if they are to perform well. A wide selection of less demanding species and less highly bred cultivars is available, and these are also well worth trying.

On sunny days in September and early October, when the flowers of the asters seem to glow in the low-angled rays of the sun, it is easy to wish that one had planted more of them. We tend to forget that during all the preceding months the foliage of most asters had been quite uninspiring. In a large garden there is no real problem, as one can have a special autumn border, or an autumn garden to celebrate these late-flowering flowers. As long as it can't be seen from the windows of the house, all is well. On the whole asters are easy to grow. Occasional division and replanting is what they need to keep them healthy, along with watering in dry periods during the growing season.

Aster laevis

ORIGIN: northwestern United States, Canada
SIZE: 60–210 × 75 cm; 2–7 × 2½ ft
FLOWERING TIME: early autumn

FLOWER COLOUR: lavender and violet
Sun
Zone 4
Useful for flower arrangement
Propagate by seed or division
Subtle impact
DESCRIPTION: A rather lax plant, elegant but untidy, well clothed in loose, open clouds of flowers. The whole plant needs support if it is not to lean unpredictably against adjacent plants. The individual flowers are similar to a Michaelmas daisy, *Aster novi-belgii*, with quite long rays and the usual yellow centre. Tolerates much drier conditions than *A. novi-belgii*, and has the advantage of being more resistant to mildew. 'Arcturus', raised about 1892, has deep rosy lilac flowers but is only 120 cm (4 ft) high; however, many plants grown and sold as it are actually 'Calliope'. There were many more varieties in the early 1900s, but these were lost to cultivation when the *A. novi-belgii* varieties became popular.

'Calliope'. Lilac purple flowers with a yellow centre, on strong, wiry stems with open branches. Quite good foliage—for an aster. Mildew resistant. Usually needs support. Raised at the Royal Horticultural Society's garden at Chiswick, before 1892. 150–200 cm (5–6½ ft).

'White Climax'. Green-tinted white flowers. Extremely late flowering, but frost resistant. Mid autumn to early winter. 200 cm (6½ ft). Not to be confused with *Aster novi-belgii* 'White Climax', a plant no longer in cultivation, nor with *A.* 'White Climax', a shorter plant circulating in the United States.

Aster laevis 'Calliope'.

Aster lanceolatus

ORIGIN: southern and eastern Canada, central and eastern United States
SIZE: 150–180 × 90 cm; 5–6 × 3 ft
FLOWERING TIME: early to mid autumn
FLOWER COLOUR: white and pale blue
Sun
Zone 4
Useful for flower arrangement
Propagate by seed or division
Subtle impact
DESCRIPTION: Small flowers, in pale violet blue or white, with pale yellow centres. Strong upright stems, with side branches, on vigorous, spreading clumps. Can be invasive. Prefers moist soil.

'Edwin Beckett'. Larger flowers, 2.5 cm (1 in) wide, with very pale violet blue petals. The stems branch into elegantly formed pyramids. A little less invasive than the species. Raised before 1902.

Aster novae-angliae

New England aster
ORIGIN: Quebec to Saskatchewan; eastern United States
SIZE: 60–165 × 60 cm; 2–5½ × 2 ft
FLOWERING TIME: late summer to late autumn
FLOWER COLOUR: pink, dark red and purple
Sun
Zone 2
Useful for flower arrangement
Propagate by seed or division
Moderate impact
DESCRIPTION: Richly coloured flowers, on plants which are sturdy, reliable and have the advantage of being mildew-free. Very attractive to butterflies. The leaves are slightly rough-textured, in an inoffensive green, but sometimes shrivel unattractively in dry weather. The stems are almost woody at the base. The clumps can remain undivided for several years—unlike *Aster novi-belgii*. Not as elegant as some asters, as the stems are stiff and straight, with the flowers clustering at the top 20 percent of the plant.

The overall flowering period is long. In bad weather the heads tend to close up, and also the seed heads of the early flowers tend to persist among the later ones, which can be annoying to the plant photographer, since it makes a perfect close-up shot hard to achieve. However, in the garden setting it is less noticeable. In spite of these small criticisms the long-lasting, easy-care nature of *Aster novae-angliae* varieties makes them preferable to most of their *A. novi-belgii* cousins. They need fertile soil which is not too dry. Specimens 300 cm (10 ft) high have been recorded on the edges of swamps in North America. Many good and well-known varieties are slightly too short to be included.

'Chilly Winds'. Masses of large white flowers, up to 3.5 cm (1½ in) wide, on a plant not as stiffly upright as some. Collected in Cattaraugus County, New York, and introduced in 2006 by Seneca Perennials, New York. Up to 200 cm (6½ ft) high.

'Lou Williams'. Large, light purple-red flowers, with twisted petals, on stems with wide branches. Early to mid autumn. 160–180 cm (5½–6 ft).

'Our Latest One'. Soft purple—almost blue. Not as stiff a grower as most others. Tolerant of damp soils. Very late: mid to late autumn. Raised by Montrose Nursery,

One of the few New England asters tall enough to be included—*Aster novae-angliae* 'Purple Cloud'.

FLOWERING TIME: early autumn
FLOWER COLOUR: blue and various
Sun
Zone 2
Useful for flower arrangement
Propagate by division
Moderate impact
DESCRIPTION: Michaelmas daisies are best grown on an open site, not overhung by trees or shaded by buildings, ideally in a south-facing border. Although they tolerate a wide range of soils, they do best in fertile and moisture-retentive ground, with plenty of organic matter. They are very easy to grow if you don't mind a less than perfect performance, but for first-rate results the whole plant should be lifted in the spring and completely replanted. Carefully break away the healthiest shoots, free of woody growth, and replant single pieces in clusters 15–22.5 cm (6–9 in) apart from each other. They should then be kept well-watered though the summer. Too much shelter should be avoided, as air movement will help to prevent mildew spores settling. Mildew is a problem with *Aster novi-belgii* varieties, though the healthier the plant the less likely it is to be attacked; the only solution is to spray them at regular intervals.

'Anita Ballard'. Medium-sized, single flowers, pale lavender blue. Strong stems with side branches, but the plant nonetheless needs support. Raised by Ernest Ballard before 1935. Early autumn. 150–180 cm (5–6 ft).

'Mount Everest'. Large, single, white flowers, on stems with many branches. Needs support. Raised by Ernest Ballard before 1930. Mid to late autumn. 165 cm (5½ ft).

North Carolina. Sometimes listed as 'Latest One'. 120–180 cm (4–6 ft).

'Purple Cloud'. Large lilac-purple flowers, on stems with wide branches. Strong, but needing support in case of wet weather weighing it down. Early to mid autumn. 160–180 cm (5½–6 ft).

'Red Cloud'. Bright, purple-pink flowers, 4 cm (1¾ in) across. A plant with very strong growth, 140 cm (4½ ft) in the first year, and can reach 200 cm (6½ ft) in subsequent years, in good soil.

Aster novi-belgii

Michaelmas daisy
ORIGIN: North America; introduced in
    Europe
SIZE: 60–150 (–180) × 45 cm; 2–5 (–6) ×
    1½ ft

'Steinebrück'. White, 4½ cm (1¾ in) across. Strong flowering sprays with many branches. Needs support. Early to mid autumn. 165 cm (5½ ft).

Aster umbellatus

ORIGIN: eastern Canada, central United States
SIZE: 140–200 × 75 cm; 4½–6½ × 2½ ft
FLOWERING TIME: late summer to early autumn
FLOWER COLOUR: creamy white
Sun
Zone 3
Useful for flower arrangement
Propagate by seed or division
Moderate impact
DESCRIPTION: This is a most atypical aster, with yellowy white, flat-topped heads, almost reminiscent of an achillea or a senecio. Strong stems with upright branches and rough-textured leaves. Support not needed. Mildew free. Can be invasive.

Boltonia

ASTERACEAE
false aster
A small genus of perennials similar and closely related to *Aster*.

Boltonia asteroides

ORIGIN: eastern United States
SIZE: 180–240 × 120–150 cm; 6–8 × 4–5 ft
FLOWERING TIME: late summer to autumn
FLOWER COLOUR: lilac, purple and white
Sun or light shade
Zone 3
Useful for flower arrangement
Propagate by division

Moderate impact
DESCRIPTION: Large panicles of small flowers, about 2 cm (¾ inch) wide, with a central yellow disc, over average, aster-like foliage. No more difficult to cultivate and propagate than a Michaelmas daisy. Often needs support. Sometimes looks dirty after a shower of rain.

var. *latisquama*. Slightly larger flowerheads.

var. *latisquama* 'Snowbank'. A clear white variety.

'Pink Beauty'. Large flowers with pink petals, white at the base. Blue-green foliage. Introduced by Montrose Nursery, North Carolina.

Brillantaisia

ACANTHACEAE
A genus of about ten species of shrubs, sub-shrubs and herbaceous plants from tropical Africa and Madagascar. Flowers often purple in colour, hooded, two-lipped, in a manner reminiscent of salvias.

Brillantaisia subulugurica

giant salvia
ORIGIN: East Africa
SIZE: 120–210 × 90–150 cm; 4–7 × 3–5 ft
FLOWERING TIME: late summer
FLOWER COLOUR: violet blue
Sun or light shade
Zone 10
Propagate by cuttings
High impact
DESCRIPTION: An "awesomely" large sub-shrubby plant, with spires of large violet blue flowers, reminiscent of an aconite or a salvia, over bold foliage with purplish stems. Loves long periods of heat and moisture.

Canna

CANNACEAE

About ten perennial species from tropical and subtropical America, with a large number of varieties. Most of the plants in cultivation are hybrids or named varieties. Cannas offer bold heads of red, yellow or orange flowers, on vertical stems, with large, oblong or elliptical leaves, creating a brilliantly coloured and showy general effect, although on close inspection they can look tacky and less than perfect. To my mind there is something slightly kitsch about cannas.

The plants die down in cooler areas in winter, but grow and flower continuously in warmer zones. They need to be well-watered, in full sun, with rich soil, improved with fertilizer and organic matter. In temperate areas, they are grown as bedding plants, planted out each year in June. They are easily propagated by division. Usually trouble-free, but young growth should be protected from snails. Cannas can be subject to virus attack, which causes stunted and twisted growth, with streaking in flowers and foliage. Infected plants should be destroyed as quickly as possible. All included here are Zone 9, unless otherwise stated.

Cannas combine somewhat awkwardly with other perennials, as their stiff upright habit and rubber-plant-like leaves need careful handling, and their brilliant colours make them look slightly brash and bold compared with many of the usual pastel-tinted inhabitants of the herbaceous border. They are best in small clusters of the same variety rather than dotted about here and there, and either contrasted with much paler, more reticent, finely textured plants, or else at the other extreme grouped with equally hot or bold competitors.

Canna ×ehemanii

(syn. *C. iridiflora*)
SIZE: 200 × 30–60 cm; 6½ × 1–2 ft
FLOWERING TIME: late summer
FLOWER COLOUR: deep pink
Sun
Zone 8
Useful for flower arrangement
Propagate by seed or division
High impact
DESCRIPTION: Deep pink, nodding flowers, trumpet-shaped, with broad leaves. Hardier than most.

Canna glauca

ORIGIN: tropical regions of the Americas
SIZE: 240 × 45–75 cm; 8 × 1½–2½ ft
FLOWERING TIME: late summer
FLOWER COLOUR: lemon yellow
Sun
Zone 9
Useful for flower arrangement
Propagate by seed or division
High impact
DESCRIPTION: Pale lemon-yellow flowers, with narrow, blue-green foliage. Requires a damp position or frequent watering.

Canna indica

ORIGIN: tropical regions of the Americas
SIZE: 90–180 × 30–60 cm; 3–6 × 1–2 ft
FLOWERING TIME: late summer
FLOWER COLOUR: red
Sun

Zones 8–9
Useful for flower arrangement
Propagate by seed or division
High impact

DESCRIPTION: A variable species, but the best are free-flowering, with cherry-red flowers, with yellow markings. Earlier flowering than most.

'Purpurea'. Small orange-red flowers over good, upright, purple foliage with green patterning. *Canna* 'Red Stripe' is possibly the same thing. 180–240 cm (6–8 ft).

'Russian Red'. Small orange flowers and purple foliage, larger than 'Purpurea' and held at a flatter angle. Zone 8.

Other *Canna* Varieties

'Annaeei'. A good foliage plant with pointed, blue-green leaves. Flowers disappointingly small, in pale orange. 300 cm (10 ft).

'Black Knight'. Dark crimson flowers, glaucous-purple foliage. 200 cm (6½ ft).

'Durban'. Large, bright red flowers, over foliage which starts off purple with pink veins, fading to orange. 160 cm (5½ ft).

'Erebus'. Pale salmon-pink flowers, over glaucous foliage, with paler edges. 160 cm (5½ ft).

'Grande'. Orange-red flowers on leafy stems up to 3 m (10 ft), over massive clumps of handsome, broad green foliage, with a hint of burgundy at the margins, up to 180 cm (6 ft) high. Very late flowering, sometimes too late. Related to 'Musifolia'.

'Intrigue'. An atypical canna, with small orange-red flowers on a plant with strongly vertical habit and narrow, pointed, purple-grey foliage. 210 cm (7 ft).

'Musifolia'. A surprising foliage plant, with bold foliage reminiscent of the leaves of a banana plant. The leaves, which can reach 90 cm (3 ft), have dark edges and mid-ribs tinted red. Flowers small, orange—but rarely seems to flower. 300 cm (10 ft). Zone 7.

'Mystique'. Small cherry-red flowers, but usually grown as an unusual coloured-foliage plant, with leaves in shades of purple, blue-green and pewter grey, colours which contrast well with the flowers. 230 cm (7½ ft).

'Pacific Beauty'. Brilliant orange flowers, over purple-grey foliage. 100–200 cm (3½–6½ ft).

'Panache'. Open trusses of graceful, soft orchid-pink and cream flowers, with narrow petals, on dark stems, above narrow, upright, pointed, grey-green leaves. An unusual variety. 150–180 cm (5–6 ft).

'Phasion' (syn. 'Tropicanna'). Sometimes listed incorrectly as 'Durban'. The quintessence of kitsch, with large, rich orange flowers, over purple-maroon leaves with pinkish red and yellow stripes. A good companion for gnomes and over-sized blue hostas. 100–200 cm (3½–6½ ft).

'Ra'. Lemon-yellow flowers, over narrow blue-green foliage. 200 cm (6½ ft).

'Roi Humbert' (syn. 'King Humbert'). Should possibly be called a group, since this name covers various plants with red flowers and dark foliage.

'Roi Soleil'. Large, frilly, bright red flowers, with yellow throat, over green foliage. 180 cm (6 ft).

'Striata' (syns. 'Bengal Tiger', 'Pretoria'). A variegated foliage plant, with large, brash

Canna 'Striata'.

Canna 'Wyoming'.

orange flowers on pink stems over finely yellow-striped foliage with a narrow maroon edge. 150–180 cm (5–6 ft).

'Stuttgart'. Peach-pink flowers, over grey-green and white variegated foliage. Leaves tend to burn at the edges, unless given some shade and kept well watered. 100–200 cm (3½–6½ ft).

'Wyoming'. Large, soft orange flowers, with very large bronze-coloured foliage. Vigorous. 210 cm (7 ft). Zone 8.

Eupatorium
ASTERACEAE

Eupatoriums have recently come into fashion, partly because they do well in meadow gardens and wild areas, and this has led to them being brought into more conventional gardens. They don't get high marks for being exciting, exotic or brilliantly coloured, but they are tough, trouble-free and generally do what they do well. Their red, pink or white flowers are in rounded or domed heads at the top of tall leafy stems. They are happy in full sun or part shade, and need soil that doesn't get too dry in the heat of summer. A few can be invasive. Many are attractive to butterflies and bees. About 40 species of perennials, subshrubs and annuals, from every continent except Australia.

Eupatorium altissimum
tall thoroughwort, tall boneset
ORIGIN: central and eastern United States
SIZE: 150–200 × 120 cm; 5–6½ × 4 ft
FLOWERING TIME: late summer to autumn
FLOWER COLOUR: white
Sun or light shade
Zone 4
Interesting seed heads
Propagate by division
Subtle impact
DESCRIPTION: White flowers in disjointed domed heads, on erect stems with long, narrow, pointed leaves. Unremarkable and harmless, and best for the wildflower meadow or semi-wild garden. Considered in many parts of the United States to be a weed. By no means the tallest species in this genus.

Eupatorium capillifolium
dog fennel
ORIGIN: southern and eastern United States
SIZE: 210–240 × 30 cm; 7–8 × 1 ft
FLOWERING TIME: autumn
FLOWER COLOUR: greenish white
Sun or light shade
Zone 5
Interesting seed heads
Propagate by seed or division
Subtle impact
DESCRIPTION: Greenish white flowers in loose vertical plumes over feathery foliage. A wilding only suitable to the garden fringes where it provides some interest very late in the year—sometimes too late, in a cold autumn. A bit too much like an enlarged version of the weed *Conyza canadensis* (Canadian fleabane) for my taste.

Eupatorium fistulosum
(syns. *Eupatoriadelphus fistulosum*, *Eutrochium fistulosum*)
trumpetweed
ORIGIN: eastern and southern United States

SIZE: 150–240 (–300) × 75 cm; 5–8 (–10 ft)–2½ ft

FLOWERING TIME: late summer to autumn

FLOWER COLOUR: deep pink

Sun or light shade

Zone 5

Interesting seed heads

Propagate by division

High impact

DESCRIPTION: Dusty pink, deep pink, or dark red flowers, on domed clusters, on erect, purple stems. Best to grow a selected form from a reliable nursery.

f. *albidum* 'Joe White'. A much-improved recent form, attractively domed in shape, creamy white with a hint of green. Early flowering. Selected by Richard Saul of Saul's Nursery, Georgia. 180–210 cm (6–7 ft).

Eupatorium glechonophyllum

(syn. *Ageratina glechonophylla*)

ORIGIN: Chile

SIZE: 165–200 × 90 cm; 5½–6½ × 3 ft

FLOWERING TIME: autumn to winter

FLOWER COLOUR: white

Sun

Zone 8

Interesting seed heads

Propagate by division

Subtle impact

DESCRIPTION: Whiskery clusters of white or pale pink flowers in loose, open heads, at the tops of reddish stems on an evergreen, subshrubby plant. Requires average to Mediterranean conditions.

Eupatorium maculatum

ORIGIN: southeastern United States

SIZE: 135–300 × 75 cm; 4½–10 × 2½ ft

FLOWERING TIME: late summer to autumn

FLOWER COLOUR: deep pink

Sun or light shade

Zone 4

Useful for flower arrangement

Interesting seed heads

Propagate by division

High impact

DESCRIPTION: A larger number of flowers. Purple-spotted stems.

Atropurpureum Group. Richer pink heads on dark red stems. The best eupatoriums for the garden. About 180 cm (6 ft). *Eupatorium maculatum* (Atropurpureum Group) 'Gateway' seems to be identical.

(Atropurpureum Group) 'Glutball'. Mauvy pink heads, rounded in shape. The name means "glow-ball." 200 cm (6½ ft) high.

(Atropurpureum Group) 'Purple Bush'. Shorter form, with smaller flowers than Atropurpureum Group. Despite its English name this was raised in the Netherlands, by Piet Oudolf. 120–150 cm (4–5 ft).

(Atropurpureum Group) 'Riesenschirm'. Massive wine-red heads, about 250 cm (8 in) wide. The name means "giant umbrella." For the best results, feed the brute.

Eupatorium purpureum

Joe Pye weed

ORIGIN: southeastern United States

SIZE: 135–300 × 75 cm; 4½–10 × 2½ ft

FLOWERING TIME: late summer to autumn

FLOWER COLOUR: deep pink

Sun or light shade
Zone 4
Useful for flower arrangement
Interesting seed heads
Propagate by division
High impact

DESCRIPTION: Deep pink flowers in domed heads, about 20 cm (8 in) wide, on leafy upright stems. Leaves pointed, 10–25 cm (4–10 in) long. Moderately shade tolerant. Prefers moist, alkaline soil, but tolerates clay. Its English name is derived from the name of a Native American who used the plant as medicine. The wild species should be passed over in favour of various cultivated varieties.

'Album'. Rather a grubby shade of off-white, fading later to brown. Smaller flowers. Passable for the wild garden.

Hedychium
ZINGIBERACEAE
ginger lily

Exotic-looking plants with upright flower spikes which sit among attractive, luxuriant foliage and are pleasantly fragrant. Growth appears quite late, not before late May, and

Shades of deep pinky red from eupatoriums and echinaceas at the Berggarten, Hannover, Germany.

arises from thick, creeping rhizomes which smell slightly of ginger. The leaves are large and smooth, borne on stout stems. There are about 45 species of perennials, from tropical Asia, the Himalayas and Madagascar, mostly Zone 9 or higher.

A hot, sunny position is best, as this will encourage the production of flowers, although light shade is quite acceptable in warmer climates. Hedychiums should be planted deeply in rich, fertile soil, and be given time to settle in. They like plenty of moisture in summer, but not in winter. As soon as the stems have been frosted in late autumn they should be cut down at the base, as this helps to eliminate pests. In cool areas the rhizomes should be protected by a thick mulch and kept reasonably dry. Care should be taken to prevent damage to the rhizomes while they are dormant, as this can easily lead to the dormant plants rotting off.

These are excellent plants for creating a subtropical look in the garden, associating well with other plants with bold foliage. Bamboos, miscanthuses, phormiums, yuccas, ricinuses, cannas, dahlias and late kniphofias would all make good companions.

Hedychium aurantiacum

(syn. *H. coccineum* var. *aurantiacum*)
ORIGIN: northern India
SIZE: 105–200 × 75–120 cm; 3½–6½ × 2½–4 ft
FLOWERING TIME: autumn
FLOWER COLOUR: red
Sun
Zone 9
Useful for flower arrangement
Propagate by seed or division
Moderate impact
DESCRIPTION: Spikes of red flowers, late flowering. Long, narrow, pointed leaves.

Hedychium coccineum

ORIGIN: Himalayas
SIZE: 105–200 × 90 cm; 3½–6½ × 3 ft
FLOWERING TIME: late summer to autumn
FLOWER COLOUR: yellow, orange and red
Sun
Zone 9
Useful for flower arrangement
Propagate by seed or division
Moderate impact
DESCRIPTION: The flowers spikes can be yellowish orange through to deep red. Long, narrow, pointed, grey-blue-green leaves, up to 45 cm (18 in) long. A variable species. One of the hardier species.

'Tara'. Large spidery spikes of orange-red flowers. A good, hardier, wild form collected in Nepal by Tony Schilling. Zone 8.

Hedychium coronarium

ORIGIN: India
SIZE: 150–200 × 90 cm; 5–6½ × 3 ft
FLOWERING TIME: summer
FLOWER COLOUR: yellow and white
Sun
Zones 8–9
Useful for flower arrangement
Propagate by division
Moderate impact
DESCRIPTION: Pleasantly scented yellow and white flowers, spikes up to 20 cm (8 in) long, but only produced in hot summers. Long, narrow, pointed leaves, up to 60 cm

(24 in) long. One of the most tender of those listed here.

Hedychium greenii

ORIGIN: western Bhutan, northern India
SIZE: 150–200 × 90 cm; 5–6½ × 3 ft
FLOWERING TIME: autumn
FLOWER COLOUR: orange and red
Sun
Zone 9
Useful for flower arrangement
Propagate by division or bulbils
Moderate impact
DESCRIPTION: Orange red or dusky red flowers, with large petals, not scented. Long, pointed, oblong leaves, 25 cm (10 in) long, maroon-red on the underside, on red stems. The bulbils which appear on the stems can be used to propagate the plant.

Hedychium spicatum

ORIGIN: Himalayas, southwestern China, Nepal
SIZE: 105–200 × 60–135 cm; 3½–6½ × 2–4½ ft
FLOWERING TIME: autumn
FLOWER COLOUR: orange and white
Sun
Zone 7
Useful for flower arrangement
Interesting seed heads
Propagate by division
Moderate impact
DESCRIPTION: Small, slightly scented orange and white flowers, with oblong or long, narrow and pointed leaves, 40 cm (16 in) long. The seed capsules split to reveal red seeds. The hardiest species, but not normally more than 105 cm (3½ ft) high.

'Singalila'. A form with broader, bronze-tinted leaves. Collected in northern India by Bleddyn and Susan Wynn-Jones. Up to 200 cm (6½ ft).

Other *Hedychium* Varieties

'Double Eagle'. Coppery gold flower in 15 cm (6 in) high spikes. Mid to late summer. 150–180 cm (5–6 ft).

'Elizabeth'. A tall hybrid with large bright orange-red flowers, scented of honeysuckle. Raised by Tom Wood of Florida. 270 cm (9 ft).

'White Starburst'. White fragrant flowers forming a ring. Early to late autumn. 180 cm (6 ft).

Hedychium greenii.

Leonotis

LAMIACEAE

lion's ear

A genus of aromatic perennials, subshrubs and annuals, with flowers in whorls, in a manner slightly reminiscent of *Phlomis*. Those in cultivation are slightly tender, as Zone 8 or 9 plants, and have orange flowers—not a colour that appeals to everyone. However, one of these species offers yellow and cream-coloured forms.

Leonotis leonurus

wild dagga

ORIGIN: South Africa

SIZE: 120–270 × 90–150 cm; 4–9 × 3–5 ft

FLOWERING TIME: autumn

FLOWER COLOUR: orange

Sun

Zone 9

Useful for flower arrangement

Propagate by seed or cuttings

Moderate impact

DESCRIPTION: A large subshrubby perennial with bright orange flowers, occurring in whorls of rising vertical flower stems. The individual florets are more or less horizontal and arching. Bushy foliage, with long, narrow, downy leaves. Apparently its narcotic properties are slight: "a bit like cannabis, but minus the fun." However, it does act as a muscle relaxant. It is used in traditional medicine, usually as a tea, for complaints ranging from snakebites, epilepsy, headaches, high blood pressure and viral hepatitis.

var. *albiflora*. White or nearly white flowers.

Leonotis nepetifolia

ORIGIN: India, tropical regions worldwide; introduced in the United States

SIZE: 60–300 × 75–150 cm; 2–10 × 2½–5 ft

FLOWERING TIME: autumn

FLOWER COLOUR: orange, yellow and white

Sun

Zone 8

Propagate by seed or cuttings

Moderate impact

DESCRIPTION: A short-lived perennial, grown as an annual in cooler areas. The flowers are in whorls, usually orange ("ginger-cat-colour"), but may also be yellow or white. The foliage is bold, coarse and downy, up to 15 cm (6 in) wide.

'Staircase'. Earlier flowering, sometimes shorter.

Leonotis ocymifolia

ORIGIN: South Africa

SIZE: 60–200 × 45–105 cm; 2–6½ × 1½–3½ ft

FLOWERING TIME: summer to autumn

FLOWER COLOUR: orange

Sun

Zone 9

Propagate by seed or cuttings

Moderate impact

DESCRIPTION: A downy, subshrubby perennial, with orange flowers in whorls, on a sparsely branched bush, woody at the base. Leaves toothed and velvety in texture.

var. *raineriana*. Earlier and longer flowering.

Leuzea

ASTERACEAE

A small genus of perennials all of which were formerly in *Centaurea*. Named for French naturalist Joseph Philippe Francois Deleuze. Three species, from the Alps, the Pyrenees, Portugal and the western Mediterranean.

Leuzea rhapontica

(syn. *Centaurea rhapontica*)
ORIGIN: Alps, Czech Republic, Slovakia
SIZE: 75–170 × 60–105 cm; 2½–5½ ×
   2–3½ ft
FLOWERING TIME: late summer to autumn
FLOWER COLOUR: lilac pink and purple
Sun

Zone 5
Useful for flower arrangement
Interesting seed heads
Propagate by division or cuttings
Moderate impact
DESCRIPTION: Large "hardhead"-type flowers, similar to centaureas, with a dark brown rounded base and a tuft of lilac-pink to purple flowers, which can be up to 10 cm (4 in) wide. Large basal leaves, deeply lobed, from which stiff upright stems arise, with only a few branches, bearing more finely divided foliage. Full sun is preferred, with well-drained soil. Good seed heads, worth retaining for a while. Sometimes sold under the name *Centaurea* 'Pulchra Major'.

Leuzea rhapontica, an attractive knapweed relation, seen here at Bressingham Gardens, Norfolk.

Persicaria

POLYGONACEAE
knotweed, bistort

Tough, long-flowering plants, with red, pink or white flowers, often held in narrow upright spikes, but sometimes in sprays or panicles. They form bold clumps of leafy upright stems, and prefer a moist or damp situation in sun or part shade. Several species spread quite vigorously, but others are well behaved. Suitable for the border or wildflower garden. Some people find that contact with the plant causes skin irritation.

All members of *Persicaria* were once in *Polygonum*. There are probably about 100 perennials and annuals in all, but the naming of many species has been in a state of flux as botanists have moved them around from one genus to another.

Persicaria mollis

(syns. *Polygonum molle, P. paniculatum*)
ORIGIN: Himalayas
SIZE: 180–240 × 150 cm; 6–8 × 5 ft
FLOWERING TIME: midsummer to autumn
FLOWER COLOUR: cream
Sun or light shade
Zone 7
Propagate by division
High impact
DESCRIPTION: Feathery clusters of tiny, creamy white flowers, often with a hint of pink, slightly fragrant, the main display in midsummer, drifting on into the autumn. It forms a leafy plant, with slightly downy foliage, leaves up to 20 cm (8 in), the stems arising from a woody rootstock.

Persicaria wallichii

(syns. *P. polystachya, Aconogonon polystachyum, Polygonum polystachyum*)
Himalayan knotweed
ORIGIN: Himalayas, western China
SIZE: 90–210 × 90–210 cm; 3–7 × 3–7 ft
FLOWERING TIME: early autumn
FLOWER COLOUR: cream and pink
Sun or light shade
Zone 4
Interesting seed heads
Propagate by division
High impact
DESCRIPTION: Wide, branching sprays of tiny, scented, creamy white or pinkish flowers, in open leafy flowerheads 30 cm (12 in) high, giving a fluffy, frothy effect overall. The plant forms a dense clump of sturdy, leafy stems, woody at the base. The large, pointed leaves have red midribs, the largest leaves being at the base of the plant, up to 30 cm (12 in) wide and 10 cm (4 in) wide. Impressive, but best reserved for the wild garden, because of its steadily invasive tendencies—or you could grow it in grass and keep it in check by mowing right up to it.

Persicaria weyrichii

(syns. *Aconogonon weyrichii, Polygonum weyrichii*)
ORIGIN: Sakhalin, Japan
SIZE: 105–180 × 105–180 cm; 3½–6 × 3½–6 ft
FLOWERING TIME: late summer
FLOWER COLOUR: greenish white
Sun or light shade
Zone 5
Interesting seed heads

Propagate by division
High impact
DESCRIPTION: Clouds of greenish white flowers held in large, branching panicles up to 40 cm (16 in) high. A tough and densely leafy plant, the lowest leaves being up to 30 × 20 cm (12 × 8 in) in size. Attractive seed case in the autumn, red-brown and papery. Some similarity to *Persicaria wallichii*, but not invasive, and flowers not scented.

Solidago
ASTERACEAE
golden rod
Perennials with bright yellow flowers in large branching sprays, held at the top of uninteresting greenery. There are a few wild white species, but these have not been seen in cultivation. The individual flowers are small, and the fact that this genus belongs to the Asteraceae is not immediately obvious to the gardener. Tough and easy to grow, sometimes a little invasive. Arguably the best varieties have been selected to be short, among other qualities, and so cannot be included here. There are about 150 species, mostly from North America, with a handful from Europe and South America.

Solidago canadensis
golden rod
ORIGIN: North America
SIZE: 135–165 (–240) × 60 cm; 4½–5½ (–8) × 2 ft
FLOWERING TIME: autumn
FLOWER COLOUR: yellow
Sun

Zone 3
Interesting seed heads
Propagate by division
Moderate impact
DESCRIPTION: The best known, but not the best species. Curving sprays of brash yellow flowers, at the top of tall leafy stems. The narrow mid-green leaves are of no value, and those at the base tend to die away early, giving the "leggy" look. But anyone who wanted this in their garden would want to plant something in front of it anyway, to hide all that greenery. Spreads and seeds itself. Widely naturalized as a weed in Europe, including Great Britain, and this has given it a bad name.

Solidago rugosa
ORIGIN: eastern United States, eastern Canada
SIZE: 105–180 × 60 cm; 3½–6 × 2 ft
FLOWERING TIME: late summer to autumn
FLOWER COLOUR: yellow
Sun
Zone 3
Useful for flower arrangement
Interesting seed heads
Propagate by division
High impact
DESCRIPTION: Clusters of graceful sprays, pointed at their ends and arching almost horizontally, in all directions. Held on erect stems bearing mid-green foliage. Probably the best tall solidago.

'Fireworks'. Longer, narrower sprays, like crowds of over-long, yellow fingers pointing in various directions.

The graceful sprays of *Solidago rugosa*, a species from the eastern United States and eastern Canada.

Solidago stricta

ORIGIN: eastern and southern United States
SIZE: 165–200 × 60 cm; 5½–6½ × 2 ft
FLOWERING TIME: summer to autumn
FLOWER COLOUR: yellow
Sun
Zone 5
Useful for flower arrangement
Interesting seed heads
Propagate by division
Moderate impact
DESCRIPTION: Long, narrow, upright inflorescences of yellow flowers, curving at their ends. The flowers don't open fully until the autumn, but are effective long before that.

Other Solidago Varieties

'Golden Wings'. A hybrid, probably with *Solidago canadensis* as one parent, and maybe *S. rugosa* as the other. The usual yellow flowers in long, large pointed clusters arch out almost horizontally. 180–200 cm (6–6½ ft).

Vernonia

ASTERACEAE
ironweed

Flattish heads of deep purple flowers, at the top of tall, leafy plants. *Vernonia noveboracensis* has quite large branching heads, but compared with the other species, the quality and quantity of the floral display doesn't

Solidago 'Golden Wings', pointing its witch's fingers at the passer-by.

seem to justify all that uninteresting green-ery. The seed heads are fairly good, but not outstanding. None of them is difficult to grow. There are more than 500 species, from the Americas, Asia, Africa and Australia, but only a few in cultivation.

Vernonia arkansana

(syn. *V. crinita*)
ORIGIN: central United States, southern Canada
SIZE: 120–240 × 90–180 cm; 4–8 × 3–6 ft
FLOWERING TIME: late summer to autumn
FLOWER COLOUR: violet
Sun or light shade
Zone 4

Propagate by seed or division
Subtle impact
DESCRIPTION: Rich violet purple heads, over a large amount of greenery.
  'Mammuth'. A form selected by Piet Oudolf, slightly larger flowers. Still not worth it.

Vernonia fasciculata

ORIGIN: northern and central United States, southern Canada
SIZE: 90–165 (–200) × 90–150 cm; 3–5½ (–6½) × 3–5 ft
FLOWERING TIME: late summer
FLOWER COLOUR: purple
Sun or light shade

Zone 3
Propagate by seed or division
Subtle impact
DESCRIPTION: Deep purple flowers on dark stems. Drought resistant.

'Albiflora'. Dirty greyish white. Shorter.

Detail of the flower of giant ironweed, *Vernonia gigantea*.

Vernonia gigantea

giant ironweed
ORIGIN: eastern and southern United States
SIZE: 150–200 × 120–180 cm; 5–6½ × 4–6 ft
FLOWERING TIME: autumn
FLOWER COLOUR: purple
Sun or light shade
Zone 4
Propagate by seed or division
Subtle impact
DESCRIPTION: Flat, deep purple heads.

Vernonia noveboracensis

ORIGIN: eastern and southeastern United States
SIZE: 150–180 × 120–150 cm; 5–6 × 4–5 ft
FLOWERING TIME: late summer to autumn
FLOWER COLOUR: purple
Sun or light shade
Zone 4
Useful for flower arrangement
Propagate by seed or division
High impact
DESCRIPTION: Widely branching heads of rich purple flowers, up to 60 cm (24 in) wide. Probably the best of the vernonias.

'Albiflora'. A form with white flowers.

CHOOSING PLANTS
for Specific Traits and Uses

Tropical effects
Angelica
Aralia
Arundo
Begonia
Beschorneria
Colocasia—some
Cyperus
Darmera
Datisca
Echium
Eryngium—some
Gunnera
Hedychium
Helianthus salicifolius
Heracleum—some
Juncus—some
Macleaya
Melianthus
Miscanthus
Osmunda
Petasites
Phormium
Polygonum—some
Rheum—some
Sambucus—some
Woodwardia

Flowers on tall stems
Acanthus
Actaea
Ampelodesmos
Angelica
Beschorneria
Calamagrostis
Dierama
Eremurus
Ferula
Hemerocallis
Kniphofia
Miscanthus—some
Molinia
Molopospermum
Opopanax
Peucedanum
Phormium—some
Rheum—some
Stipa—some

Foliage plants
Acanthus
Actaea
Amicia
Angelica
Aralia
Artemisia
Arundo
Begonia
Colocasia
Cynara
Cyperus
Darmera
Datisca
Echinops
Elymus
Eryngium—some
Euphorbia—some
Ferula
Filipendula
Foeniculum
Gunnera
Helianthus salicifolius
Heracleum—some
Ischyrolepis

Juncus
Leymus
Ligularia
Macleaya
Melanoselinum
Melianthus
Miscanthus
Molinia
Molopospermum
Onopordum
Osmunda
Panicum
Petasites
Phormium
Polygonum—some
Restio—some
Rheum—some
Romneya
Sambucus
Sinacalia
Tanacetum—some
Thalictrum
Valeriana
Woodwardia

Coloured foliage
Actaea—some
Artemisia
Calamagrostis—some
Canna—some
Chionochloa
Colocasia—some
Elymus
Foeniculum—some
Juncus—some
Leymus
Melianthus
Miscanthus—some
Molinia—some

Panicum—some
Rheum—some
Zizania (autumn)

Specimen plants
Acanthus
Actaea—some
Amicia
Ampelodesmos
Angelica
Aralia
Artemisia—some
Aruncus
Arundo
Chionochloa—some
Colocasia
Conium
Cortaderia
Cynara
Datisca
Delphinium—some
Echium
Eryngium—some
Euphorbia—some
Ferula
Ferulago
Foeniculum
Gunnera
Helianthus salicifolius
Heracleum—some
Ligularia—some
Macleaya
Melianthus
Miscanthus
Molinia—some
Onopordum
Osmunda
Phormium
Salvia—some

Sambucus
Stipa—some
Thalictrum
Valeriana
Verbascum
Veronicastrum
Woodwardia

Spiky plants
Acanthus
Beschorneria
Echinops
Eryngium
Kniphofia—some
Onopordum
Phormium

Statuesque and architectural plants
Acanthus
Agastache—some
Alcea—some
Althea—some
Angelica
Calopsis
Conium
Cortaderia
Cynara
Echinops
Echium
Elegia
Eryngium—some
Ferula
Ferulago
Heracleum—some
Inula
Kniphofia
Molinia—some
Molopospermum

Onopordum
Opopanax
Rhodocoma
Thamnochortus
Verbascum

Dry garden plants

Acanthus
Achillea
Althaea—some
Artemisia
Boltonia
Centaurea—some
Cirsium—some
Cynara
Dierama
Echinops—some
Echium
Eremurus
Eryngium—some
Euphorbia—some
Ferula
Ferulago
Foeniculum—some
Kitaibelia
Kniphofia—some
Leuzea
Onopordum
Romneya
Salvia
Sida
Silphium—some
Stipa
Verbascum

Damp garden plants

Aruncus
Chionochloa
Cyperus

Darmera
Elegia—some
Equisetum—some
Eupatorium
Filipendula
Gunnera
Inula—some
Juncus
Ligularia
Molinia
Osmunda
Persicaria
Petasites
Polygonum—some
Restio—some
Rheum—some
Saccharum—some
Sanguisorba
Schoenoplectus
Sinacalia
Telekia
Valeriana
Woodwardia

Waterside and aquatic plants

Calopsis
Cyperus
Darmera
Elegia—some
Equisetum—some
Gunnera
Inula—some
Osmunda
Phragmites
Polygonum—some
Schoenoplectus
Telekia
Typha

Herb garden plants

Angelica
Foeniculum
Leonurus
Leonotis—some
Levisticum
Opopanax
Valeriana

Meadow garden plants

Calamagrostis
Centaurea—some
Cirsium
Conium
Digitalis
Elymus
Eupatorium
Heracleum—some
Liatris
Lysimachia—some
Onopordum
Petasites
Peucedanum
Rudbeckia—some
Verbascum

Wild garden plants

Acanthus
Achillea—some
Agrimonia
Aralia
Aruncus
Calamagrostis
Chamerion
Cirsium
Conium
Cortaderia
Darmera
Datisca

Digitalis
Eupatorium
Filipendula
Gunnera
Helenium—some
Helianthus—some
Heracleum—some
Leuzea
Liatris
Ligularia
Lysimachia—some
Macleaya
Meconopsis
Miscanthus
Molinia
Onopordum
Osmunda
Persicaria
Petasites
Peucedanum
Phormium
Polygonum—some
Rheum—some
Rudbeckia
Sambucus
Sanguisorba
Senecio—some
Stipa
Valeriana
Verbascum

Shade tolerant

Aconitum—some
Actaea
Aralia
Aruncus
Digitalis
Equisetum
Meconopsis

Osmunda
Petasites
Polygonatum
Polygonum
Sinacalia
Woodwardia

Evergreen

Beschorneria
Cortaderia
Cynara
Eryngium—some
Leymus
Melianthus
Phormium

Short-lived perennials and biennials

Althaea—some
Angelica
Campanula—some
Cirsium—some
Conium
Echium
Ferula
Ferulago
Heracleum
Kitaibelia
Lavatera—some
Leonotis—some
Melanoselinum
Onopordum
Peucedanum
Verbascum

Die down early in the season

Crambe—some
Eremurus

Ferula
Molopospermum

Self-seeders (benign— in most situations)

Alcea—some
Angelica
Aruncus
Conium
Elymus—some
Ferulago
Heracleum—some
Leonurus
Onopordum
Phytolacca
Valeriana
Verbascum

Self-seeders (aggressive)

Cephalaria
Cirsium
Echium
Elymus
Foeniculum

Staking required

Achillea—some
Aconitum—some
Boltonia
Delphinium
Helenium—some
Helianthus—some
Heliopsis—some
Leucanthemella
Rudbeckia—some
Salvia uliginosa
Sanguisorba—some

HARDINESS ZONES

USDA Plant Hardiness Zones Average Annual Minimum Temperature

ZONE	TEMPERATURE (DEG. F)			TEMPERATURE (DEG. C)		
1		below −50		−45.6	and below	
2a	−45	to	−50	−42.8	to	−45.5
2b	−40	to	−45	−40.0	to	−42.7
3a	−35	to	−40	−37.3	to	−40.0
3b	−30	to	−35	−34.5	to	−37.2
4a	−25	to	−30	−31.7	to	−34.4
4b	−20	to	−25	−28.9	to	−31.6
5a	−15	to	−20	−26.2	to	−28.8
5b	−10	to	−15	−23.4	to	−26.1
6a	−5	to	−10	−20.6	to	−23.3
6b	0	to	−5	−17.8	to	−20.5
7a	5	to	0	−15.0	to	−17.7
7b	10	to	5	−12.3	to	−15.0
8a	15	to	10	−9.5	to	−12.2
8b	20	to	15	−6.7	to	−9.4
9a	25	to	20	−3.9	to	−6.6
9b	30	to	25	−1.2	to	−3.8
10a	35	to	30	1.6	to	−1.1
10b	40	to	35	4.4	to	1.7
11	40	and above		4.5	and above	

To see the USDA Hardiness Zone Map, go to the U.S. National Arboretum site at http://www.usna.usda.gov/Hardzone/ushzmap.html.

Temperatures

$°C = 5/9 \times (°F–32)$

$°F = (9/5 \times °C) + 32$

INDEX

Page numbers in *italic* type refer to photographs.